THE XXL
AIR FRYER
Recipes Cookbook

— 600 —

No-Fuss and Tasty British Recipes for Busy
People to Easily Make The Most of Your Air Fryer

George Barrett

Table of Contents

INTRODUCTION

One of the most popular kitchen appliances in 2022 has to be the Air Fryer. If you don't own an air fryer, you are missing out. A lot of cooking videos on social media had an Air Fryer making a special appearance. Everyone loves and uses them. If it is a question of whether it is worth the hype, "Yeah, definitcly!" I can't believe it took me so long to decide to get one. Whatever my motivation for getting the air fryer was, I'm happy I did! Peer pressure is never a good reason to make a decision, but let's say it was a good thing this one time. Nobody likes to jump on a bandwagon, at least not me, but I have to hand it to the band this time; they were on point! The air fryer is my best single kitchen appliance purchase in a long time, and I buy a lot of kitchen appliances, so that says a lot.

Air fryers are now a must-have cooking appliance in the UK. The global market capitalization for air fryers in 2018 was $894.3 million, and experts are predicting that the market size could reach $1.4 billion by 2026 with a Compound Annual Growth Rate (from 2019-2026) of 6.1%. The accelerated growth of the hospitality sector is predicted to improve the market growth of air fryers. The functionality and continuous innovation of air fryers will attract more consumers over time. The ease and versatility of air fryers are second to none. With air fryers, you can bake, fry, and roast chicken with a small amount of oil. Its multifunctionality is truly impressive.

When the pandemic hit, more and more people were spending more time at home, and, as such, there were not many options regarding the purchase of food. This forced most people to prepare their meals. People were always looking for easier and faster ways to prepare their favourite meals, and the air fryer provided the solution. Don't even get me started on how good foods that are air-fried taste. They come out so crispy and chewy that you would not want to eat another meal that is fried traditionally or deep-fried. Air flying is safer and healthier, and requires no oil to fry. At this point, if you don't have an air fryer in your kitchen, you need to do something about that.

Every day, people are looking for more meal recipes they can try out with their air fryers. Just as air fryers have become popular, air fryer cookbooks have also become sought after in the market. If you don't have many options regarding meals you can prepare using an air fryer, or you just want to do more with your air fryer, stick around. This cookbook has a lot of mouth-watering recipes that you could try. This book offers a wide variety of recipes with easy-to-get ingredients and easy-to-make steps. Boring and repetitive meals will be a thing of the past with this book.

Chapter 1 Air Fryer Basic Guide

Chapter 1 Air Fryer Basic Guide

An air fryer is ideal when making meals for the whole family because it comes with enough capacity. The air fryer saves up to 50% on energy bills compared to an oven. It cooks meals in at least 15 minutes. That's 30% faster and with 99% less oil. Its rapid air circulation means that your meals are evenly cooked, and its four options of baking, grilling, frying, and roasting mean more meal choices for your family.

How Do Air Fryers Work?

Air fryers use convection heat to cook foods. It circulates hot air to cook the food. The basket in which the foods in the air fryer are placed to cook comes in various styles, and they are usually perforated with holes. These holes in the pan make sure the hot air circulates the food properly without restriction. It soft cooks the food first, gets it to be golden brown and delicious, and then the moisture settles. There are even air fryers with automatically stirred food options where you don't have to turn the food to the other side manually to cook. That's why air-fried meals always come out with perfect brown tones and the best textures. It does this with little oil as well, and that's why air fryers have a reputation for being a healthier way to prepare high-fat foods.

This method is not only easier but way less messy than when you deep fry your meals. So long as the temperature high is more than 320F, your foods will turn brown and cook well. It doesn't "fry" the food, but just uses all that heat around the food to cook it. Classic heat transfer by convection.

5 Features of the Air Fryer

Less Fat

This is why the Air Fryer is a much better option than other traditional frying methods like deep frying. When you deep fry, you fully immerse the food into that sizzling hot oil and leave it to cook. Think of all the fat in the oil that is been added to that food, plus the fat that is originally contained in the food. When you use this air fryer, you'll be able to have your foods cooked with 99% less fat. You lose the fat, but not the flavour. Now you can enjoy your favourite foods without thinking about all that extra fat you'll be consuming. I mean, you can still enjoy fried chicken without the guilt of how much oil is used to cook it and with 99% less fat. Who wouldn't want to be a part of that?

Faster Meals

With the air fryers, you can cook deliciously crisp and golden meals in about 15 minutes. Nobody wants to spend hours cooking a meal they'll finish in minutes. Certainly not me. You'll cut your meal preparation time in half with this air fryer, so you have more time to do other fun things. No one wants to spend more time in the kitchen, and when given an option to cut that time down, you should take it with both hands. That's what you'll get with an air fryer.

More Meal Choices

Whether you want to grill, bake, roast, or fry, the air fryer has got you. Just imagine how much wider this will make your meal options now. From vegetables like broccoli, potatoes, zucchini, mushrooms, and onions, to proteins like tofu, meatballs, chicken drumsticks, pork chops, and fried chicken. All these are just some of the meals that are perfectly cooked with air fryers. Even appetizers like jalapenó poppers and spinach artichoke are great options that are cooked well with air fryers. It completely changed the game when it comes to the meals you can make.

Less Energy

Air fryers save up to 50% on energy. That's a massive saving if you decide to switch to air-fry cooking. This is just another reason why air-fry cooking is an absolute no-brainer addition to your kitchen countertop.

Enough Capacity

Air Fryer's capacity lets you cook enough food to serve your whole family. It's perfectly suited to serve your family's food needs. This is one of those times when bigger is indeed better. This capacity also means you have enough space to place your food in the air fryer pan, and it's not clustered together.

Different Types of Air Fryers

Basket Air Fryer

Just as the name goes, basket air fryers always come with a basket to accommodate the food. This basket comes with holes surrounding them, so the heat can easily circulate the food and make sure it comes out well cooked. These baskets also come with a handle, so you can easily toss your food when cooking. They come in different shapes; they are cylindrical, square, or round. No matter what shape they come in, they all come with a removable basket you use to keep the food inside. This basket air fryer is one of the most popular types of air fryers on the market today.

Features of Basket Air Fryer:

- Small space - The basket air fryer is small and portable. It won't take up space on your kitchen countertop.
- Quick Heating up - Basket Air fryers do not take long to heat up and cook meals. This is because of the perforated baskets that allow better circulation of heat around the food.
- Easy to clean - The baskets in these air fryers are easy to clean and maintain. You can easily toss them in a dishwasher.

Paddle Air Fryer

This air fryer comes with a self-stirring paddle that stirs the food as it cooks to make sure that all of the food is properly cooked. It's similar to the basket air fryer because it also has a removable basket, but the self-stirring feature of the paddle air fryer is what sets it apart from the basket air fryer. This is the air fryer you'll set and forget, and not have to check it while cooking because it will do all the cooking work for you.

Features of the Paddle Air Fryer:

- Automatic stirring - the rotating paddle ensures that your food is thoroughly cooked.
- Digital countdown timer - so you can easily monitor the time and temperature of the air frying.
- Little to no oil used - you may only need a tablespoon of oil for your cooking.

Oven Air Fryer

This is another popular type of air fryer. It's also very similar to the other two mentioned above, but the distinguishing feature is its shape. It's shaped almost like a toaster oven with square or rectangular shapes, while the other air fryers have a more cylindrical shape. They also have racks and baking trays.

They are very versatile; you can bake, roast, boil, or even dehydrate your food. Because it is designed with racks, you can have different dishes in an oven air fryer and have all of them cook at the same time. That's one of the sterling features of the oven air fryer.

Features of the Oven Air Fryer:

- Large capacity - If you're in the market for an air fryer with a large capacity, then the oven air fryer is your choice. It has a larger capacity than the two other air fryers we've mentioned.
- Cook more than one meal at a time - Because of its racks, you can place different meals on different racks and cook them all at the same time.
- Glass doors - the oven air fryers have glass doors where you can monitor your food easily.

Halogen Air Fryer

This uses a different mechanism, it uses halogen light to produce heat and circulate the food. This one also comes with glass doors, which you can use to monitor your food.

Features of Halogen Air Fryer:

- Large capacity - You can grill a whole turkey in a halogen air fryer.
- Glass doors - You get to watch your meal as it's been cooked.
- Less Oil - The halogen air fryer doesn't cook with so much oil.

Microwave Air Fryer

This is a combination of a microwave and an air fryer. You can roast, boil, steam, and reheat your food.

Features of the Microwave Air Fryer:

- Energy saving technology- It saves energy with LED light and ECO mode.
- More cooking options - You can fit more than one dish inside the Microwave Air Fryer.

Air Fryer Cooking Tips

Add Water to the Air Fryer When Cooking Fatty Foods

When you add water to the basket before you cook, it prevents the grease from getting too hot and starting smoking.

Don't Overfill the Basket

You want the food pieces to have enough space to breathe and cook properly, right? So don't cluster the basket.

Flip Foods Occasionally

Just like with a traditional grill, when cooking with an air fryer, you should also flip it so that both sides of the food are evenly cooked. Eating unevenly baked cookies is no fun.

Shake the Basket

While cooking, you may want to shake the basket just to allow the ingredients to mix well. It will help to redistribute the spices and make sure they come out evenly brown and crispy.

Occasionally Check for Doneness

As your food cooks in the air fryer, you should check it from time to time to see how cooked it is and put it off when you're satisfied with the doneness. You want to do this to avoid your food being overcooked or worse, burnt.

Adjust the Temperatures for Certain Foods

You may think getting your air fryer's temperature as high as possible would make it cook faster, but that's not always the best way to go about it.

Spray with Oil Halfway Through the Cooking

This works magic, I tell you! Spraying your food with oil halfway while cooking makes your food come out deliciously crispy. Simple, yet effective.

Use Foil

Line the base of your basket with foil paper. And when you're done cooking, you could just take the foil off. When cooking with a lot of spices and ingredients, the inside of your fryer can get messy. Using foil to coat the base of your basket would save you a lot of that work.

Care and Cleaning

After every use, you want to make sure to unplug your air fryer. The trick to maintaining your air fryer is to clean it after every use. After you use your air fryer, it's going to be hot, so you want to leave it to cool for a while. When it's cool, you should take out the basket of the air fryer and soak it in warm water and soap for about 15 minutes. If there's any hard grease or stains left in the basket, you want to scrub this off with a non-abrasive brush with warm water and soap solution till it comes off. Leaving stains in your basket is never a good idea.

When you're done with the basket, now you want to clean the interior of the air fryer itself. Take a damp cloth or sponge with a small amount of dish soap and clean the interior of the air fryer till there are no stains left. Once you have done this, turn the air fryer upside down for it to dry. You must allow all parts of the air fryer to completely dry before reassembling them.

Air Fryer Q&A

Q: Is Air Fryer Healthier Than Deep Frying?

Yes, significantly healthier. Instead of using tons of oil, you'll only have to use drops of oil with an air fryer. That's one of the main reasons the air fryer is such a better substitute for deep frying.

Q: Do I Have To PreHeat My Air Fryer?

Air fryers heat up faster than ovens, so there isn't much difference in the overall time you'll spend cooking the meal when you preheat it versus when you don't. There's no hard and fast rule as to whether or not you should preheat your air fryer because it varies between different models and types of air fryers. Some air fryers come with automatic preheating settings, while others don't. Ultimately, you should follow what the manual for your air fryer says.

Q: How Often Should I Clean My Air Fryer?

The ideal time is after every usage. You should try and make your air fryer clean all the time, that means you clean it after you use it every time. This prevents your air fryer from having lingering odours that could now spill into the subsequent dishes you'll make using your air fryer.

Q: Can I Cook All My Foods With My Air Fryer?

According to experts, an air fryer can cook nearly all types of food. But that doesn't mean it's okay to cook all types of food in an air fryer. Certain foods are best prepared in an air fryer, but not so much for others. So while your air fryer can cook anything, it probably shouldn't.

Chapter 2 Breakfasts

Chapter 2 Breakfasts

Parmesan Ranch Risotto

Prep time: 10 minutes | Cook time: 30 minutes | Serves 2

1 tablespoon olive oil	180 ml Arborio rice
1 clove garlic, minced	475 ml chicken stock, boiling
1 tablespoon unsalted butter	120 ml Parmesan cheese, grated
1 onion, diced	

Preheat the air fryer to 200°C.
Grease a round baking tin with olive oil and stir in the garlic, butter, and onion.
Transfer the tin to the air fryer and bake for 4 minutes. Add the rice and bake for 4 more minutes.
Turn the air fryer to 160°C and pour in the chicken stock. Cover and bake for 22 minutes.
Scatter with cheese and serve.

Classic British Breakfast

Prep time: 5 minutes | Cook time: 25 minutes | Serves 2

235 ml potatoes, sliced and diced	1 tablespoon olive oil
475 ml baked beans	1 sausage
2 eggs	Salt, to taste

Preheat the air fryer to 200°C and allow to warm.
Break the eggs onto a baking dish and sprinkle with salt.
Lay the beans on the dish, next to the eggs.
In a bowl, coat the potatoes with the olive oil. Sprinkle with salt.
Transfer the bowl of potato slices to the air fryer and bake for 10 minutes.
Swap out the bowl of potatoes for the dish containing the eggs and beans. Bake for another 10 minutes. Cover the potatoes with parchment paper.
Slice up the sausage and throw the slices on top of the beans and eggs. Bake for another 5 minutes.
Serve with the potatoes.

Portobello Eggs Benedict

Prep time: 10 minutes | Cook time: 10 to 14 minutes | Serves 2

1 tablespoon olive oil	pepper, to taste
2 cloves garlic, minced	2 large eggs
¼ teaspoon dried thyme	2 tablespoons grated Pecorino
2 portobello mushrooms, stems removed and gills scraped out	Romano cheese
2 plum tomatoes, halved lengthwise	1 tablespoon chopped fresh parsley, for garnish
Salt and freshly ground black	1 teaspoon truffle oil (optional)

Preheat the air fryer to 204°C.
In a small bowl, combine the olive oil, garlic, and thyme. Brush the mixture over the mushrooms and tomatoes until thoroughly coated. Season to taste with salt and freshly ground black pepper.
Arrange the vegetables, cut side up, in the air fryer basket. Crack an egg into the center of each mushroom and sprinkle with cheese. Air fry for 10 to 14 minutes until the vegetables are tender and the whites are firm. When cool enough to handle, coarsely chop the tomatoes and place on top of the eggs. Scatter parsley on top and drizzle with truffle oil, if desired, just before serving.

Ham and Cheese Crescents

Prep time: 5 minutes | Cook time: 7 minutes | Makes 8 rolls

Oil, for spraying	8 cheese slices
1 (230 g) can ready-to-bake croissants	2 tablespoons unsalted butter, melted
4 slices wafer-thin ham	

Line the air fryer basket with parchment and spray lightly with oil.
Separate the dough into 8 pieces.
Tear the ham slices in half and place 1 piece on each piece of dough. Top each with 1 slice of cheese.
Roll up each piece of dough, starting on the wider side.
Place the rolls in the prepared basket. Brush with the melted butter.
Air fry at 160°C for 6 to 7 minutes, or until puffed and golden brown and the cheese is melted.

Scotch Eggs

Prep time: 10 minutes | Cook time: 20 to 25 minutes | Serves 4

2 tablespoons flour, plus extra for coating	1 tablespoon water
450 g sausage meat	Oil for misting or cooking spray
4 hard-boiled eggs, peeled	Crumb Coating:
1 raw egg	180 ml panko bread crumbs
	180 ml flour

Combine flour with sausage meat and mix thoroughly.
Divide into 4 equal portions and mold each around a hard-boiled egg so the sausage completely covers the egg.
In a small bowl, beat together the raw egg and water.
Dip sausage-covered eggs in the remaining flour, then the egg mixture, then roll in the crumb coating.
Air fry at 182°C for 10 minutes. Spray eggs, turn, and spray other side.
Continue cooking for another 10 to 15 minutes or until sausage is well done.

Homemade Toaster Pastries

Prep time: 10 minutes | Cook time: 11 minutes | Makes 6 pastries

Oil, for spraying
1 (425 g) package refrigerated piecrust
6 tablespoons jam or preserves of choice

475 ml icing sugar
3 tablespoons milk
1 to 2 tablespoons sprinkles of choice

Preheat the air fryer to 176ºC. Line the air fryer basket with parchment and spray lightly with oil.

Cut the piecrust into 12 rectangles, about 3 by 4 inches each. You will need to reroll the dough scraps to get 12 rectangles.

Spread 1 tablespoon of jam in the center of 6 rectangles, leaving ¼ inch around the edges.

Pour some water into a small bowl. Use your finger to moisten the edge of each rectangle.

Top each rectangle with another and use your fingers to press around the edges. Using the tines of a fork, seal the edges of the dough and poke a few holes in the top of each one. Place the pastries in the prepared basket.

Air fry for 11 minutes. Let cool completely.

In a medium bowl, whisk together the icing sugar and milk. Spread the icing over the tops of the pastries and add sprinkles. Serve immediately.

Fried Chicken Wings with Waffles

Prep time: 10 minutes | Cook time: 30 minutes | Serves 4

8 whole chicken wings
1 teaspoon garlic powder
Chicken seasoning, for preparing the chicken
Freshly ground black pepper, to taste

120 ml plain flour
Cooking oil spray
8 frozen waffles
Pure maple syrup, for serving (optional)

In a medium bowl, combine the chicken and garlic powder and season with chicken seasoning and pepper. Toss to coat.

Transfer the chicken to a resealable plastic bag and add the flour. Seal the bag and shake it to coat the chicken thoroughly.

Insert the crisper plate into the basket and the basket into the unit. Preheat the unit by selecting AIR FRY, setting the temperature to 204ºC, and setting the time to 3 minutes. Select START/STOP to begin.

Once the unit is preheated, spray the crisper plate with cooking oil. Using tongs, transfer the chicken from the bag to the basket. It is okay to stack the chicken wings on top of each other. Spray them with cooking oil.

Select AIR FRY, set the temperature to 204ºC, and set the time to 20 minutes. Select START/STOP to begin.

After 5 minutes, remove the basket and shake the wings. Reinsert the basket to resume cooking. Remove and shake the basket every 5 minutes until the chicken is fully cooked.

When the cooking is complete, remove the cooked chicken from the basket; cover to keep warm.

Rinse the basket and crisper plate with warm water. Insert them back into the unit.

Select AIR FRY, set the temperature to 182ºC, and set the time to 3 minutes. Select START/STOP to begin.

1Once the unit is preheated, spray the crisper plate with cooking spray. Working in batches, place the frozen waffles into the basket. Do not stack them. Spray the waffles with cooking oil.

1Select AIR FRY, set the temperature to 182ºC, and set the time to 6 minutes. Select START/STOP to begin.

1When the cooking is complete, repeat steps 10 and 11 with the remaining waffles.

1Serve the waffles with the chicken and a touch of maple syrup, if desired.

Three-Berry Dutch Pancake

Prep time: 10 minutes | Cook time: 12 to 16 minutes | Serves 4

2 egg whites
1 egg
120 ml wholemeal plain flour plus 1 tablespoon cornflour
120 ml semi-skimmed milk
1 teaspoon pure vanilla extract

1 tablespoon unsalted butter, melted
235 ml sliced fresh strawberries
120 ml fresh blueberries
120 ml fresh raspberries

In a medium bowl, use an eggbeater or hand mixer to quickly mix the egg whites, egg, flour, milk, and vanilla until well combined.

Use a pastry brush to grease the bottom of a baking pan with the melted butter. Immediately pour in the batter and put the basket back in the fryer. Bake at 166ºC for 12 to 16 minutes, or until the pancake is puffed and golden brown.

Remove the pan from the air fryer; the pancake will fall. Top with the strawberries, blueberries, and raspberries. Serve immediately.

Cinnamon Rolls

Prep time: 10 minutes | Cook time: 20 minutes | Makes 12 rolls

600 ml shredded Mozzarella cheese
60 g cream cheese, softened
235 ml blanched finely ground almond flour

½ teaspoon vanilla extract
120 ml icing sugar-style sweetener
1 tablespoon ground cinnamon

In a large microwave-safe bowl, combine Mozzarella cheese, cream cheese, and flour. Microwave the mixture on high 90 seconds until cheese is melted.

Add vanilla extract and sweetener, and mix 2 minutes until a dough forms.

Once the dough is cool enough to work with your hands, about 2 minutes, spread it out into a 12 × 4-inch rectangle on ungreased parchment paper. Evenly sprinkle dough with cinnamon.

Starting at the long side of the dough, roll lengthwise to form a log. Slice the log into twelve even pieces.

Divide rolls between two ungreased round nonstick baking dishes. Place one dish into air fryer basket. Adjust the temperature to 192ºC and bake for 10 minutes.

Cinnamon rolls will be done when golden around the edges and mostly firm. Repeat with second dish. Allow rolls to cool in dishes 10 minutes before serving.

Maple Granola

Prep time: 5 minutes | Cook time: 40 minutes | Makes 475 ml

235 ml rolled oats
3 tablespoons pure maple syrup
1 tablespoon sugar
1 tablespoon neutral-flavored oil, such as refined coconut or

sunflower
¼ teaspoon sea salt
¼ teaspoon ground cinnamon
¼ teaspoon vanilla extract

Insert the crisper plate into the basket and the basket into the unit. Preheat the unit by selecting BAKE, setting the temperature to 120°C, and setting the time to 3 minutes. Select START/STOP to begin.

In a medium bowl, stir together the oats, maple syrup, sugar, oil, salt, cinnamon, and vanilla until thoroughly combined. Transfer the granola to a 6-by-2-inch round baking pan.

Once the unit is preheated, place the pan into the basket.

Select BAKE, set the temperature to 120°C and set the time to 40 minutes. Select START/STOP to begin.

After 10 minutes, stir the granola well. Resume cooking, stirring the granola every 10 minutes, for a total of 40 minutes, or until the granola is lightly browned and mostly dry.

When the cooking is complete, place the granola on a plate to cool. It will become crisp as it cools. Store the completely cooled granola in an airtight container in a cool, dry place for 1 to 2 weeks.

Breakfast Meatballs

Prep time: 10 minutes | Cook time: 15 minutes | Makes 18 meatballs

450 g pork sausage meat, removed from casings
½ teaspoon salt
¼ teaspoon ground black pepper

120 ml shredded sharp Cheddar cheese
30 g cream cheese, softened
1 large egg, whisked

Combine all ingredients in a large bowl. Form mixture into eighteen 1-inch meatballs.

Place meatballs into ungreased air fryer basket. Adjust the temperature to 204°C and air fry for 15 minutes, shaking basket three times during cooking. Meatballs will be browned on the outside and have an internal temperature of at least 64°C when completely cooked. Serve warm.

Cauliflower Avocado Toast

Prep time: 15 minutes | Cook time: 8 minutes | Serves 2

1 (40 g) steamer bag cauliflower
1 large egg
120 ml shredded Mozzarella cheese

1 ripe medium avocado
½ teaspoon garlic powder
¼ teaspoon ground black pepper

Cook cauliflower according to package instructions. Remove from bag and place into cheesecloth or clean towel to remove excess moisture.

Place cauliflower into a large bowl and mix in egg and Mozzarella. Cut a piece of parchment to fit your air fryer basket. Separate the cauliflower mixture into two, and place it on the parchment in two mounds. Press out the cauliflower mounds into a ¼-inch-thick rectangle. Place the parchment into the air fryer basket.

Adjust the temperature to 204°C and set the timer for 8 minutes.

Flip the cauliflower halfway through the cooking time.

When the timer beeps, remove the parchment and allow the cauliflower to cool 5 minutes.

Cut open the avocado and remove the pit. Scoop out the inside, place it in a medium bowl, and mash it with garlic powder and pepper. Spread onto the cauliflower. Serve immediately.

Turkey Sausage Breakfast Pizza

Prep time: 15 minutes | Cook time: 24 minutes | Serves 2

4 large eggs, divided
1 tablespoon water
½ teaspoon garlic powder
½ teaspoon onion granules
½ teaspoon dried oregano
2 tablespoons coconut flour
3 tablespoons grated Parmesan cheese

120 ml shredded low-moisture Mozzarella or other melting cheese
1 link cooked turkey sausage, chopped (about 60 g)
2 sun-dried tomatoes, finely chopped
2 spring onions, thinly sliced

Preheat the air fryer to 204°C. Line a cake pan with parchment paper and lightly coat the paper with olive oil.

In a large bowl, whisk 2 of the eggs with the water, garlic powder, onion granules, and dried oregano. Add the coconut flour, breaking up any lumps with your hands as you add it to the bowl. Stir the coconut flour into the egg mixture, mixing until smooth. Stir in the Parmesan cheese. Allow the mixture to rest for a few minutes until thick and dough-like.

Transfer the mixture to the prepared pan. Use a spatula to spread it evenly and slightly up the sides of the pan. Air fry until the crust is set but still light in color, about 10 minutes. Top with the cheeses, sausage, and sun-dried tomatoes.

Break the remaining 2 eggs into a small bowl, then slide them onto the pizza. Return the pizza to the air fryer. Air fry 10 to 14 minutes until the egg whites are set and the yolks are the desired doneness. Top with the scallions and allow to rest for 5 minutes before serving.

Cheesy Bell Pepper Eggs

Prep time: 10 minutes | Cook time: 15 minutes | Serves 4

4 medium green peppers
85 g cooked ham, chopped
¼ medium onion, peeled and

chopped
8 large eggs
235 ml mild Cheddar cheese

Cut the tops off each pepper. Remove the seeds and the white membranes with a small knife. Place ham and onion into each pepper.

Crack 2 eggs into each pepper. Top with 60 ml cheese per pepper. Place into the air fryer basket.

Adjust the temperature to 200°C and air fry for 15 minutes.

When fully cooked, peppers will be tender and eggs will be firm. Serve immediately.

Potatoes Lyonnaise

Prep time: 10 minutes | Cook time: 31 minutes | Serves 4

1 sweet/mild onion, sliced	thick
1 teaspoon butter, melted	1 tablespoon vegetable oil
1 teaspoon brown sugar	Salt and freshly ground black
2 large white potatoes (about	pepper, to taste
450 g in total), sliced ½-inch	

Preheat the air fryer to 188°C.

Toss the sliced onions, melted butter and brown sugar together in the air fryer basket. Air fry for 8 minutes, shaking the basket occasionally to help the onions cook evenly.

While the onions are cooking, bring a saucepan of salted water to a boil on the stovetop. Par-cook the potatoes in boiling water for 3 minutes. Drain the potatoes and pat them dry with a clean kitchen towel.

Add the potatoes to the onions in the air fryer basket and drizzle with vegetable oil. Toss to coat the potatoes with the oil and season with salt and freshly ground black pepper.

Increase the air fryer temperature to 204°C and air fry for 20 minutes, tossing the vegetables a few times during the cooking time to help the potatoes brown evenly.

Season with salt and freshly ground black pepper and serve warm.

Apple Rolls

Prep time: 20 minutes | Cook time: 20 to 24 minutes | Makes 12 rolls

Apple Rolls:

475 ml plain flour, plus more for dusting	1 teaspoon ground cinnamon
2 tablespoons granulated sugar	1 large Granny Smith apple, peeled and diced
1 teaspoon salt	1 to 2 tablespoons oil
3 tablespoons butter, at room temperature	Icing:
180 ml milk, whole or semi-skimmed	120 ml icing sugar
	½ teaspoon vanilla extract
120 ml packed light brown sugar	2 to 3 tablespoons milk, whole or semi-skimmed

Make the Apple Rolls In a large bowl, whisk the flour, granulated sugar, and salt until blended. Stir in the butter and milk briefly until a sticky dough forms.

In a small bowl, stir together the brown sugar, cinnamon, and apple. Place a piece of parchment paper on a work surface and dust it with flour. Roll the dough on the prepared surface to ¼ inch thickness.

Spread the apple mixture over the dough. Roll up the dough jelly roll-style, pinching the ends to seal. Cut the dough into 12 rolls.

Preheat the air fryer to 160°C.

Line the air fryer basket with parchment paper and spritz it with oil. Place 6 rolls on the prepared parchment.

Bake for 5 minutes. Flip the rolls and bake for 5 to 7 minutes more until lightly browned. Repeat with the remaining rolls. Make the Icing

In a medium bowl, whisk the icing sugar, vanilla, and milk until blended.

Drizzle over the warm rolls.

Bourbon Vanilla French Toast

Prep time: 15 minutes | Cook time: 6 minutes | Serves 4

2 large eggs	2 tablespoons bourbon
2 tablespoons water	1 teaspoon vanilla extract
160 ml whole or semi-skimmed milk	8 (1-inch-thick) French bread slices
1 tablespoon butter, melted	Cooking spray

Preheat the air fryer to 160°C. Line the air fryer basket with parchment paper and spray it with cooking spray.

Beat the eggs with the water in a shallow bowl until combined. Add the milk, melted butter, bourbon, and vanilla and stir to mix well.

Dredge 4 slices of bread in the batter, turning to coat both sides evenly. Transfer the bread slices onto the parchment paper.

Bake for 6 minutes until nicely browned. Flip the slices halfway through the cooking time.

Remove from the basket to a plate and repeat with the remaining 4 slices of bread.

Serve warm.

Vanilla Granola

Prep time: 5 minutes | Cook time: 40 minutes | Serves 4

235 ml rolled oats	¼ teaspoon vanilla
3 tablespoons maple syrup	¼ teaspoon cinnamon
1 tablespoon sunflower oil	¼ teaspoon sea salt
1 tablespoon coconut sugar	

Preheat the air fryer to 120°C.

Mix together the oats, maple syrup, sunflower oil, coconut sugar, vanilla, cinnamon, and sea salt in a medium bowl and stir to combine. Transfer the mixture to a baking pan.

Place the pan in the air fryer basket and bake for 40 minutes, or until the granola is mostly dry and lightly browned. Stir the granola four times during cooking.

Let the granola stand for 5 to 10 minutes before serving.

Bunless Breakfast Turkey Burgers

Prep time: 5 minutes | Cook time: 15 minutes | Serves 4

450 g turkey sausage meat, removed from casings	pepper
	2 tablespoons mayonnaise
½ teaspoon salt	1 medium avocado, peeled,
¼ teaspoon ground black pepper	pitted, and sliced
60 ml seeded and chopped green	

In a large bowl, mix sausage meat with salt, black pepper, bell pepper, and mayonnaise. Form meat into four patties.

Place patties into ungreased air fryer basket. Adjust the temperature to 188°C and air fry for 15 minutes, turning patties halfway through cooking. Burgers will be done when dark brown and they have an internal temperature of at least 74°C.

Serve burgers topped with avocado slices on four medium plates.

Easy Buttermilk Biscuits

Prep time: 5 minutes | Cook time: 18 minutes | Makes 16 biscuits

600 ml plain flour	½ teaspoon baking soda
1 tablespoon baking powder	8 tablespoons (1 stick) unsalted
1 teaspoon coarse or flaky salt	butter, at room temperature
1 teaspoon sugar	235 ml buttermilk, chilled

Stir together the flour, baking powder, salt, sugar, and baking powder in a large bowl.

Add the butter and stir to mix well. Pour in the buttermilk and stir with a rubber spatula just until incorporated.

Place the dough onto a lightly floured surface and roll the dough out to a disk, ½ inch thick. Cut out the biscuits with a 2-inch round cutter and re-roll any scraps until you have 16 biscuits.

Preheat the air fryer to 164ºC.

Working in batches, arrange the biscuits in the air fryer basket in a single layer. Bake for about 18 minutes until the biscuits are golden brown.

Remove from the basket to a plate and repeat with the remaining biscuits.

Serve hot.

Double-Dipped Mini Cinnamon Biscuits

Prep time: 15 minutes | Cook time: 13 minutes | Makes 8 biscuits

475 ml blanched almond flour	1 large egg
120 ml liquid or powdered	1 teaspoon vanilla extract
sweetener	3 teaspoons ground cinnamon
1 teaspoon baking powder	Glaze:
½ teaspoon fine sea salt	120 ml powdered sweetener
60 ml plus 2 tablespoons (¾	60 ml double cream or
stick) very cold unsalted butter	unsweetened, unflavoured
60 ml unsweetened, unflavoured	almond milk
almond milk	

Preheat the air fryer to 176ºC. Line a pie pan that fits into your air fryer with parchment paper.

In a medium-sized bowl, mix together the almond flour, sweetener (if powdered; do not add liquid sweetener), baking powder, and salt. Cut the butter into ½-inch squares, then use a hand mixer to work the butter into the dry ingredients. When you are done, the mixture should still have chunks of butter.

In a small bowl, whisk together the almond milk, egg, and vanilla extract (if using liquid sweetener, add it as well) until blended. Using a fork, stir the wet ingredients into the dry ingredients until large clumps form. Add the cinnamon and use your hands to swirl it into the dough.

Form the dough into sixteen 1-inch balls and place them on the prepared pan, spacing them about ½ inch apart. (If you're using a smaller air fryer, work in batches if necessary.) Bake in the air fryer until golden, 10 to 13 minutes. Remove from the air fryer and let cool on the pan for at least 5 minutes.

While the biscuits bake, make the glaze: Place the powdered sweetener in a small bowl and slowly stir in the heavy cream with a fork.

When the biscuits have cooled somewhat, dip the tops into the glaze, allow it to dry a bit, and then dip again for a thick glaze.

Serve warm or at room temperature. Store unglazed biscuits in an airtight container in the refrigerator for up to 3 days or in the freezer for up to a month. Reheat in a preheated 176ºC air fryer for 5 minutes, or until warmed through, and dip in the glaze as instructed above.

Bacon, Egg, and Cheese Roll Ups

Prep time: 15 minutes | Cook time: 15 minutes | Serves 4

2 tablespoons unsalted butter	12 slices bacon
60 ml chopped onion	235 ml shredded sharp Cheddar
½ medium green pepper, seeded	cheese
and chopped	120 ml mild salsa, for dipping
6 large eggs	

In a medium skillet over medium heat, melt butter. Add onion and pepper to the skillet and sauté until fragrant and onions are translucent, about 3 minutes.

Whisk eggs in a small bowl and pour into skillet. Scramble eggs with onions and peppers until fluffy and fully cooked, about 5 minutes. Remove from heat and set aside.

On work surface, place three slices of bacon side by side, overlapping about ¼ inch. Place 60 ml scrambled eggs in a heap on the side closest to you and sprinkle 60 ml cheese on top of the eggs. Tightly roll the bacon around the eggs and secure the seam with a toothpick if necessary. Place each roll into the air fryer basket.

Adjust the temperature to 176ºC and air fry for 15 minutes. Rotate the rolls halfway through the cooking time.

Bacon will be brown and crispy when completely cooked. Serve immediately with salsa for dipping.

All-in-One Toast

Prep time: 10 minutes | Cook time: 10 minutes | Serves 1

1 strip bacon, diced	pepper, to taste
1 slice 1-inch thick bread	60 ml grated Monterey Jack or
1 egg	Chedday cheese
Salt and freshly ground black	

Preheat the air fryer to 204ºC.

Air fry the bacon for 3 minutes, shaking the basket once or twice while it cooks. Remove the bacon to a paper towel lined plate and set aside.

Use a sharp paring knife to score a large circle in the middle of the slice of bread, cutting halfway through, but not all the way through to the cutting board. Press down on the circle in the center of the bread slice to create an indentation.

Transfer the slice of bread, hole side up, to the air fryer basket. Crack the egg into the center of the bread, and season with salt and pepper.

Adjust the air fryer temperature to 192ºC and air fry for 5 minutes. Sprinkle the grated cheese around the edges of the bread, leaving the center of the yolk uncovered, and top with the cooked bacon. Press the cheese and bacon into the bread lightly to help anchor it to the bread and prevent it from blowing around in the air fryer.

Air fry for one or two more minutes, just to melt the cheese and finish cooking the egg. Serve immediately.

Breakfast Sammies

Prep time: 15 minutes | Cook time: 20 minutes | Serves 5

Biscuits:
6 large egg whites
475 ml blanched almond flour, plus more if needed
1½ teaspoons baking powder
½ teaspoon fine sea salt
60 ml (½ stick) very cold unsalted butter (or lard for dairy-free), cut into ¼-inch

pieces
Eggs:
5 large eggs
½ teaspoon fine sea salt
¼ teaspoon ground black pepper
5 (30 g) slices Cheddar cheese (omit for dairy-free)
10 thin slices ham

Spray the air fryer basket with avocado oil. Preheat the air fryer to 176ºC. Grease two pie pans or two baking pans that will fit inside your air fryer.
Make the biscuits: In a medium-sized bowl, whip the egg whites with a hand mixer until very stiff. Set aside.
In a separate medium-sized bowl, stir together the almond flour, baking powder, and salt until well combined. Cut in the butter. Gently fold the flour mixture into the egg whites with a rubber spatula. If the dough is too wet to form into mounds, add a few tablespoons of almond flour until the dough holds together well.
Using a large spoon, divide the dough into 5 equal portions and drop them about 1 inch apart on one of the greased pie pans. (If you're using a smaller air fryer, work in batches if necessary.) Place the pan in the air fryer and bake for 11 to 14 minutes, until the biscuits are golden brown. Remove from the air fryer and set aside to cool.
Make the eggs: Set the air fryer to 192ºC. Crack the eggs into the remaining greased pie pan and sprinkle with the salt and pepper. Place the eggs in the air fryer to bake for 5 minutes, or until they are cooked to your liking.
Open the air fryer and top each egg yolk with a slice of cheese (if using). Bake for another minute, or until the cheese is melted.
Once the biscuits are cool, slice them in half lengthwise. Place 1 cooked egg topped with cheese and 2 slices of ham in each biscuit. Store leftover biscuits, eggs, and ham in separate airtight containers in the fridge for up to 3 days. Reheat the biscuits and eggs on a baking sheet in a preheated 176ºC air fryer for 5 minutes, or until warmed through.

Cheddar-Ham-Corn Muffins

Prep time: 10 minutes | Cook time: 6 to 8 minutes per batch | Makes 8 muffins

180 ml cornmeal/polenta
60 ml flour
1½ teaspoons baking powder
¼ teaspoon salt
1 egg, beaten
2 tablespoons rapeseed oil
120 ml milk

120 ml shredded sharp Cheddar cheese
120 ml diced ham
8 foil muffin cups, liners removed and sprayed with cooking spray

Preheat the air fryer to 200ºC.
In a medium bowl, stir together the cornmeal, flour, baking powder, and salt.
Add egg, oil, and milk to dry ingredients and mix well.
Stir in shredded cheese and diced ham.

Divide batter among the muffin cups.
Place 4 filled muffin cups in air fryer basket and bake for 5 minutes.
Reduce temperature to 166ºC and bake for 1 to 2 minutes or until toothpick inserted in center of muffin comes out clean.
Repeat steps 6 and 7 to cook remaining muffins.

Oat and Chia Porridge

Prep time: 10 minutes | Cook time: 5 minutes | Serves 4

2 tablespoons peanut butter
4 tablespoons honey
1 tablespoon butter, melted

1 L milk
475 ml oats
235 ml chia seeds

Preheat the air fryer to 200ºC.
Put the peanut butter, honey, butter, and milk in a bowl and stir to mix. Add the oats and chia seeds and stir.
Transfer the mixture to a bowl and bake in the air fryer for 5 minutes. Give another stir before serving.

Baked Egg and Mushroom Cups

Prep time: 5 minutes | Cook time: 15 minutes | Serves 6

Olive oil cooking spray
6 large eggs
1 garlic clove, minced
½ teaspoon salt
½ teaspoon black pepper

Pinch red pepper flakes
230 g baby mushrooms, sliced
235 ml fresh baby spinach
2 spring onions, white parts and green parts, diced

Preheat the air fryer to 160ºC. Lightly coat the inside of six silicone muffin cups or a six-cup muffin tin with olive oil cooking spray.
In a large bowl, beat the eggs, garlic, salt, pepper, and red pepper flakes for 1 to 2 minutes, or until well combined.
Fold in the mushrooms, spinach, and spring onions.
Divide the mixture evenly among the muffin cups.
Place into the air fryer and bake for 12 to 15 minutes, or until the eggs are set.
Remove and allow to cool for 5 minutes before serving.

BLT Breakfast Wrap

Prep time: 5 minutes | Cook time: 10 minutes | Serves 4

230 g reduced-salt bacon
8 tablespoons mayonnaise
8 large romaine lettuce leaves

4 plum tomatoes, sliced
Salt and freshly ground black pepper, to taste

Arrange the bacon in a single layer in the air fryer basket. (It's OK if the bacon sits a bit on the sides.) Set the air fryer to 176ºC and air fry for 10 minutes. Check for crispiness and air fry for 2 to 3 minutes longer if needed. Cook in batches, if necessary, and drain the grease in between batches.
Spread 1 tablespoon of mayonnaise on each of the lettuce leaves and top with the tomatoes and cooked bacon. Season to taste with salt and freshly ground black pepper. Roll the lettuce leaves as you would a burrito, securing with a toothpick if desired.

Tomato and Cheddar Rolls

Prep time: 30 minutes | Cook time: 25 minutes | Makes 12 rolls

4 plum tomatoes	2 teaspoons sugar
½ clove garlic, minced	2 teaspoons salt
1 tablespoon olive oil	1 tablespoon olive oil
¼ teaspoon dried thyme	235 ml grated Cheddar cheese,
Salt and freshly ground black pepper, to taste	plus more for sprinkling at the end
1 L plain flour	350 ml water
1 teaspoon active dry yeast	

Cut the tomatoes in half, remove the seeds with your fingers and transfer to a bowl. Add the garlic, olive oil, dried thyme, salt and freshly ground black pepper and toss well.
Preheat the air fryer to 200ºC.
Place the tomatoes, cut side up in the air fryer basket and air fry for 10 minutes. The tomatoes should just start to brown. Shake the basket to redistribute the tomatoes, and air fry for another 5 to 10 minutes at 166ºC until the tomatoes are no longer juicy. Let the tomatoes cool and then rough chop them.
Combine the flour, yeast, sugar and salt in the bowl of a stand mixer. Add the olive oil, chopped roasted tomatoes and Cheddar cheese to the flour mixture and start to mix using the dough hook attachment. As you're mixing, add 300 ml of the water, mixing until the dough comes together. Continue to knead the dough with the dough hook for another 10 minutes, adding enough water to the dough to get it to the right consistency.
Transfer the dough to an oiled bowl, cover with a clean kitchen towel and let it rest and rise until it has doubled in volume, about 1 to 2 hours. Then, divide the dough into 12 equal portions. Roll each portion of dough into a ball. Lightly coat each dough ball with oil and let the dough balls rest and rise a second time, covered lightly with plastic wrap for 45 minutes. (Alternately, you can place the rolls in the refrigerator overnight and take them out 2 hours before you bake them.)
Preheat the air fryer to 182ºC.
Spray the dough balls and the air fryer basket with a little olive oil. Place three rolls at a time in the basket and bake for 10 minutes. Add a little grated Cheddar cheese on top of the rolls for the last 2 minutes of air frying for an attractive finish.

Canadian Bacon Muffin Sandwiches

Prep time: 5 minutes | Cook time: 8 minutes | Serves 4

4 English muffins, split	4 slices cheese
8 slices back bacon	Cooking spray

Preheat the air fryer to 188ºC.
Make the sandwiches: Top each of 4 muffin halves with 2 slices of bacon, 1 slice of cheese, and finish with the remaining muffin half.
Put the sandwiches in the air fryer basket and spritz the tops with cooking spray.
Bake for 4 minutes. Flip the sandwiches and bake for another 4 minutes.
Divide the sandwiches among four plates and serve warm.

Homemade Cherry Breakfast Tarts

Prep time: 15 minutes | Cook time: 20 minutes | Serves 6

Tarts:	Frosting:
2 refrigerated piecrusts	120 ml vanilla yoghurt
80 ml cherry preserves	30 g cream cheese
1 teaspoon cornflour	1 teaspoon stevia
Cooking oil	Rainbow sprinkles

Make the Tarts Place the piecrusts on a flat surface. Using a knife or pizza cutter, cut each piecrust into 3 rectangles, for 6 total. (I discard the unused dough left from slicing the edges.)
In a small bowl, combine the preserves and cornflour. Mix well.
Scoop 1 tablespoon of the preserves mixture onto the top half of each piece of piecrust.
Fold the bottom of each piece up to close the tart. Using the back of a fork, press along the edges of each tart to seal.
Spray the breakfast tarts with cooking oil and place them in the air fryer. I do not recommend stacking the breakfast tarts. They will stick together if stacked. You may need to prepare them in two batches. Bake at 375ºF for 10 minutes.
Allow the breakfast tarts to cool fully before removing from the air fryer.
If necessary, repeat steps 5 and 6 for the remaining breakfast tarts.
Make the Frosting
In a small bowl, combine the yoghurt, cream cheese, and stevia. Mix well.
Spread the breakfast tarts with frosting and top with sprinkles, and serve.

Baked Potato Breakfast Boats

Prep time: 10 minutes | Cook time: 20 minutes | Serves 4

2 large white potatoes, scrubbed	2 tablespoons chopped, cooked bacon
Olive oil	235 ml shredded Cheddar cheese
Salt and freshly ground black pepper, to taste	
4 eggs	

Poke holes in the potatoes with a fork and microwave on full power for 5 minutes.
Turn potatoes over and cook an additional 3 to 5 minutes, or until the potatoes are fork-tender.
Cut the potatoes in half lengthwise and use a spoon to scoop out the inside of the potato. Be careful to leave a layer of potato so that it makes a sturdy "boat."
Preheat the air fryer to 176ºC.
Lightly spray the air fryer basket with olive oil. Spray the skin side of the potatoes with oil and sprinkle with salt and pepper to taste.
Place the potato skins in the air fryer basket, skin-side down. Crack one egg into each potato skin.
Sprinkle ½ tablespoon of bacon pieces and 60 ml shredded cheese on top of each egg. Sprinkle with salt and pepper to taste.
Air fry until the yolk is slightly runny, 5 to 6 minutes, or until the yolk is fully cooked, 7 to 10 minutes.

Spinach and Bacon Roll-ups

Prep time: 5 minutes | Cook time: 8 to 9 minutes | Serves 4

4 flour tortillas (6- or 7-inch size)
4 slices Swiss cheese
235 ml baby spinach leaves
4 slices turkey bacon
Special Equipment:
4 toothpicks, soak in water for at least 30 minutes

Preheat the air fryer to 200ºC.
On a clean work surface, top each tortilla with one slice of cheese and 60 ml spinach, then tightly roll them up.
Wrap each tortilla with a strip of turkey bacon and secure with a toothpick.
Arrange the roll-ups in the air fryer basket, leaving space between each roll-up.
Air fry for 4 minutes. Flip the roll-ups with tongs and rearrange them for more even cooking. Air fry for another 4 to 5 minutes until the bacon is crisp.
Rest for 5 minutes and remove the toothpicks before serving.

Pancake Cake

Prep time: 10 minutes | Cook time: 7 minutes | Serves 4

120 ml blanched finely ground almond flour
60 ml powdered erythritol
½ teaspoon baking powder
2 tablespoons unsalted butter,
softened
1 large egg
½ teaspoon unflavoured gelatin
½ teaspoon vanilla extract
½ teaspoon ground cinnamon

In a large bowl, mix almond flour, erythritol, and baking powder. Add butter, egg, gelatin, vanilla, and cinnamon. Pour into a round baking pan.
Place pan into the air fryer basket.
Adjust the temperature to 150ºC and set the timer for 7 minutes.
When the cake is completely cooked, a toothpick will come out clean. Cut cake into four and serve.

Bacon-and-Eggs Avocado

Prep time: 5 minutes | Cook time: 17 minutes | Serves 1

1 large egg
1 avocado, halved, peeled, and pitted
2 slices bacon
Fresh parsley, for serving (optional)
Sea salt flakes, for garnish (optional)

Spray the air fryer basket with avocado oil. Preheat the air fryer to 160ºC. Fill a small bowl with cool water.
Soft-boil the egg: Place the egg in the air fryer basket. Air fry for 6 minutes for a soft yolk or 7 minutes for a cooked yolk. Transfer the egg to the bowl of cool water and let sit for 2 minutes. Peel and set aside.
Use a spoon to carve out extra space in the center of the avocado halves until the cavities are big enough to fit the soft-boiled egg.
Place the soft-boiled egg in the center of one half of the avocado and replace the other half of the avocado on top, so the avocado appears whole on the outside.
Starting at one end of the avocado, wrap the bacon around the avocado to completely cover it. Use toothpicks to hold the bacon in place.
Place the bacon-wrapped avocado in the air fryer basket and air fry for 5 minutes. Flip the avocado over and air fry for another 5 minutes, or until the bacon is cooked to your liking. Serve on a bed of fresh parsley, if desired, and sprinkle with salt flakes, if desired. Best served fresh. Store extras in an airtight container in the fridge for up to 4 days. Reheat in a preheated 160ºC air fryer for 4 minutes, or until heated through.

Spinach and Mushroom Mini Quiche

Prep time: 10 minutes | Cook time: 15 minutes | Serves 4

1 teaspoon olive oil, plus more for spraying
235 ml coarsely chopped mushrooms
235 ml fresh baby spinach, shredded
4 eggs, beaten
120 ml shredded Cheddar cheese
120 ml shredded Mozzarella cheese
¼ teaspoon salt
¼ teaspoon black pepper

Spray 4 silicone baking cups with olive oil and set aside.
In a medium sauté pan over medium heat, warm 1 teaspoon of olive oil. Add the mushrooms and sauté until soft, 3 to 4 minutes.
Add the spinach and cook until wilted, 1 to 2 minutes. Set aside.
In a medium bowl, whisk together the eggs, Cheddar cheese, Mozzarella cheese, salt, and pepper.
Gently fold the mushrooms and spinach into the egg mixture.
Pour ¼ of the mixture into each silicone baking cup.
Place the baking cups into the air fryer basket and air fry at 176ºC for 5 minutes. Stir the mixture in each ramekin slightly and air fry until the egg has set, an additional 3 to 5 minutes.

Buffalo Chicken Breakfast Muffins

Prep time: 7 minutes | Cook time: 13 to 16 minutes | Serves 10

170 g shredded cooked chicken
85 g blue cheese, crumbled
2 tablespoons unsalted butter, melted
80 ml Buffalo hot sauce, such as Frank's RedHot
1 teaspoon minced garlic
6 large eggs
Sea salt and freshly ground black pepper, to taste
Avocado oil spray

In a large bowl, stir together the chicken, blue cheese, melted butter, hot sauce, and garlic.
In a medium bowl or large liquid measuring cup, beat the eggs. Season with salt and pepper.
Spray 10 silicone muffin cups with oil. Divide the chicken mixture among the cups, and pour the egg mixture over top.
Place the cups in the air fryer and set to 150ºC. Bake for 13 to 16 minutes, until the muffins are set and cooked through. (Depending on the size of your air fryer, you may need to cook the muffins in batches.)

Wholemeal Blueberry Muffins

Prep time: 10 minutes | Cook time: 15 minutes | Serves 6

Olive oil cooking spray
120 ml unsweetened applesauce
60 ml honey
120 ml non-fat plain Greek yoghurt
1 teaspoon vanilla extract
1 large egg
350 ml plus 1 tablespoon wholemeal, divided
½ teaspoon baking soda
½ teaspoon baking powder
½ teaspoon salt
120 ml blueberries, fresh or frozen

Preheat the air fryer to 182°C. Lightly coat the inside of six silicone muffin cups or a six-cup muffin tin with olive oil cooking spray.

In a large bowl, combine the applesauce, honey, yoghurt, vanilla, and egg and mix until smooth.

Sift in 350 ml of the flour, the baking soda, baking powder, and salt into the wet mixture, then stir until just combined.

In a small bowl, toss the blueberries with the remaining 1 tablespoon flour, then fold the mixture into the muffin batter.

Divide the mixture evenly among the prepared muffin cups and place into the basket of the air fryer. Bake for 12 to 15 minutes, or until golden brown on top and a toothpick inserted into the middle of one of the muffins comes out clean.

Allow to cool for 5 minutes before serving.

Strawberry Toast

Prep time: 10 minutes | Cook time: 8 minutes | Makes 4 toasts

4 slices bread, ½-inch thick
Butter-flavoured cooking spray
235 ml sliced strawberries
1 teaspoon sugar

Spray one side of each bread slice with butter-flavored cooking spray. Lay slices sprayed side down.

Divide the strawberries among the bread slices.

Sprinkle evenly with the sugar and place in the air fryer basket in a single layer.

Air fry at 200°C for 8 minutes. The bottom should look brown and crisp and the top should look glazed.

Sausage and Egg Breakfast Burrito

Prep time: 5 minutes | Cook time: 30 minutes | Serves 6

6 eggs
Salt and pepper, to taste
Cooking oil
120 ml chopped red pepper
120 ml chopped green pepper
230 g chicken sausage meat
(removed from casings)
120 ml salsa
6 medium (8-inch) flour tortillas
120 ml shredded Cheddar cheese

In a medium bowl, whisk the eggs. Add salt and pepper to taste.

Place a skillet on medium-high heat. Spray with cooking oil. Add the eggs. Scramble for 2 to 3 minutes, until the eggs are fluffy. Remove the eggs from the skillet and set aside.

If needed, spray the skillet with more oil. Add the chopped red and green bell peppers. Cook for 2 to 3 minutes, until the peppers are soft.

Add the sausage meat to the skillet. Break the sausage into smaller pieces using a spatula or spoon. Cook for 3 to 4 minutes, until the sausage is brown.

Add the salsa and scrambled eggs. Stir to combine. Remove the skillet from heat.

Spoon the mixture evenly onto the tortillas.

To form the burritos, fold the sides of each tortilla in toward the middle and then roll up from the bottom. You can secure each burrito with a toothpick. Or you can moisten the outside edge of the tortilla with a small amount of water. I prefer to use a cooking brush, but you can also dab with your fingers.

Spray the burritos with cooking oil and place them in the air fryer. Do not stack. Cook the burritos in batches if they do not all fit in the basket. Air fry at 204°C for 8 minutes.

Open the air fryer and flip the burritos. Cook for an additional 2 minutes or until crisp.

1If necessary, repeat steps 8 and 9 for the remaining burritos.

1Sprinkle the Cheddar cheese over the burritos. Cool before serving.

Chapter 3 Vegetarian Mains

Chapter 3 Vegetarian Mains

Spaghetti Squash Alfredo

Prep time: 10 minutes | Cook time: 15 minutes | Serves 2

½ large cooked spaghetti squash
2 tablespoons salted butter, melted
120 ml low-carb Alfredo sauce
60 ml grated vegetarian Parmesan cheese
½ teaspoon garlic powder
1 teaspoon dried parsley
¼ teaspoon ground peppercorn
120 ml shredded Italian blend cheese

Using a fork, remove the strands of spaghetti squash from the shell.
Place into a large bowl with butter and Alfredo sauce.
Sprinkle with Parmesan, garlic powder, parsley, and peppercorn.
Pour into a 1 L round baking dish and top with shredded cheese.
Place dish into the air fryer basket.
Adjust the temperature to 160°C and bake for 15 minutes. When finished, cheese will be golden and bubbling.
Serve immediately.

Crustless Spinach Cheese Pie

Prep time: 10 minutes | Cook time: 20 minutes | Serves 4

6 large eggs
60 ml double cream
235 ml frozen chopped spinach, drained
235 ml shredded sharp Cheddar cheese
60 ml diced brown onion

In a medium bowl, whisk eggs and add cream.
Add remaining ingredients to bowl.
Pour into a round baking dish.
Place into the air fryer basket.
Adjust the temperature to 160°C and bake for 20 minutes. Eggs will be firm and slightly browned when cooked.
Serve immediately.

White Cheddar and Mushroom Soufflés

Prep time: 15 minutes | Cook time: 12 minutes | Serves 4

3 large eggs, whites and yolks separated
120 ml extra mature white Cheddar cheese
85 g soft white cheese
¼ teaspoon cream of tartar
¼ teaspoon salt
¼ teaspoon ground black pepper
120 ml chestnut mushrooms, sliced

In a large bowl, whip egg whites until stiff peaks form, about 2 minutes.
In a separate large bowl, beat Cheddar, egg yolks, soft white cheese, cream of tartar, salt, and pepper together until combined.
Fold egg whites into cheese mixture, being careful not to stir.

Fold in mushrooms, then pour mixture evenly into four ungreased ramekins.
Place ramekins into air fryer basket.
Adjust the temperature to 176°C and bake for 12 minutes. Eggs will be browned on the top and firm in the centre when done.
Serve warm.

Crispy Fried Okra with Chilli

Prep time: 5 minutes | Cook time: 10 minutes | Serves 4

3 tablespoons sour cream
2 tablespoons flour
2 tablespoons semolina
½ teaspoon red chilli powder
Salt and black pepper, to taste
450 g okra, halved
Cooking spray

Preheat the air fryer to 204°C.
Spray the air fryer basket with cooking spray.
In a shallow bowl, place the sour cream.
In another shallow bowl, thoroughly combine the flour, semolina, red chilli powder, salt, and pepper.
Dredge the okra in the sour cream, then roll in the flour mixture until evenly coated.
Arrange the okra in the air fryer basket and air fry for 10 minutes, flipping the okra halfway through, or until golden brown and crispy.
Cool for 5 minutes before serving.

Super Vegetable Burger

Prep time: 15 minutes | Cook time: 12 minutes | Serves 8

230 g cauliflower, steamed and diced, rinsed and drained
2 teaspoons coconut oil, melted
2 teaspoons minced garlic
60 ml desiccated coconut
120 ml oats
3 tablespoons flour
1 tablespoon flaxseeds plus 3
tablespoons water, divided
1 teaspoon mustard powder
2 teaspoons thyme
2 teaspoons parsley
2 teaspoons chives
Salt and ground black pepper, to taste
235 ml breadcrumbs

Preheat the air fryer to 200°C.
Combine the cauliflower with all the ingredients, except for the breadcrumbs, incorporating everything well.
Using the hands, shape 8 equal-sized amounts of the mixture into burger patties.
Coat the patties in breadcrumbs before putting them in the air fryer basket in a single layer.
Air fry for 12 minutes or until crispy.
Serve hot.

Courgette and Spinach Croquettes

Prep time: 9 minutes | Cook time: 7 minutes | Serves 6

4 eggs, slightly beaten
120 ml almond flour
120 ml goat cheese, crumbled
1 teaspoon fine sea salt
4 garlic cloves, minced
235 ml baby spinach

120 ml Parmesan cheese, grated
⅓ teaspoon red pepper flakes
450 g courgette, peeled and grated
⅓ teaspoon dried dill weed

Thoroughly combine all ingredients in a bowl.
Now, roll the mixture to form small croquettes.
Air fry at 172°C for 7 minutes or until golden.
Taste, adjust for seasonings and serve warm.

Super Veg Rolls

Prep time: 20 minutes | Cook time: 10 minutes | Serves 6

2 potatoes, mashed
60 ml peas
60 ml mashed carrots
1 small cabbage, sliced
60 ml beans
2 tablespoons sweetcorn

1 small onion, chopped
120 ml breadcrumbs
1 packet spring roll sheets
120 ml cornflour slurry (mix 40 ml cornflour with 80 ml water)

Preheat the air fryer to 200°C.
Boil all the vegetables in water over a low heat.
Rinse and allow to dry.
Unroll the spring roll sheets and spoon equal amounts of vegetable onto the centre of each one.
Fold into spring rolls and coat each one with the slurry and breadcrumbs.
Air fry the rolls in the preheated air fryer for 10 minutes.
Serve warm.

Whole Roasted Lemon Cauliflower

Prep time: 5 minutes | Cook time: 15 minutes | Serves 4

1 medium head cauliflower
2 tablespoons salted butter, melted

1 medium lemon
½ teaspoon garlic powder
1 teaspoon dried parsley

Remove the leaves from the head of cauliflower and brush it with melted butter.
Cut the lemon in half and zest one half onto the cauliflower.
Squeeze the juice of the zested lemon half and pour it over the cauliflower.
Sprinkle with garlic powder and parsley.
Place cauliflower head into the air fryer basket.
Adjust the temperature to 176°C and air fry for 15 minutes.
Check cauliflower every 5 minutes to avoid overcooking.
It should be fork tender.
To serve, squeeze juice from other lemon half over cauliflower.
Serve immediately.

Cheese Stuffed Courgette

Prep time: 20 minutes | Cook time: 8 minutes | Serves 4

1 large courgette, cut into four pieces
2 tablespoons olive oil
235 ml Ricotta cheese, room temperature
2 tablespoons spring onions, chopped
1 heaping tablespoon fresh

parsley, roughly chopped
1 heaping tablespoon coriander, minced
60 g Cheddar cheese, preferably freshly grated
1 teaspoon celery seeds
½ teaspoon salt
½ teaspoon garlic pepper

Cook your courgette in the air fryer basket for approximately 10 minutes at 176°C.
Check for doneness and cook for 2-3 minutes longer if needed.
Meanwhile, make the stuffing by mixing the other items.
When your courgette is thoroughly cooked, open them up.
Divide the stuffing among all courgette pieces and bake an additional 5 minutes.

Air Fryer Veggies with Halloumi

Prep time: 5 minutes | Cook time: 14 minutes | Serves 2

2 courgettes, cut into even chunks
1 large aubergine, peeled, cut into chunks
1 large carrot, cut into chunks

170 g halloumi cheese, cubed
2 teaspoons olive oil
Salt and black pepper, to taste
1 teaspoon dried mixed herbs

Preheat the air fryer to 172°C.
Combine the courgettes, aubergine, carrot, cheese, olive oil, salt, and pepper in a large bowl and toss to coat well.
Spread the mixture evenly in the air fryer basket and air fry for 14 minutes until crispy and golden, shaking the basket once during cooking.
Serve topped with mixed herbs.

Air Fryer Winter Vegetables

Prep time: 5 minutes | Cook time: 16 minutes | Serves 2

1 parsnip, sliced
235 ml sliced butternut squash
1 small red onion, cut into wedges
½ chopped celery stalk

1 tablespoon chopped fresh thyme
2 teaspoons olive oil
Salt and black pepper, to taste

Preheat the air fryer to 192°C.
Toss all the ingredients in a large bowl until the vegetables are well coated.
Transfer the vegetables to the air fryer basket and air fry for 16 minutes, shaking the basket halfway through, or until the vegetables are golden brown and tender.
Remove from the basket and serve warm.

Chapter 4 Beef, Pork, and Lamb

Mushroom in Bacon-Wrapped Filets Mignons

Prep time: 10 minutes | Cook time: 13 minutes per batch | Serves 8

ried porcini mushrooms
poon granulated white
poon salt

½ teaspoon ground white pepper
8 (110 g) filets mignons or beef fillet steaks
8 thin-cut bacon strips

at the air fryer to 204ºC.
e mushrooms, sugar, salt, and white pepper in a spice grinder
ind to combine.
clean work surface, rub the filets mignons with the mushroom
re, then wrap each filet with a bacon strip. Secure with
icks if necessary.
ge the bacon-wrapped filets mignons in the preheated air fryer
t, seam side down. Work in batches to avoid overcrowding.
y for 13 minutes or until medium rare. Flip the filets halfway
gh.
immediately.

ice-Coated Steaks with Cucumber and Snap Pea Salad

Prep time: 15 minutes | Cook time: 15 to 20 minutes | Serves 4

0 g) boneless rump steak,
ned and halved crosswise
aspoons chili powder
aspoons ground cumin
spoon ground coriander
spoon cayenne pepper
spoon ground cinnamon
aspoons plus ⅛ teaspoon
divided
spoon plus ⅛ teaspoon
d black pepper, divided
spoon plus 1½ tablespoons
-virgin olive oil, divided

3 tablespoons mayonnaise
1½ tablespoons white wine vinegar
1 tablespoon minced fresh dill
1 small garlic clove, minced
230 g sugar snap peas, strings removed and cut in half on bias
½ cucumber, halved lengthwise and sliced thin
2 radishes, trimmed, halved and sliced thin
475 ml baby rocket

at the air fryer to 204ºC.
bowl, mix chili powder, cumin, coriander, cayenne pepper,
amon, 1¼ teaspoons salt and ½ teaspoon pepper until well
ined.
the steaks to another bowl and pat dry with paper towels.
h with 1 teaspoon oil and transfer to the bowl of spice mixture.
over to coat thoroughly.
nge the coated steaks in the air fryer basket, spaced evenly
t. Air fry for 15 to 20 minutes, or until an instant-read
nometer inserted in the thickest part of the meat registers at
64ºC. Flip halfway through to ensure even cooking.

Transfer the steaks to a clean work surface and wrap with aluminum foil. Let stand while preparing salad.
Make the salad: In a large bowl, stir together 1½ tablespoons olive oil, mayonnaise, vinegar, dill, garlic, ⅛ teaspoon salt, and ⅛ teaspoon pepper. Add snap peas, cucumber, radishes and rocket. Toss to blend well.
Slice the steaks and serve with the salad.

Bacon Wrapped Pork with Apple Gravy

Prep time: 10 minutes | Cook time: 25 minutes | Serves 4

Pork:
1 tablespoons Dijon mustard
1 pork tenderloin
3 strips bacon
Apple Gravy:
3 tablespoons ghee, divided

1 small shallot, chopped
2 apples
1 tablespoon almond flour
235 ml vegetable stock
½ teaspoon Dijon mustard

Preheat the air fryer to 182ºC.
Spread Dijon mustard all over tenderloin and wrap with strips of bacon.
Put into air fryer and air fry for 12 minutes. Use a meat thermometer to check for doneness.
To make sauce, heat 1 tablespoons of ghee in a pan and add shallots. Cook for 1 minute.
Then add apples, cooking for 4 minutes until softened.
Add flour and 2 tablespoons of ghee to make a roux. Add stock and mustard, stirring well to combine.
When sauce starts to bubble, add 235 ml of sautéed apples, cooking until sauce thickens.
Once pork tenderloin is cooked, allow to sit 8 minutes to rest before slicing.
Serve topped with apple gravy.

Spinach and Mozzarella Steak Rolls

Prep time: 10 minutes | Cook time: 12 minutes | Makes 8 rolls

1 (450 g) bavette or skirt steak, butterflied
8 (30 g, ¼-inch-thick) slices low-moisture Mozzarella or

other melting cheese
235 ml fresh spinach leaves
½ teaspoon salt
¼ teaspoon ground black pepper

Place steak on a large plate. Place Mozzarella slices to cover steak, leaving 1-inch at the edges. Lay spinach leaves over cheese. Gently roll steak and tie with kitchen twine or secure with toothpicks. Carefully slice into eight pieces. Sprinkle each with salt and pepper. Place rolls into ungreased air fryer basket, cut side up. Adjust the temperature to 204ºC and air fry for 12 minutes. Steak rolls will be browned and cheese will be melted when done and have an internal temperature of at least 64ºC for medium steak and 82ºC for well-done steak. Serve warm.

Baked Turnip and Courgette

Prep time: 5 minutes | Cook time: 15 to 20 minutes | Serves 4

3 turnips, sliced
1 large courgette, sliced
1 large red onion, cut into rings

2 cloves garlic, crushed
1 tablespoon olive oil
Salt and black pepper, to taste

Preheat the air fryer to 166ºC.
Put the turnips, courgette, red onion, and garlic in a baking pan.
Drizzle the olive oil over the top and sprinkle with the salt and pepper.
Place the baking pan in the preheated air fryer and bake for 15 to 20 minutes, or until the vegetables are tender.
Remove from the basket and serve on a plate.

Vegetable Burgers

Prep time: 10 minutes | Cook time: 12 minutes | Serves 4

227 g cremini or chestnut mushrooms
2 large egg yolks
½ medium courgette, trimmed and chopped
60 ml peeled and chopped

brown onion
1 clove garlic, peeled and finely minced
½ teaspoon salt
¼ teaspoon ground black pepper

Place all ingredients into a food processor and pulse twenty times until finely chopped and combined.
Separate mixture into four equal sections and press each into a burger shape.
Place burgers into ungreased air fryer basket.
Adjust the temperature to 192ºC and air fry for 12 minutes, turning burgers halfway through cooking. Burgers will be browned and firm when done.
Place burgers on a large plate and let cool 5 minutes before serving.

Baked Courgette

Prep time: 10 minutes | Cook time: 8 minutes | Serves 4

2 tablespoons salted butter
60 ml diced white onion
½ teaspoon minced garlic
120 ml double cream

60 g full fat soft white cheese
235 ml shredded extra mature Cheddar cheese
2 medium courgette, spiralized

In a large saucepan over medium heat, melt butter.
Add onion and sauté until it begins to soften, 1 to 3 minutes.
Add garlic and sauté for 30 seconds, then pour in cream and add soft white cheese.
Remove the pan from heat and stir in Cheddar.
Add the courgette and toss in the sauce, then put into a round baking dish.
Cover the dish with foil and place into the air fryer basket.
Adjust the temperature to 188ºC and set the timer for 8 minutes.
After 6 minutes remove the foil and let the top brown for remaining cooking time.
Stir and serve.

Mushroom and Pepper Pizza Squares

Prep time: 10 minutes | Cook time: 10 minutes | Serves 10

1 pizza dough, cut into squares
235 ml chopped oyster mushrooms
1 shallot, chopped

¼ red pepper, chopped
2 tablespoons parsley
Salt and ground black pepper, to taste

Preheat the air fryer to 204ºC.
In a bowl, combine the oyster mushrooms, shallot, pepper and parsley.
Sprinkle some salt and pepper as desired.
Spread this mixture on top of the pizza squares.
Bake in the air fryer for 10 minutes.
Serve warm.

Teriyaki Cauliflower

Prep time: 5 minutes | Cook time: 14 minutes | Serves 4

120 ml soy sauce
80 ml water
1 tablespoon brown sugar
1 teaspoon sesame oil
1 teaspoon cornflour

2 cloves garlic, chopped
½ teaspoon chilli powder
1 big cauliflower head, cut into florets

Preheat the air fryer to 172ºC.
Make the teriyaki sauce: In a small bowl, whisk together the soy sauce, water, brown sugar, sesame oil, cornflour, garlic, and chilli powder until well combined.
Place the cauliflower florets in a large bowl and drizzle the top with the prepared teriyaki sauce and toss to coat well.
Put the cauliflower florets in the air fryer basket and air fry for 14 minutes, shaking the basket halfway through, or until the cauliflower is crisp-tender.
Let the cauliflower cool for 5 minutes before serving.

Cheese Stuffed Peppers

Prep time: 20 minutes | Cook time: 15 minutes | Serves 2

1 red pepper, top and seeds removed
1 yellow pepper, top and seeds removed

Salt and pepper, to taste
235 ml Cottage cheese
4 tablespoons mayonnaise
2 pickles, chopped

Arrange the peppers in the lightly greased air fryer basket.
Cook in the preheated air fryer at 204ºC for 15 minutes, turning them over halfway through the cooking time.
Season with salt and pepper.
Then, in a mixing bowl, combine the soft white cheese with the mayonnaise and chopped pickles.
Stuff the pepper with the soft white cheese mixture and serve.
Enjoy!

Courgette-Ricotta Tart

Prep time: 15 minutes | Cook time: 60 minutes | Serves 6

120 ml grated Parmesan cheese, divided	1 courgette, thinly sliced (about 475 ml)
350 ml almond flour	235 ml ricotta cheese
1 tablespoon coconut flour	3 eggs
½ teaspoon garlic powder	2 tablespoons double cream
¾ teaspoon salt, divided	2 cloves garlic, minced
60 ml unsalted butter, melted	½ teaspoon dried tarragon

Preheat the air fryer to 166ºC.

Coat a round pan with olive oil and set aside.

In a large bowl, whisk 60 ml Parmesan with the almond flour, coconut flour, garlic powder, and ¼ teaspoon of the salt.

Stir in the melted butter until the dough resembles coarse crumbs.

Press the dough firmly into the bottom and up the sides of the prepared pan.

Air fry for 12 to 15 minutes until the crust begins to brown.

Let cool to room temperature.

Meanwhile, place the courgette in a colander and sprinkle with the remaining ½ teaspoon salt.

Toss gently to distribute the salt and let sit for 30 minutes.

Use paper towels to pat the courgette dry.

In a large bowl, whisk together the ricotta, eggs, double cream, garlic, and tarragon. Gently stir in the courgette slices.

Pour the cheese mixture into the cooled crust and sprinkle with the remaining 60 ml Parmesan.

Increase the air fryer to 176ºC.

Place the pan in the air fryer basket and air fry for 45 to 50 minutes, or until set and a tester inserted into the centre of the tart comes out clean.

Serve warm or at room temperature.

Greek Stuffed Aubergine

Prep time: 15 minutes | Cook time: 20 minutes | Serves 2

1 large aubergine	235 ml fresh spinach
2 tablespoons unsalted butter	2 tablespoons diced red pepper
¼ medium brown onion, diced	120 ml crumbled feta
60 ml chopped artichoke hearts	

Slice aubergine in half lengthwise and scoop out flesh, leaving enough inside for shell to remain intact.

Take aubergine that was scooped out, chop it, and set aside.

In a medium skillet over medium heat, add butter and onion.

Sauté until onions begin to soften, about 3 to 5 minutes.

Add chopped aubergine, artichokes, spinach, and pepper.

Continue cooking 5 minutes until peppers soften and spinach wilts.

Remove from the heat and gently fold in the feta.

Place filling into each aubergine shell and place into the air fryer basket.

Adjust the temperature to 160ºC and air fry for 20 minutes.

Aubergine will be tender when done.

Serve warm.

Broccoli-Cheese Fritters

Prep time: 5 minutes | Cook time: 20 to 25 minutes | Serves 4

235 ml broccoli florets	1 teaspoon garlic powder
235 ml shredded Mozzarella cheese	Salt and freshly ground black pepper, to taste
180 ml almond flour	2 eggs, lightly beaten
120 ml milled flaxseed, divided	120 ml ranch dressing
2 teaspoons baking powder	

Preheat the air fryer to 204ºC.

In a food processor fitted with a metal blade, pulse the broccoli until very finely chopped.

Transfer the broccoli to a large bowl and add the Mozzarella, almond flour, 60 ml milled flaxseed, baking powder, and garlic powder. Stir until thoroughly combined.

Season to taste with salt and black pepper

Add the eggs and stir again to form a sticky dough.

Shape the dough into 1¼-inch fritters.

Place the remaining 60 ml milled flaxseed in a shallow bowl and roll the fritters in the meal to form an even coating.

Working in batches if necessary, arrange the fritters in a single layer in the basket of the air fryer and spray generously with olive oil.

Pausing halfway through the cooking time to shake the basket, air fry for 20 to 25 minutes until the fritters are golden brown and crispy.

Serve with the ranch dressing for dipping.

Chapter 4 Beef, Pork, and L

Baked Turnip and Courgette

Prep time: 5 minutes | Cook time: 15 to 20 minutes | Serves 4

3 turnips, sliced	2 cloves garlic, crushed
1 large courgette, sliced	1 tablespoon olive oil
1 large red onion, cut into rings	Salt and black pepper, to taste

Preheat the air fryer to 166ºC.
Put the turnips, courgette, red onion, and garlic in a baking pan.
Drizzle the olive oil over the top and sprinkle with the salt and pepper.
Place the baking pan in the preheated air fryer and bake for 15 to 20 minutes, or until the vegetables are tender.
Remove from the basket and serve on a plate.

Vegetable Burgers

Prep time: 10 minutes | Cook time: 12 minutes | Serves 4

227 g cremini or chestnut mushrooms	brown onion
2 large egg yolks	1 clove garlic, peeled and finely minced
½ medium courgette, trimmed and chopped	½ teaspoon salt
60 ml peeled and chopped	¼ teaspoon ground black pepper

Place all ingredients into a food processor and pulse twenty times until finely chopped and combined.
Separate mixture into four equal sections and press each into a burger shape.
Place burgers into ungreased air fryer basket.
Adjust the temperature to 192ºC and air fry for 12 minutes, turning burgers halfway through cooking. Burgers will be browned and firm when done.
Place burgers on a large plate and let cool 5 minutes before serving.

Baked Courgette

Prep time: 10 minutes | Cook time: 8 minutes | Serves 4

2 tablespoons salted butter	60 g full fat soft white cheese
60 ml diced white onion	235 ml shredded extra mature Cheddar cheese
½ teaspoon minced garlic	
120 ml double cream	2 medium courgette, spiralized

In a large saucepan over medium heat, melt butter.
Add onion and sauté until it begins to soften, 1 to 3 minutes.
Add garlic and sauté for 30 seconds, then pour in cream and add soft white cheese.
Remove the pan from heat and stir in Cheddar.
Add the courgette and toss in the sauce, then put into a round baking dish.
Cover the dish with foil and place into the air fryer basket.
Adjust the temperature to 188ºC and set the timer for 8 minutes.
After 6 minutes remove the foil and let the top brown for remaining cooking time.
Stir and serve.

Mushroom and Pepper Pizza Squares

Prep time: 10 minutes | Cook time: 10 minutes | Serves 10

1 pizza dough, cut into squares	¼ red pepper, chopped
235 ml chopped oyster mushrooms	2 tablespoons parsley
1 shallot, chopped	Salt and ground black pepper, to taste

Preheat the air fryer to 204ºC.
In a bowl, combine the oyster mushrooms, shallot, pepper and parsley.
Sprinkle some salt and pepper as desired.
Spread this mixture on top of the pizza squares.
Bake in the air fryer for 10 minutes.
Serve warm.

Teriyaki Cauliflower

Prep time: 5 minutes | Cook time: 14 minutes | Serves 4

120 ml soy sauce	2 cloves garlic, chopped
80 ml water	½ teaspoon chilli powder
1 tablespoon brown sugar	1 big cauliflower head, cut into florets
1 teaspoon sesame oil	
1 teaspoon cornflour	

Preheat the air fryer to 172ºC.
Make the teriyaki sauce: In a small bowl, whisk together the soy sauce, water, brown sugar, sesame oil, cornflour, garlic, and chilli powder until well combined.
Place the cauliflower florets in a large bowl and drizzle the top with the prepared teriyaki sauce and toss to coat well.
Put the cauliflower florets in the air fryer basket and air fry for 14 minutes, shaking the basket halfway through, or until the cauliflower is crisp-tender.
Let the cauliflower cool for 5 minutes before serving.

Cheese Stuffed Peppers

Prep time: 20 minutes | Cook time: 15 minutes | Serves 2

1 red pepper, top and seeds removed	Salt and pepper, to taste
	235 ml Cottage cheese
1 yellow pepper, top and seeds removed	4 tablespoons mayonnaise
	2 pickles, chopped

Arrange the peppers in the lightly greased air fryer basket.
Cook in the preheated air fryer at 204ºC for 15 minutes, turning them over halfway through the cooking time.
Season with salt and pepper.
Then, in a mixing bowl, combine the soft white cheese with the mayonnaise and chopped pickles.
Stuff the pepper with the soft white cheese mixture and serve.
Enjoy!

Courgette-Ricotta Tart

Prep time: 15 minutes | Cook time: 60 minutes | Serves 6

120 ml grated Parmesan cheese, divided
350 ml almond flour
1 tablespoon coconut flour
½ teaspoon garlic powder
¾ teaspoon salt, divided
60 ml unsalted butter, melted

1 courgette, thinly sliced (about 475 ml)
235 ml ricotta cheese
3 eggs
2 tablespoons double cream
2 cloves garlic, minced
½ teaspoon dried tarragon

Preheat the air fryer to 166°C.
Coat a round pan with olive oil and set aside.
In a large bowl, whisk 60 ml Parmesan with the almond flour, coconut flour, garlic powder, and ¼ teaspoon of the salt.
Stir in the melted butter until the dough resembles coarse crumbs.
Press the dough firmly into the bottom and up the sides of the prepared pan.
Air fry for 12 to 15 minutes until the crust begins to brown.
Let cool to room temperature.
Meanwhile, place the courgette in a colander and sprinkle with the remaining ½ teaspoon salt.
Toss gently to distribute the salt and let sit for 30 minutes.
Use paper towels to pat the courgette dry.
In a large bowl, whisk together the ricotta, eggs, double cream, garlic, and tarragon. Gently stir in the courgette slices.
Pour the cheese mixture into the cooled crust and sprinkle with the remaining 60 ml Parmesan.
Increase the air fryer to 176°C.
Place the pan in the air fryer basket and air fry for 45 to 50 minutes, or until set and a tester inserted into the centre of the tart comes out clean.
Serve warm or at room temperature.

Greek Stuffed Aubergine

Prep time: 15 minutes | Cook time: 20 minutes | Serves 2

1 large aubergine
2 tablespoons unsalted butter
¼ medium brown onion, diced
60 ml chopped artichoke hearts

235 ml fresh spinach
2 tablespoons diced red pepper
120 ml crumbled feta

Slice aubergine in half lengthwise and scoop out flesh, leaving enough inside for shell to remain intact.
Take aubergine that was scooped out, chop it, and set aside.
In a medium skillet over medium heat, add butter and onion.
Sauté until onions begin to soften, about 3 to 5 minutes.
Add chopped aubergine, artichokes, spinach, and pepper.
Continue cooking 5 minutes until peppers soften and spinach wilts.
Remove from the heat and gently fold in the feta.
Place filling into each aubergine shell and place into the air fryer basket.
Adjust the temperature to 160°C and air fry for 20 minutes.
Aubergine will be tender when done.
Serve warm.

Broccoli-Cheese Fritters

Prep time: 5 minutes | Cook time: 20 to 25 minutes | Serves 4

235 ml broccoli florets
235 ml shredded Mozzarella cheese
180 ml almond flour
120 ml milled flaxseed, divided
2 teaspoons baking powder

1 teaspoon garlic powder
Salt and freshly ground black pepper, to taste
2 eggs, lightly beaten
120 ml ranch dressing

Preheat the air fryer to 204°C.
In a food processor fitted with a metal blade, pulse the broccoli until very finely chopped.
Transfer the broccoli to a large bowl and add the Mozzarella, almond flour, 60 ml milled flaxseed, baking powder, and garlic powder. Stir until thoroughly combined.
Season to taste with salt and black pepper.
Add the eggs and stir again to form a sticky dough.
Shape the dough into 1¼-inch fritters.
Place the remaining 60 ml milled flaxseed in a shallow bowl and roll the fritters in the meal to form an even coating.
Working in batches if necessary, arrange the fritters in a single layer in the basket of the air fryer and spray generously with olive oil.
Pausing halfway through the cooking time to shake the basket, air fry for 20 to 25 minutes until the fritters are golden brown and crispy.
Serve with the ranch dressing for dipping.

Chapter 4 Beef, Pork, and Lamb

Chapter 4 Beef, Pork, and Lamb

Mushroom in Bacon-Wrapped Filets Mignons

Prep time: 10 minutes | Cook time: 13 minutes per batch | Serves 8

30 g dried porcini mushrooms
½ teaspoon granulated white sugar
½ teaspoon salt
½ teaspoon ground white pepper
8 (110 g) filets mignons or beef fillet steaks
8 thin-cut bacon strips

Preheat the air fryer to 204ºC.
Put the mushrooms, sugar, salt, and white pepper in a spice grinder and grind to combine.
On a clean work surface, rub the filets mignons with the mushroom mixture, then wrap each filet with a bacon strip. Secure with toothpicks if necessary.
Arrange the bacon-wrapped filets mignons in the preheated air fryer basket, seam side down. Work in batches to avoid overcrowding.
Air fry for 13 minutes or until medium rare. Flip the filets halfway through.
Serve immediately.

Spice-Coated Steaks with Cucumber and Snap Pea Salad

Prep time: 15 minutes | Cook time: 15 to 20 minutes | Serves 4

1 (680 g) boneless rump steak, trimmed and halved crosswise
1½ teaspoons chili powder
1½ teaspoons ground cumin
¾ teaspoon ground coriander
⅛ teaspoon cayenne pepper
⅛ teaspoon ground cinnamon
1¼ teaspoons plus ⅛ teaspoon salt, divided
½ teaspoon plus ⅛ teaspoon ground black pepper, divided
1 teaspoon plus 1½ tablespoons extra-virgin olive oil, divided
3 tablespoons mayonnaise
1½ tablespoons white wine vinegar
1 tablespoon minced fresh dill
1 small garlic clove, minced
230 g sugar snap peas, strings removed and cut in half on bias
½ cucumber, halved lengthwise and sliced thin
2 radishes, trimmed, halved and sliced thin
475 ml baby rocket

Preheat the air fryer to 204ºC.
In a bowl, mix chili powder, cumin, coriander, cayenne pepper, cinnamon, 1¼ teaspoons salt and ½ teaspoon pepper until well combined.
Add the steaks to another bowl and pat dry with paper towels. Brush with 1 teaspoon oil and transfer to the bowl of spice mixture. Roll over to coat thoroughly.
Arrange the coated steaks in the air fryer basket, spaced evenly apart. Air fry for 15 to 20 minutes, or until an instant-read thermometer inserted in the thickest part of the meat registers at least 64ºC. Flip halfway through to ensure even cooking.
Transfer the steaks to a clean work surface and wrap with aluminum foil. Let stand while preparing salad.
Make the salad: In a large bowl, stir together 1½ tablespoons olive oil, mayonnaise, vinegar, dill, garlic, ⅛ teaspoon salt, and ⅛ teaspoon pepper. Add snap peas, cucumber, radishes and rocket. Toss to blend well.
Slice the steaks and serve with the salad.

Bacon Wrapped Pork with Apple Gravy

Prep time: 10 minutes | Cook time: 25 minutes | Serves 4

Pork:
1 tablespoons Dijon mustard
1 pork tenderloin
3 strips bacon
Apple Gravy:
3 tablespoons ghee, divided
1 small shallot, chopped
2 apples
1 tablespoon almond flour
235 ml vegetable stock
½ teaspoon Dijon mustard

Preheat the air fryer to 182ºC.
Spread Dijon mustard all over tenderloin and wrap with strips of bacon.
Put into air fryer and air fry for 12 minutes. Use a meat thermometer to check for doneness.
To make sauce, heat 1 tablespoons of ghee in a pan and add shallots. Cook for 1 minute.
Then add apples, cooking for 4 minutes until softened.
Add flour and 2 tablespoons of ghee to make a roux. Add stock and mustard, stirring well to combine.
When sauce starts to bubble, add 235 ml of sautéed apples, cooking until sauce thickens.
Once pork tenderloin is cooked, allow to sit 8 minutes to rest before slicing.
Serve topped with apple gravy.

Spinach and Mozzarella Steak Rolls

Prep time: 10 minutes | Cook time: 12 minutes | Makes 8 rolls

1 (450 g) bavette or skirt steak, butterflied
8 (30 g, ¼-inch-thick) slices low-moisture Mozzarella or
other melting cheese
235 ml fresh spinach leaves
½ teaspoon salt
¼ teaspoon ground black pepper

Place steak on a large plate. Place Mozzarella slices to cover steak, leaving 1-inch at the edges. Lay spinach leaves over cheese. Gently roll steak and tie with kitchen twine or secure with toothpicks. Carefully slice into eight pieces. Sprinkle each with salt and pepper. Place rolls into ungreased air fryer basket, cut side up. Adjust the temperature to 204ºC and air fry for 12 minutes. Steak rolls will be browned and cheese will be melted when done and have an internal temperature of at least 64ºC for medium steak and 82ºC for well-done steak. Serve warm.

Crescent Dogs

Prep time: 15 minutes | Cook time: 8 minutes | Makes 24 crescent dogs

Oil, for spraying
1 (230 g) can ready-to-bake croissants
8 slices Cheddar cheese, cut into thirds
24 cocktail sausages or 8 (6-inch) hot dogs, cut into thirds
2 tablespoons unsalted butter, melted
1 tablespoon sea salt flakes

Line the air fryer basket with parchment and spray lightly with oil.
Separate the dough into 8 triangles. Cut each triangle into 3 narrow triangles so you have 24 total triangles.
Top each triangle with 1 piece of cheese and 1 cocktail sausage.
Roll up each piece of dough, starting at the wide end and rolling toward the point.
Place the rolls in the prepared basket in a single layer. You may need to cook in batches, depending on the size of your air fryer.
Air fry at 164°C for 3 to 4 minutes, flip, and cook for another 3 to 4 minutes, or until golden brown.
Brush with the melted butter and sprinkle with the sea salt flakes before serving.

Ham Hock Mac and Cheese

Prep time: 20 minutes | Cook time: 25 minutes | Serves 4

2 large eggs, beaten
475 ml cottage cheese, full-fat or low-fat
475 ml grated sharp Cheddar cheese, divided
235 ml sour cream
½ teaspoon salt
1 teaspoon freshly ground black pepper
475 ml uncooked elbow macaroni
2 ham hocks (about 310 g each), meat removed and diced
1 to 2 tablespoons oil

In a large bowl, stir together the eggs, cottage cheese, 235 ml of the Cheddar cheese, sour cream, salt, and pepper.
Stir in the macaroni and the diced meat.
Preheat the air fryer to 182°C. Spritz a baking pan with oil.
Pour the macaroni mixture into the prepared pan, making sure all noodles are covered with sauce.
Cook for 12 minutes. Stir in the remaining 235 ml of Cheddar cheese, making sure all the noodles are covered with sauce. Cook for 13 minutes more, until the noodles are tender. Let rest for 5 minutes before serving.

Bacon-Wrapped Cheese Pork

Prep time: 10 minutes | Cook time: 20 minutes | Serves 4

4 (1-inch-thick) boneless pork chops
2 (150 g) packages Boursin
cheese
8 slices thin-cut bacon

Spray the air fryer basket with avocado oil. Preheat the air fryer to 204°C.
Place one of the chops on a cutting board. With a sharp knife held parallel to the cutting board, make a 1-inch-wide incision on the top edge of the chop. Carefully cut into the chop to form a large pocket, leaving a ½-inch border along the sides and bottom. Repeat with the other 3 chops.
Snip the corner of a large resealable plastic bag to form a ¾-inch hole. Place the Boursin cheese in the bag and pipe the cheese into the pockets in the chops, dividing the cheese evenly among them.
Wrap 2 slices of bacon around each chop and secure the ends with toothpicks. Place the bacon-wrapped chops in the air fryer basket and cook for 10 minutes, then flip the chops and cook for another 8 to 10 minutes, until the bacon is crisp, the chops are cooked through, and the internal temperature reaches 64°C.
Store leftovers in an airtight container in the refrigerator for up to 3 days. Reheat in a preheated 204°C air fryer for 5 minutes, or until warmed through.

Beef and Tomato Sauce Meatloaf

Prep time: 15 minutes | Cook time: 25 minutes | Serves 4

680 g beef mince
235 ml tomato sauce
120 ml breadcrumbs
2 egg whites
120 ml grated Parmesan cheese
1 diced onion
2 tablespoons chopped parsley
2 tablespoons minced ginger
2 garlic cloves, minced
½ teaspoon dried basil
1 teaspoon cayenne pepper
Salt and ground black pepper, to taste
Cooking spray

Preheat the air fryer to 182°C. Spritz a meatloaf pan with cooking spray.
Combine all the ingredients in a large bowl. Stir to mix well.
Pour the meat mixture in the prepared meatloaf pan and press with a spatula to make it firm.
Arrange the pan in the preheated air fryer and bake for 25 minutes or until the beef is well browned.
Serve immediately.

Marinated Steak Tips with Mushrooms

Prep time: 30 minutes | Cook time: 10 minutes | Serves 4

680 g rump steak, trimmed and cut into 1-inch pieces
230 g brown mushrooms, halved
60 ml Worcestershire sauce
1 tablespoon Dijon mustard
1 tablespoon olive oil
1 teaspoon paprika
1 teaspoon crushed red pepper flakes
2 tablespoons chopped fresh parsley (optional)

Place the beef and mushrooms in a gallon-size resealable bag. In a small bowl, whisk together the Worcestershire, mustard, olive oil, paprika, and red pepper flakes. Pour the marinade into the bag and massage gently to ensure the beef and mushrooms are evenly coated. Seal the bag and refrigerate for at least 4 hours, preferably overnight. Remove from the refrigerator 30 minutes before cooking.
Preheat the air fryer to 204°C.
Drain and discard the marinade. Arrange the steak and mushrooms in the air fryer basket. Air fry for 10 minutes, pausing halfway through the baking time to shake the basket. Transfer to a serving plate and top with the parsley, if desired.

Spicy Bavette Steak with Zhoug

Prep time: 30 minutes | Cook time: 8 minutes | Serves 4

Marinade and Steak:
120 ml dark beer or orange juice
60 ml fresh lemon juice
3 cloves garlic, minced
2 tablespoons extra-virgin olive oil
2 tablespoons Sriracha
2 tablespoons brown sugar
2 teaspoons ground cumin
2 teaspoons smoked paprika
1 tablespoon coarse or flaky salt
1 teaspoon black pepper
680 g bavette or skirt steak,
trimmed and cut into 3 pieces
Zhoug:
235 ml packed fresh coriander leaves
2 cloves garlic, peeled
2 jalapeño or green chiles, stemmed and coarsely chopped
½ teaspoon ground cumin
¼ teaspoon ground coriander
¼ teaspoon coarse or flaky salt
2 to 4 tablespoons extra-virgin olive oil

For the marinade and steak: In a small bowl, whisk together the beer, lemon juice, garlic, olive oil, Sriracha, brown sugar, cumin, paprika, salt, and pepper. Place the steak in a large resealable plastic bag. Pour the marinade over the steak, seal the bag, and massage the steak to coat. Marinate in the refrigerator for 1 hour or up to 24 hours, turning the bag occasionally.

Meanwhile, for the zhoug: In a food processor, combine the coriander, garlic, jalapeños, cumin, coriander, and salt. Process until finely chopped. Add 2 tablespoons olive oil and pulse to form a loose paste, adding up to 2 tablespoons more olive oil if needed. Transfer the zhoug to a glass container. Cover and store in the refrigerator until 30 minutes before serving if marinating more than 1 hour.

Remove the steak from the marinade and discard the marinade. Place the steak in the air fryer basket and set the air fryer to 204°C for 8 minutes. Use a meat thermometer to ensure the steak has reached an internal temperature of 64°C (for medium).

Transfer the steak to a cutting board and let rest for 5 minutes. Slice the steak across the grain and serve with the zhoug.

Rack of Lamb with Pistachio Crust

Prep time: 10 minutes | Cook time: 19 minutes | Serves 2

120 ml finely chopped pistachios
3 tablespoons panko bread crumbs
1 teaspoon chopped fresh rosemary
2 teaspoons chopped fresh
oregano
Salt and freshly ground black pepper, to taste
1 tablespoon olive oil
1 rack of lamb, bones trimmed of fat and frenched
1 tablespoon Dijon mustard

Preheat the air fryer to 192°C.

Combine the pistachios, bread crumbs, rosemary, oregano, salt and pepper in a small bowl. (This is a good job for your food processor if you have one.) Drizzle in the olive oil and stir to combine.

Season the rack of lamb with salt and pepper on all sides and transfer it to the air fryer basket with the fat side facing up. Air fry the lamb for 12 minutes. Remove the lamb from the air fryer and brush the fat side of the lamb rack with the Dijon mustard. Coat the rack with the pistachio mixture, pressing the bread crumbs onto the lamb with your hands and rolling the bottom of the rack in any of

the crumbs that fall off.

Return the rack of lamb to the air fryer and air fry for another 3 to 7 minutes or until an instant read thermometer reads 60°C for medium. Add or subtract a couple of minutes for lamb that is more or less well cooked. (Your time will vary depending on how big the rack of lamb is.)

Let the lamb rest for at least 5 minutes. Then, slice into chops and serve.

Spicy Lamb Sirloin Chops

Prep time: 30 minutes | Cook time: 15 minutes | Serves 4

½ brown onion, coarsely chopped
4 coin-size slices peeled fresh ginger
5 garlic cloves
1 teaspoon garam masala
1 teaspoon ground fennel
1 teaspoon ground cinnamon
1 teaspoon ground turmeric
½ to 1 teaspoon cayenne pepper
½ teaspoon ground cardamom
1 teaspoon coarse or flaky salt
450 g lamb sirloin chops

In a blender, combine the onion, ginger, garlic, garam masala, fennel, cinnamon, turmeric, cayenne, cardamom, and salt. Pulse until the onion is finely minced and the mixture forms a thick paste, 3 to 4 minutes.

Place the lamb chops in a large bowl. Slash the meat and fat with a sharp knife several times to allow the marinade to penetrate better. Add the spice paste to the bowl and toss the lamb to coat. Marinate at room temperature for 30 minutes or cover and refrigerate for up to 24 hours.

Place the lamb chops in a single layer in the air fryer basket. Set the air fryer to 164°C for 15 minutes, turning the chops halfway through the cooking time. Use a meat thermometer to ensure the lamb has reached an internal temperature of 64°C (medium-rare).

Stuffed Beef Fillet with Feta Cheese

Prep time: 10 minutes | Cook time: 10 minutes | Serves 4

680 g beef fillet, pounded to ¼ inch thick
3 teaspoons sea salt
1 teaspoon ground black pepper
60 g creamy goat cheese
120 ml crumbled feta cheese
60 ml finely chopped onions
2 cloves garlic, minced
Cooking spray

Preheat the air fryer to 204°C. Spritz the air fryer basket with cooking spray.

Unfold the beef on a clean work surface. Rub the salt and pepper all over the beef to season.

Make the filling for the stuffed beef fillet: Combine the goat cheese, feta, onions, and garlic in a medium bowl. Stir until well blended.

Spoon the mixture in the center of the fillet. Roll the fillet up tightly like rolling a burrito and use some kitchen twine to tie the fillet.

Arrange the fillet in the air fryer basket and air fry for 10 minutes, flipping the fillet halfway through to ensure even cooking, or until an instant-read thermometer inserted in the center of the fillet registers 57°C for medium-rare.

Transfer to a platter and serve immediately.

Honey-Baked Pork Loin

Prep time: 30 minutes | Cook time: 22 to 25 minutes | Serves 6

60 ml honey
60 ml freshly squeezed lemon juice
2 tablespoons soy sauce
1 teaspoon garlic powder
1 (900 g) pork loin
2 tablespoons vegetable oil

In a medium bowl, whisk together the honey, lemon juice, soy sauce, and garlic powder. Reserve half of the mixture for basting during cooking.

Cut 5 slits in the pork loin and transfer it to a resealable bag. Add the remaining honey mixture. Seal the bag and refrigerate to marinate for at least 2 hours.

Preheat the air fryer to 204ºC. Line the air fryer basket with parchment paper.

Remove the pork from the marinade, and place it on the parchment. Spritz with oil, then baste with the reserved marinade.

Cook for 15 minutes. Flip the pork, baste with more marinade and spritz with oil again. Cook for 7 to 10 minutes more until the internal temperature reaches 64ºC. Let rest for 5 minutes before serving.

BBQ Pork Steaks

Prep time: 5 minutes | Cook time: 15 minutes | Serves 4

4 pork steaks
1 tablespoon Cajun seasoning
2 tablespoons BBQ sauce
1 tablespoon vinegar
1 teaspoon soy sauce
120 ml brown sugar
120 ml ketchup

Preheat the air fryer to 143ºC.
Sprinkle pork steaks with Cajun seasoning.
Combine remaining ingredients and brush onto steaks.
Add coated steaks to air fryer. Air fry 15 minutes until just browned.
Serve immediately.

Barbecue Ribs

Prep time: 5 minutes | Cook time: 30 minutes | Serves 4

1 (900 g) rack baby back ribs
1 teaspoon onion granules
1 teaspoon garlic powder
1 teaspoon light brown sugar
1 teaspoon dried oregano
Salt and freshly ground black pepper, to taste
Cooking oil spray
120 ml barbecue sauce

Use a sharp knife to remove the thin membrane from the back of the ribs. Cut the rack in half, or as needed, so the ribs fit in the air fryer basket. The best way to do this is to cut the ribs into 4- or 5-rib sections.

In a small bowl, stir together the onion granules, garlic powder, brown sugar, and oregano and season with salt and pepper. Rub the spice seasoning onto the front and back of the ribs.

Cover the ribs with plastic wrap or foil and let sit at room temperature for 30 minutes.

Insert the crisper plate into the basket and the basket into the unit. Preheat the unit by selecting AIR ROAST, setting the temperature to 182ºC, and setting the time to 3 minutes. Select START/STOP to begin.

Once the unit is preheated, spray the crisper plate with cooking oil. Place the ribs into the basket. It is okay to stack them.

Select AIR ROAST, set the temperature to 182ºC, and set the time to 30 minutes. Select START/STOP to begin.

After 15 minutes, flip the ribs. Resume cooking for 15 minutes, or until a food thermometer registers 88ºC.

When the cooking is complete, transfer the ribs to a serving dish. Drizzle the ribs with the barbecue sauce and serve.

Blackened Steak Nuggets

Prep time: 10 minutes | Cook time: 7 minutes | Serves 2

450 g rib eye steak, cut into 1-inch cubes
2 tablespoons salted butter, melted
½ teaspoon paprika
½ teaspoon salt
¼ teaspoon garlic powder
¼ teaspoon onion granules
¼ teaspoon ground black pepper
⅛ teaspoon cayenne pepper

Place steak into a large bowl and pour in butter. Toss to coat. Sprinkle with remaining ingredients.

Place bites into ungreased air fryer basket. Adjust the temperature to 204ºC and air fry for 7 minutes, shaking the basket three times during cooking. Steak will be crispy on the outside and browned when done and internal temperature is at least 64ºC for medium and 82ºC for well-done. Serve warm.

Herbed Lamb Steaks

Prep time: 30 minutes | Cook time: 15 minutes | Serves 4

½ medium onion
2 tablespoons minced garlic
2 teaspoons ground ginger
1 teaspoon ground cinnamon
1 teaspoon onion granules
1 teaspoon cayenne pepper
1 teaspoon salt
4 (170 g) boneless lamb sirloin steaks
Oil, for spraying

In a blender, combine the onion, garlic, ginger, cinnamon, onion granules, cayenne pepper, and salt and pulse until the onion is minced.

Place the lamb steaks in a large bowl or zip-top plastic bag and sprinkle the onion mixture over the top. Turn the steaks until they are evenly coated. Cover with plastic wrap or seal the bag and refrigerate for 30 minutes.

Preheat the air fryer to 164ºC. Line the air fryer basket with parchment and spray lightly with oil.

Place the lamb steaks in a single layer in the prepared basket, making sure they don't overlap. You may need to work in batches, depending on the size of your air fryer.

Cook for 8 minutes, flip, and cook for another 7 minutes, or until the internal temperature reaches 68ºC.

Pork Shoulder with Garlicky Coriander-Parsley Sauce

Prep time: 1 hour 15 minutes | Cook time: 30 minutes | Serves 4

1 teaspoon flaxseed meal	taste
1 egg white, well whisked	Garlicky Coriander-Parsley
1 tablespoon soy sauce	Sauce:
1 teaspoon lemon juice,	3 garlic cloves, minced
preferably freshly squeezed	80 ml fresh coriander leaves
1 tablespoon olive oil	80 ml fresh parsley leaves
450 g pork shoulder, cut into	1 teaspoon lemon juice
pieces 2-inches long	½ tablespoon salt
Salt and ground black pepper, to	80 ml extra-virgin olive oil

Combine the flaxseed meal, egg white, soy sauce, lemon juice, salt, black pepper, and olive oil in a large bowl. Dunk the pork strips in and press to submerge.

Wrap the bowl in plastic and refrigerate to marinate for at least an hour.

Preheat the air fryer to 192ºC.

Arrange the marinated pork strips in the preheated air fryer and air fry for 30 minutes or until cooked through and well browned. Flip the strips halfway through.

Meanwhile, combine the ingredients for the sauce in a small bowl. Stir to mix well. Arrange the bowl in the refrigerator to chill until ready to serve.

Serve the air fried pork strips with the chilled sauce.

Spinach and Beef Braciole

Prep time: 25 minutes | Cook time: 1 hour 32 minutes | Serves 4

½ onion, finely chopped	680 g)
1 teaspoon olive oil	salt and freshly ground black
80 ml red wine	pepper
475 ml crushed tomatoes	475 ml fresh spinach, chopped
1 teaspoon Italian seasoning	1 clove minced garlic
½ teaspoon garlic powder	120 ml roasted red peppers,
¼ teaspoon crushed red pepper	julienned
flakes	120 ml grated pecorino cheese
2 tablespoons chopped fresh	60 ml pine nuts, toasted and
parsley	roughly chopped
2 bavette or skirt steaks (about	2 tablespoons olive oil

Preheat the air fryer to 204ºC.

Toss the onions and olive oil together in a baking pan or casserole dish. Air fry at 204ºC for 5 minutes, stirring a couple times during the cooking process. Add the red wine, crushed tomatoes, Italian seasoning, garlic powder, red pepper flakes and parsley and stir. Cover the pan tightly with aluminum foil, lower the air fryer temperature to 176ºC and continue to air fry for 15 minutes.

While the sauce is simmering, prepare the beef. Using a meat mallet, pound the beef until it is ¼-inch thick. Season both sides of the beef with salt and pepper. Combine the spinach, garlic, red peppers, pecorino cheese, pine nuts and olive oil in a medium bowl. Season with salt and freshly ground black pepper. Disperse the mixture over the steaks. Starting at one of the short ends, roll the beef around the filling, tucking in the sides as you roll to ensure the

filling is completely enclosed. Secure the beef rolls with toothpicks. Remove the baking pan with the sauce from the air fryer and set it aside. Preheat the air fryer to 204ºC.

Brush or spray the beef rolls with a little olive oil and air fry at 204ºC for 12 minutes, rotating the beef during the cooking process for even browning. When the beef is browned, submerge the rolls into the sauce in the baking pan, cover the pan with foil and return it to the air fryer. Reduce the temperature of the air fryer to 121ºC and air fry for 60 minutes.

Remove the beef rolls from the sauce. Cut each roll into slices and serve, ladling some sauce overtop.

Buttery Pork Chops

Prep time: 5 minutes | Cook time: 12 minutes | Serves 4

4 (110 g) boneless pork chops	2 tablespoons salted butter,
½ teaspoon salt	softened
¼ teaspoon ground black pepper	

Sprinkle pork chops on all sides with salt and pepper. Place chops into ungreased air fryer basket in a single layer. Adjust the temperature to 204ºC and air fry for 12 minutes. Pork chops will be golden and have an internal temperature of at least 64ºC when done.

Use tongs to remove cooked pork chops from air fryer and place onto a large plate. Top each chop with ½ tablespoon butter and let sit 2 minutes to melt. Serve warm.

Nigerian Peanut-Crusted Bavette Steak

Prep time: 30 minutes | Cook time: 8 minutes | Serves 4

Suya Spice Mix:	1 teaspoon coarse or flaky salt
60 ml dry-roasted peanuts	½ teaspoon cayenne pepper
1 teaspoon cumin seeds	Steak:
1 teaspoon garlic powder	450 g bavette or skirt steak
1 teaspoon smoked paprika	2 tablespoons vegetable oil
½ teaspoon ground ginger	

For the spice mix: In a clean coffee grinder or spice mill, combine the peanuts and cumin seeds. Process until you get a coarse powder. (Do not overprocess or you will wind up with peanut butter! Alternatively, you can grind the cumin with 80 ml ready-made peanut powder instead of the peanuts.)

Pour the peanut mixture into a small bowl, add the garlic powder, paprika, ginger, salt, and cayenne, and stir to combine. This recipe makes about 120 ml suya spice mix. Store leftovers in an airtight container in a cool, dry place for up to 1 month.

For the steak: Cut the steak into ½-inch-thick slices, cutting against the grain and at a slight angle. Place the beef strips in a resealable plastic bag and add the oil and 2½ to 3 tablespoons of the spice mixture. Seal the bag and massage to coat all of the meat with the oil and spice mixture. Marinate at room temperature for 30 minutes or in the refrigerator for up to 24 hours.

Place the beef strips in the air fryer basket. Set the air fryer to 204ºC for 8 minutes, turning the strips halfway through the cooking time.

Transfer the meat to a serving platter. Sprinkle with additional spice mix, if desired.

Pork and Pinto Bean Gorditas

Prep timePork and Pinto Bean Gorditas

450 g lean pork mince	pepper, to taste
2 tablespoons chili powder	475 ml grated Cheddar cheese
2 tablespoons ground cumin	5 (12-inch) flour tortillas
1 teaspoon dried oregano	4 (8-inch) crispy corn taco
2 teaspoons paprika	shells
1 teaspoon garlic powder	1 L shredded lettuce
120 ml water	1 tomato, diced
1 (425 g) can pinto beans,	80 ml sliced black olives
drained and rinsed	Sour cream, for serving
120 ml salsa	Tomato salsa, for serving
Salt and freshly ground black	Cooking spray

Preheat the air fryer to 204ºC. Spritz the air fryer basket with cooking spray.

Put the pork in the air fryer basket and air fry at 204ºC for 10 minutes, stirring a few times to gently break up the meat. Combine the chili powder, cumin, oregano, paprika, garlic powder and water in a small bowl. Stir the spice mixture into the browned pork. Stir in the beans and salsa and air fry for an additional minute. Transfer the pork mixture to a bowl. Season with salt and freshly ground black pepper.

Sprinkle 120 ml of the grated cheese in the center of the flour tortillas, leaving a 2-inch border around the edge free of cheese and filling. Divide the pork mixture among the four tortillas, placing it on top of the cheese. Put a taco shell on top of the pork and top with shredded lettuce, diced tomatoes, and black olives. Cut the remaining flour tortilla into 4 quarters. These quarters of tortilla will serve as the bottom of the gordita. Put one quarter tortilla on top of each gordita and fold the edges of the bottom flour tortilla up over the sides, enclosing the filling. While holding the seams down, brush the bottom of the gordita with olive oil and place the seam side down on the countertop while you finish the remaining three gorditas.

Adjust the temperature to 192ºC.

Air fry one gordita at a time. Transfer the gordita carefully to the air fryer basket, seam side down. Brush or spray the top tortilla with oil and air fry for 5 minutes. Carefully turn the gordita over and air fry for an additional 4 to 5 minutes until both sides are browned. When finished air frying all four gorditas, layer them back into the air fryer for an additional minute to make sure they are all warm before serving with sour cream and salsa.

Beef Mince Taco Rolls

Prep time: 20 minutes | Cook time: 10 minutes | Serves 4

230 g 80/20 beef mince	2 tablespoons chopped coriander
80 ml water	355 ml shredded Mozzarella
1 tablespoon chili powder	cheese
2 teaspoons cumin	120 ml blanched finely ground
½ teaspoon garlic powder	almond flour
¼ teaspoon dried oregano	60 g full-fat cream cheese
60 ml tinned diced tomatoes	1 large egg

In a medium skillet over medium heat, brown the beef mince about 7 to 10 minutes. When meat is fully cooked, drain.

Add water to skillet and stir in chili powder, cumin, garlic powder,

oregano, and tomatoes. Add coriander. Bring to a boil, then reduce heat to simmer for 3 minutes.

In a large microwave-safe bowl, place Mozzarella, almond flour, cream cheese, and egg. Microwave for 1 minute. Stir the mixture quickly until smooth ball of dough forms.

Cut a piece of parchment for your work surface. Press the dough into a large rectangle on the parchment, wetting your hands to prevent the dough from sticking as necessary. Cut the dough into eight rectangles.

On each rectangle place a few spoons of the meat mixture. Fold the short ends of each roll toward the center and roll the length as you would a burrito.

Cut a piece of parchment to fit your air fryer basket. Place taco rolls onto the parchment and place into the air fryer basket.

Adjust the temperature to 182ºC and air fry for 10 minutes.

Flip halfway through the cooking time.

Allow to cool 10 minutes before serving.

Italian Sausage and Cheese Meatballs

Prep time: 10 minutes | Cook time: 20 minutes | Serves 4

230 g sausage meat with Italian	cheese
seasoning added to taste	½ teaspoon onion granules
230 g 85% lean beef mince	½ teaspoon garlic powder
120 ml shredded sharp Cheddar	½ teaspoon black pepper

In a large bowl, gently mix the sausage meat, beef mince, cheese, onion granules, garlic powder, and pepper until well combined. Form the mixture into 16 meatballs. Place the meatballs in a single layer in the air fryer basket. Set the air fryer to 176ºC for 20 minutes, turning the meatballs halfway through the cooking time. Use a meat thermometer to ensure the meatballs have reached an internal temperature of 72ºC (medium).

Teriyaki Rump Steak with Broccoli and Capsicum

Prep time: 5 minutes | Cook time: 13 minutes | Serves 4

230 g rump steak	2 red peppers, sliced
80 ml teriyaki marinade	Fine sea salt and ground black
1½ teaspoons sesame oil	pepper, to taste
½ head broccoli, cut into florets	Cooking spray

Toss the rump steak in a large bowl with teriyaki marinade. Wrap the bowl in plastic and refrigerate to marinate for at least an hour.

Preheat the air fryer to 204ºC and spritz with cooking spray.

Discard the marinade and transfer the steak in the preheated air fryer. Spritz with cooking spray.

Air fry for 13 minutes or until well browned. Flip the steak halfway through.

Meanwhile, heat the sesame oil in a nonstick skillet over medium heat. Add the broccoli and red pepper. Sprinkle with salt and ground black pepper. Sauté for 5 minutes or until the broccoli is tender.

Transfer the air fried rump steak on a plate and top with the sautéed broccoli and pepper. Serve hot.

Bean and Beef Meatball Taco Pizza

Prep time: 10 minutes | Cook time: 7 to 9 minutes per batch | Serves 4

180 ml refried beans (from a 450 g can)
120 ml salsa
10 frozen precooked beef meatballs, thawed and sliced
1 jalapeño pepper, sliced

4 whole-wheat pitta breads
235 ml shredded chilli cheese
120 ml shredded Monterey Jack or Cheddar cheese
Cooking oil spray
80 ml sour cream

In a medium bowl, stir together the refried beans, salsa, meatballs, and jalapeño.

Insert the crisper plate into the basket and the basket into the unit. Preheat the unit by selecting BAKE, setting the temperature to 192ºC, and setting the time to 3 minutes. Select START/STOP to begin.

Top the pittas with the refried bean mixture and sprinkle with the cheeses.

Once the unit is preheated, spray the crisper plate with cooking oil. Working in batches, place the pizzas into the basket. Select BAKE, set the temperature to 192ºC, and set the time to 9 minutes. Select START/STOP to begin.

After about 7 minutes, check the pizzas. They are done when the cheese is melted and starts to brown. If not ready, resume cooking.

When the cooking is complete, top each pizza with a dollop of sour cream and serve warm.

Smoky Pork Tenderloin

Prep time: 5 minutes | Cook time: 19 to 22 minutes | Serves 6

680 g pork tenderloin
1 tablespoon avocado oil
1 teaspoon chili powder
1 teaspoon smoked paprika

1 teaspoon garlic powder
1 teaspoon sea salt
1 teaspoon freshly ground black pepper

Pierce the tenderloin all over with a fork and rub the oil all over the meat.

In a small dish, stir together the chili powder, smoked paprika, garlic powder, salt, and pepper.

Rub the spice mixture all over the tenderloin.

Set the air fryer to 204ºC. Place the pork in the air fryer basket and air fry for 10 minutes. Flip the tenderloin and cook for 9 to 12 minutes more, until an instant-read thermometer reads at least 64ºC. Allow the tenderloin to rest for 5 minutes, then slice and serve.

Almond and Caraway Crust Steak

Prep time: 16 minutes | Cook time: 10 minutes | Serves 4

80 ml almond flour
2 eggs
2 teaspoons caraway seeds
4 beef steaks

2 teaspoons garlic powder
1 tablespoon melted butter
Fine sea salt and cayenne pepper, to taste

Generously coat steaks with garlic powder, caraway seeds, salt, and cayenne pepper.

In a mixing dish, thoroughly combine melted butter with seasoned crumbs. In another bowl, beat the eggs until they're well whisked. First, coat steaks with the beaten egg; then, coat beef steaks with the buttered crumb mixture. Place the steaks in the air fryer basket; cook for 10 minutes at 179ºC. Bon appétit!

Chicken-Fried Steak

Prep time: 20 minutes | Cook time: 14 minutes | Serves 2

Steak:
Oil, for spraying
180 ml all-purpose flour
1 teaspoon salt
1 teaspoon freshly ground black pepper
½ teaspoon paprika
½ teaspoon onion granules
1 teaspoon granulated garlic
180 ml buttermilk

½ teaspoon hot sauce
2 (140 g) minute steaks
Gravy:
2 tablespoons unsalted butter
2 tablespoons all-purpose flour
235 ml milk
½ teaspoon salt
½ teaspoon freshly ground black pepper

Make the Steak Line the air fryer basket with parchment and spray lightly with oil.

In a medium bowl, mix together the flour, salt, black pepper, paprika, onion granules, and garlic.

In another bowl, whisk together the buttermilk and hot sauce.

Dredge the steaks in the flour mixture, dip in the buttermilk mixture, and dredge again in the flour until completely coated. Shake off any excess flour.

Place the steaks in the prepared basket and spray liberally with oil.

Air fry at 204ºC for 7 minutes, flip, spray with oil, and cook for another 6 to 7 minutes, or until crispy and browned. Make the Gravy

In a small saucepan, whisk together the butter and flour over medium heat until the butter is melted. Slowly add the milk, salt, and black pepper, increase the heat to medium-high, and continue to cook, stirring constantly, until the mixture thickens. Remove from the heat.

Transfer the steaks to plates and pour the gravy over the top. Serve immediately.

Chinese-Style Baby Back Ribs

Prep time: 30 minutes | Cook time: 30 minutes | Serves 4

1 tablespoon toasted sesame oil
1 tablespoon fermented black bean paste
1 tablespoon Shaoxing wine (rice cooking wine)
1 tablespoon dark soy sauce

1 tablespoon agave nectar or honey
1 teaspoon minced garlic
1 teaspoon minced fresh ginger
1 (680 g) slab baby back ribs, cut into individual ribs

In a large bowl, stir together the sesame oil, black bean paste, wine, soy sauce, agave, garlic, and ginger. Add the ribs and toss well to coat. Marinate at room temperature for 30 minutes, or cover and refrigerate for up to 24 hours.

Place the ribs in the air fryer basket; discard the marinade. Set the air fryer to 176ºC for 30 minutes.

Mustard Lamb Chops

Prep time: 5 minutes | Cook time: 14 minutes | Serves 4

Oil, for spraying
1 tablespoon Dijon mustard
2 teaspoons lemon juice
½ teaspoon dried tarragon
¼ teaspoon salt
¼ teaspoon freshly ground black pepper
4 (1¼-inch-thick) loin lamb chops

Preheat the air fryer to 200°C. Line the air fryer basket with parchment and spray lightly with oil.

In a small bowl, mix together the mustard, lemon juice, tarragon, salt, and black pepper.

Pat dry the lamb chops with a paper towel. Brush the chops on both sides with the mustard mixture.

Place the chops in the prepared basket. You may need to work in batches, depending on the size of your air fryer.

Cook for 8 minutes, flip, and cook for another 6 minutes, or until the internal temperature reaches 52°C for rare, 64°C for medium-rare, or 68°C for medium.

Swedish Meatloaf

Prep time: 10 minutes | Cook time: 35 minutes | Serves 8

680 g beef mince (85% lean)
110 g pork mince
1 large egg (omit for egg-free)
120 ml minced onions
60 ml tomato sauce
2 tablespoons mustard powder
2 cloves garlic, minced
2 teaspoons fine sea salt
1 teaspoon ground black pepper, plus more for garnish

Sauce:
120 ml (1 stick) unsalted butter
120 ml shredded Swiss or mild Cheddar cheese (about 60 g)
60 g cream cheese (60 ml), softened
80 ml beef stock
⅛ teaspoon ground nutmeg
Halved cherry tomatoes, for serving (optional)

Preheat the air fryer to 200°C.

In a large bowl, combine the beef, pork, egg, onions, tomato sauce, mustard powder, garlic, salt, and pepper. Using your hands, mix until well combined.

Place the meatloaf mixture in a loaf pan and place it in the air fryer. Bake for 35 minutes, or until cooked through and the internal temperature reaches 64°C. Check the meatloaf after 25 minutes; if it's getting too brown on the top, cover it loosely with foil to prevent burning.

While the meatloaf cooks, make the sauce: Heat the butter in a saucepan over medium-high heat until it sizzles and brown flecks appear, stirring constantly to keep the butter from burning. Turn the heat down to low and whisk in the Swiss cheese, cream cheese, stock, and nutmeg. Simmer for at least 10 minutes. The longer it simmers, the more the flavors open up.

When the meatloaf is done, transfer it to a serving tray and pour the sauce over it. Garnish with ground black pepper and serve with cherry tomatoes, if desired. Allow the meatloaf to rest for 10 minutes before slicing so it doesn't crumble apart.

Store leftovers in an airtight container in the fridge for 3 days or in the freezer for up to a month. Reheat in a preheated 176°C air fryer for 4 minutes, or until heated through.

Short Ribs with Chimichurri

Prep time: 30 minutes | Cook time: 13 minutes | Serves 4

450 g boneless short ribs
1½ teaspoons sea salt, divided
½ teaspoon freshly ground black pepper, divided
120 ml fresh parsley leaves
120 ml fresh coriander leaves
1 teaspoon minced garlic
1 tablespoon freshly squeezed lemon juice
½ teaspoon ground cumin
¼ teaspoon red pepper flakes
2 tablespoons extra-virgin olive oil
Avocado oil spray

Pat the short ribs dry with paper towels. Sprinkle the ribs all over with 1 teaspoon salt and ¼ teaspoon black pepper. Let sit at room temperature for 45 minutes.

Meanwhile, place the parsley, coriander, garlic, lemon juice, cumin, red pepper flakes, the remaining ½ teaspoon salt, and the remaining ¼ teaspoon black pepper in a blender or food processor. With the blender running, slowly drizzle in the olive oil. Blend for about 1 minute, until the mixture is smooth and well combined.

Set the air fryer to 204°C. Spray both sides of the ribs with oil. Place in the basket and air fry for 8 minutes. Flip and cook for another 5 minutes, until an instant-read thermometer reads 52°C for medium-rare (or to your desired doneness).

Allow the meat to rest for 5 to 10 minutes, then slice. Serve warm with the chimichurri sauce.

Lebanese Malfouf (Stuffed Cabbage Rolls)

Prep time: 15 minutes | Cook time: 33 minutes | Serves 4

1 head green cabbage
450 g lean beef mince
120 ml long-grain brown rice
4 garlic cloves, minced
1 teaspoon salt
½ teaspoon black pepper
1 teaspoon ground cinnamon
2 tablespoons chopped fresh mint
Juice of 1 lemon
Olive oil cooking spray
120 ml beef stock
1 tablespoon olive oil

Cut the cabbage in half and remove the core. Remove 12 of the larger leaves to use for the cabbage rolls.

Bring a large pot of salted water to a boil, then drop the cabbage leaves into the water, boiling them for 3 minutes. Remove from the water and set aside.

In a large bowl, combine the beef, rice, garlic, salt, pepper, cinnamon, mint, and lemon juice, and mix together until combined. Divide this mixture into 12 equal portions.

Preheat the air fryer to 182°C. Lightly coat a small casserole dish with olive oil cooking spray.

Place a cabbage leaf on a clean work surface. Place a spoonful of the beef mixture on one side of the leaf, leaving space on all other sides. Fold the two perpendicular sides inward and then roll forward, tucking tightly as rolled (similar to a burrito roll). Place the finished rolls into the baking dish, stacking them on top of each other if needed.

Pour the beef stock over the top of the cabbage rolls so that it soaks down between them, and then brush the tops with the olive oil.

Place the casserole dish into the air fryer basket and bake for 30 minutes.

Sweet and Spicy Country-Style Ribs

Prep time: 10 minutes | Cook time: 25 minutes | Serves 4

2 tablespoons brown sugar	1 teaspoon coarse or flaky salt
2 tablespoons smoked paprika	1 teaspoon black pepper
1 teaspoon garlic powder	¼ to ½ teaspoon cayenne pepper
1 teaspoon onion granules	680 g boneless pork steaks
1 teaspoon mustard powder	235 ml barbecue sauce
1 teaspoon ground cumin	

In a small bowl, stir together the brown sugar, paprika, garlic powder, onion granules, mustard powder, cumin, salt, black pepper, and cayenne. Mix until well combined.

Pat the ribs dry with a paper towel. Generously sprinkle the rub evenly over both sides of the ribs and rub in with your fingers.

Place the ribs in the air fryer basket. Set the air fryer to 176ºC for 15 minutes. Turn the ribs and brush with 120 ml of the barbecue sauce. Cook for an additional 10 minutes. Use a meat thermometer to ensure the pork has reached an internal temperature of 64ºC.

Serve with remaining barbecue sauce.

Parmesan Herb Filet Mignon

Prep time: 20 minutes | Cook time: 13 minutes | Serves 4

450 g filet mignon	1 teaspoon dried rosemary
Sea salt and ground black pepper, to taste	1 teaspoon dried thyme
½ teaspoon cayenne pepper	1 tablespoon sesame oil
1 teaspoon dried basil	1 small-sized egg, well-whisked
	120 ml Parmesan cheese, grated

Season the filet mignon with salt, black pepper, cayenne pepper, basil, rosemary, and thyme. Brush with sesame oil.

Put the egg in a shallow plate. Now, place the Parmesan cheese in another plate.

Coat the filet mignon with the egg; then lay it into the Parmesan cheese. Set the air fryer to 182ºC.

Cook for 10 to 13 minutes or until golden. Serve with mixed salad leaves and enjoy!

Italian Sausages with Peppers and Onions

Prep time: 5 minutes | Cook time: 28 minutes | Serves 3

1 medium onion, thinly sliced	coconut oil
1 yellow or orange pepper, thinly sliced	1 teaspoon fine sea salt
1 red pepper, thinly sliced	6 Italian-seasoned sausages
60 ml avocado oil or melted	Dijon mustard, for serving (optional)

Preheat the air fryer to 204ºC.

Place the onion and peppers in a large bowl. Drizzle with the oil and toss well to coat the veggies. Season with the salt.

Place the onion and peppers in a pie pan and cook in the air fryer for 8 minutes, stirring halfway through. Remove from the air fryer and set aside.

Spray the air fryer basket with avocado oil. Place the sausages in the air fryer basket and air fry for 20 minutes, or until crispy and golden brown. During the last minute or two of cooking, add the onion and peppers to the basket with the sausages to warm them through.

Place the onion and peppers on a serving platter and arrange the sausages on top. Serve Dijon mustard on the side, if desired.

Store leftovers in an airtight container in the fridge for up to 7 days or in the freezer for up to a month. Reheat in a preheated 200ºC air fryer for 3 minutes, or until heated through.

Mediterranean Beef Steaks

Prep time: 20 minutes | Cook time: 20 minutes | Serves 4

2 tablespoons soy sauce or tamari	pepper
3 heaping tablespoons fresh chives	½ teaspoon dried basil
2 tablespoons olive oil	½ teaspoon dried rosemary
3 tablespoons dry white wine	1 teaspoon freshly ground black pepper
4 small-sized beef steaks	1 teaspoon sea salt, or more to taste
2 teaspoons smoked cayenne	

Firstly, coat the steaks with the cayenne pepper, black pepper, salt, basil, and rosemary.

Drizzle the steaks with olive oil, white wine, and soy sauce.

Finally, roast in the air fryer for 20 minutes at 172ºC. Serve garnished with fresh chives. Bon appétit!

Saucy Beef Fingers

Prep time: 30 minutes | Cook time: 14 minutes | Serves 4

680 g rump steak	Coarse sea salt and ground black pepper, to taste
60 ml red wine	1 teaspoon red pepper flakes
60 ml fresh lime juice	2 eggs, lightly whisked
1 teaspoon garlic powder	235 ml Parmesan cheese
1 teaspoon onion granules	1 teaspoon paprika
1 teaspoon celery salt	
1 teaspoon mustard seeds	

Place the steak, red wine, lime juice, garlic powder, onion granules, celery salt, mustard seeds, salt, black pepper, and red pepper in a large ceramic bowl; let it marinate for 3 hours.

Tenderize the steak by pounding with a mallet; cut into 1-inch strips.

In a shallow bowl, whisk the eggs. In another bowl, mix the Parmesan cheese and paprika.

Dip the beef pieces into the whisked eggs and coat on all sides. Now, dredge the beef pieces in the Parmesan mixture.

Cook at 204ºC for 14 minutes, flipping halfway through the cooking time.

Meanwhile, make the sauce by heating the reserved marinade in a saucepan over medium heat; let it simmer until thoroughly warmed. Serve the steak fingers with the sauce on the side. Enjoy!

Chapter 5 Fish and Seafood

Chapter 5 Fish and Seafood

Crab Legs

Prep time: 5 minutes | Cook time: 15 minutes | Serves 4

60 g salted butter, melted and divided
1.4 kg crab legs

¼ teaspoon garlic powder
Juice of ½ medium lemon

In a large bowl, drizzle 2 tablespoons butter over crab legs. Place crab legs into the air fryer basket.
Adjust the temperature to 204°C and air fry for 15 minutes.
Shake the air fryer basket to toss the crab legs halfway through the cooking time.
In a small bowl, mix remaining butter, garlic powder, and lemon juice.
To serve, crack open crab legs and remove meat. Dip in lemon butter.

Coconut Cream Mackerel

Prep time: 10 minutes | Cook time: 6 minutes | Serves 4

900 g mackerel fillet
240 ml coconut cream
1 teaspoon ground coriander

1 teaspoon cumin seeds
1 garlic clove, peeled, chopped

Chop the mackerel roughly and sprinkle it with coconut cream, ground coriander, cumin seeds, and garlic.
Then put the fish in the air fryer and cook at 204°C for 6 minutes.

Marinated Salmon Fillets

Prep time: 10 minutes | Cook time: 15 to 20 minutes | Serves 4

60 ml soy sauce
60 ml rice wine vinegar
1 tablespoon brown sugar
1 tablespoon olive oil
1 teaspoon mustard powder
1 teaspoon ground ginger

½ teaspoon freshly ground black pepper
½ teaspoon minced garlic
4 salmon fillets, 170 g each, skin-on
Cooking spray

In a small bowl, combine the soy sauce, rice wine vinegar, brown sugar, olive oil, mustard powder, ginger, black pepper, and garlic to make a marinade.
Place the fillets in a shallow baking dish and pour the marinade over them. Cover the baking dish and marinate for at least 1 hour in the refrigerator, turning the fillets occasionally to keep them coated in the marinade.
Preheat the air fryer to 188°C. Spray the air fryer basket lightly with cooking spray.
Shake off as much marinade as possible from the fillets and place them, skin-side down, in the air fryer basket in a single layer. You may need to cook the fillets in batches.
Air fry for 15 to 20 minutes for well done. The minimum internal temperature should be 64°C at the thickest part of the fillets.
Serve hot.

Scallops Gratiné with Parmesan

Prep time: 10 minutes | Cook time: 9 minutes | Serves 2

Scallops:
120 ml single cream
45 g grated Parmesan cheese
235 g thinly sliced spring onions
5 g chopped fresh parsley
3 cloves garlic, minced
½ teaspoon kosher or coarse sea salt
½ teaspoon black pepper

455 g sea scallops
Topping:
30 g panko bread crumbs
20 g grated Parmesan cheese
Vegetable oil spray
For Serving:
Lemon wedges
Crusty French bread (optional)

For the scallops: In a baking pan, combine the single cream, cheese, spring onions, parsley, garlic, salt, and pepper. Stir in the scallops.
For the topping: In a small bowl, combine the bread crumbs and cheese. Sprinkle evenly over the scallops. Spray the topping with vegetable oil spray.
Place the pan in the air fryer basket. Set the air fryer to 164°C for 6 minutes. Set the air fryer to 204°C for 3 minutes until the topping has browned.
To serve: Squeeze the lemon wedges over the gratin and serve with crusty French bread, if desired.

Snapper with Shallot and Tomato

Prep time: 20 minutes | Cook time: 15 minutes | Serves 2

2 snapper fillets
1 shallot, peeled and sliced
2 garlic cloves, halved
1 bell pepper, sliced
1 small-sized serrano pepper, sliced
1 tomato, sliced

1 tablespoon olive oil
¼ teaspoon freshly ground black pepper
½ teaspoon paprika
Sea salt, to taste
2 bay leaves

Place two baking paper sheets on a working surface. Place the fish in the center of one side of the baking paper.
Top with the shallot, garlic, peppers, and tomato. Drizzle olive oil over the fish and vegetables. Season with black pepper, paprika, and salt. Add the bay leaves.
Fold over the other half of the baking paper. Now, fold the paper around the edges tightly and create a half moon shape, sealing the fish inside.
Cook in the preheated air fryer at 200°C for 15 minutes. Serve warm.

Prawn Bake

400 g prawns, peeled and deveined	120 g Cheddar cheese, shredded
1 egg, beaten	½ teaspoon coconut oil
120 ml coconut milk	1 teaspoon ground coriander

In the mixing bowl, mix prawns with egg, coconut milk, Cheddar cheese, coconut oil, and ground coriander.

Then put the mixture in the baking ramekins and put in the air fryer.

Cook the prawns at 204°C for 5 minutes.

Blackened Fish

1 large egg, beaten	4 tilapia fillets, 110g each
Blackened seasoning, as needed	Cooking spray
2 tablespoons light brown sugar	

In a shallow bowl, place the beaten egg. In a second shallow bowl, stir together the Blackened seasoning and the brown sugar.

One at a time, dip the fish fillets in the egg, then the brown sugar mixture, coating thoroughly.

Preheat the air fryer to 150°C. Line the air fryer basket with baking paper.

Place the coated fish on the baking paper and spritz with oil.

Bake for 4 minutes. Flip the fish, spritz it with oil, and bake for 4 to 6 minutes more until the fish is white inside and flakes easily with a fork.

Serve immediately.

Browned Prawns Patties

230 g raw prawns, peeled, deveined and chopped finely	sauce
500 g cooked sushi rice	½ teaspoon salt
35 g chopped red bell pepper	½ teaspoon garlic powder
35 g chopped celery	½ teaspoon Old Bay seasoning
35 g chopped spring onion	75 g plain bread crumbs
2 teaspoons Worcestershire	Cooking spray

Preheat the air fryer to 200°C.

Put all the ingredients except the bread crumbs and oil in a large bowl and stir to incorporate.

Scoop out the prawn mixture and shape into 8 equal-sized patties with your hands, no more than ½-inch thick. Roll the patties in the bread crumbs on a plate and spray both sides with cooking spray.

Place the patties in the air fryer basket. You may need to work in batches to avoid overcrowding.

Air fry for 10 to 12 minutes, flipping the patties halfway through, or until the outside is crispy brown.

Divide the patties among four plates and serve warm.

Dukkah-Crusted Halibut

Dukkah:	¼ teaspoon black pepper
1 tablespoon coriander seeds	Fish:
1 tablespoon sesame seeds	2 halibut fillets, 140 g each
1½ teaspoons cumin seeds	2 tablespoons mayonnaise
50 g roasted mixed nuts	Vegetable oil spray
¼ teaspoon kosher or coarse sea salt	Lemon wedges, for serving

For the Dukkah: Combine the coriander, sesame seeds, and cumin in a small baking pan. Place the pan in the air fryer basket. Set the air fryer to 204°C for 5 minutes. Toward the end of the cooking time, you will hear the seeds popping. Transfer to a plate and let cool for 5 minutes.

Transfer the toasted seeds to a food processor or spice grinder and add the mixed nuts. Pulse until coarsely chopped. Add the salt and pepper and stir well.

For the fish: Spread each fillet with 1 tablespoon of the mayonnaise. Press a heaping tablespoon of the Dukkah into the mayonnaise on each fillet, pressing lightly to adhere.

Spray the air fryer basket with vegetable oil spray. Place the fish in the basket. Cook for 12 minutes, or until the fish flakes easily with a fork.

Serve the fish with lemon wedges.

Lemon-Tarragon Fish en Papillote

2 tablespoons salted butter, melted	435 g julienned fennel, or 1 stalk julienned celery
1 tablespoon fresh lemon juice	75 g thinly sliced red bell pepper
½ teaspoon dried tarragon, crushed, or 2 sprigs fresh tarragon	2 cod fillets, 170 g each, thawed if frozen
1 teaspoon kosher or coarse sea salt	Vegetable oil spray
85 g julienned carrots	½ teaspoon black pepper

In a medium bowl, combine the butter, lemon juice, tarragon, and ½ teaspoon of the salt. Whisk well until you get a creamy sauce. Add the carrots, fennel, and bell pepper and toss to combine; set aside.

Cut two squares of baking paper each large enough to hold one fillet and half the vegetables. Spray the fillets with vegetable oil spray. Season both sides with the remaining ½ teaspoon salt and the black pepper.

Lay one fillet down on each baking paper square. Top each with half the vegetables. Pour any remaining sauce over the vegetables.

Fold over the baking paper and crimp the sides in small, tight folds to hold the fish, vegetables, and sauce securely inside the packet. Place the packets in the air fryer basket. Set the air fryer to 176°C for 15 minutes.

Transfer each packet to a plate. Cut open with scissors just before serving (be careful, as the steam inside will be hot).

Quick Prawns Skewers

Prep time: 10 minutes | Cook time: 5 minutes | Serves 5

1.8kg prawns, peeled and deveined
1 tablespoon dried rosemary

1 tablespoon avocado oil
1 teaspoon apple cider vinegar

Mix the prawns with dried rosemary, avocado oil, and apple cider vinegar.
Then thread the prawns onto skewers and put in the air fryer.
Cook the prawns at 204°C for 5 minutes.

Tilapia with Pecans

Prep time: 20 minutes | Cook time: 16 minutes | Serves 5

2 tablespoons ground flaxseeds
1 teaspoon paprika
Sea salt and white pepper, to taste
1 teaspoon garlic paste

2 tablespoons extra-virgin olive oil
65 g pecans, ground
5 tilapia fillets, sliced into halves

Combine the ground flaxseeds, paprika, salt, white pepper, garlic paste, olive oil, and ground pecans in a sealable freezer bag. Add the fish fillets and shake to coat well.
Spritz the air fryer basket with cooking spray. Cook in the preheated air fryer at 204°C for 10 minutes; turn them over and cook for 6 minutes more. Work in batches.
Serve with lemon wedges, if desired. Enjoy!

Cod with Creamy Mustard Sauce

Prep time: 10 minutes | Cook time: 10 minutes | Serves 4

Fish:
Olive or vegetable oil, for spraying
455 g cod fillets
2 tablespoons olive oil
1 tablespoon lemon juice
1 teaspoon salt

½ teaspoon freshly ground black pepper
Mustard Sauce:
120 ml heavy cream
3 tablespoons Dijon mustard
1 tablespoon unsalted butter
1 teaspoon salt

Make the Fish: Line the air fryer basket with baking paper and spray lightly with oil.
Rub the cod with the olive oil and lemon juice. Season with the salt and black pepper.
Place the cod in the prepared basket. You may need to work in batches, depending on the size of your air fryer.
Roast at 176°C for 5 minutes. Increase the temperature to 204°C and cook for another 5 minutes, until flaky and the internal temperature reaches 64°C. Make the Mustard Sauce:
In a small saucepan, mix together the heavy cream, mustard, butter, and salt and bring to a simmer over low heat. Cook for 3 to 4 minutes, or until the sauce starts to thicken.
Transfer the cod to a serving plate and drizzle with the mustard sauce. Serve immediately.

Mediterranean-Style Cod

Prep time: 5 minutes | Cook time: 12 minutes | Serves 4

4 cod fillets, 170 g each
3 tablespoons fresh lemon juice
1 tablespoon olive oil
¼ teaspoon salt

6 cherry tomatoes, halved
45 g pitted and sliced kalamata olives

Place cod into an ungreased round nonstick baking dish. Pour lemon juice into dish and drizzle cod with olive oil. Sprinkle with salt. Place tomatoes and olives around baking dish in between fillets.
Place dish into air fryer basket. Adjust the temperature to 176°C and bake for 12 minutes, carefully turning cod halfway through cooking. Fillets will be lightly browned, easily flake, and have an internal temperature of at least 64°C when done. Serve warm.

Scallops and Spinach with Cream Sauce

Prep time: 5 minutes | Cook time: 10 minutes | Serves 2

Vegetable oil spray
280 g frozen spinach, thawed and drained
8 jumbo sea scallops
Kosher or coarse sea salt, and black pepper, to taste

180 ml heavy cream
1 tablespoon tomato paste
1 tablespoon chopped fresh basil
1 teaspoon minced garlic

Spray a baking pan with vegetable oil spray. Spread the thawed spinach in an even layer in the bottom of the pan.
Spray both sides of the scallops with vegetable oil spray. Season lightly with salt and pepper. Arrange the scallops on top of the spinach.
In a small bowl, whisk together the cream, tomato paste, basil, garlic, ½ teaspoon salt, and ½ teaspoon pepper. Pour the sauce over the scallops and spinach.
Place the pan in the air fryer basket. Set the air fryer to 176°C for 10 minutes. Use a meat thermometer to ensure the scallops have an internal temperature of 56°C.

Italian Baked Cod

Prep time: 5 minutes | Cook time: 12 minutes | Serves 4

4 cod fillets, 170 g each
2 tablespoons salted butter, melted
1 teaspoon Italian seasoning

¼ teaspoon salt
120 ml tomato-based pasta sauce

Place cod into an ungreased round nonstick baking dish. Pour butter over cod and sprinkle with Italian seasoning and salt. Top with pasta sauce.
Place dish into air fryer basket. Adjust the temperature to 176°C and bake for 12 minutes. Fillets will be lightly browned, easily flake, and have an internal temperature of at least 64°C when done. Serve warm.

Prawn Dejonghe Skewers

Prep time: 10 minutes | Cook time: 15 minutes | Serves 4

2 teaspoons sherry, or apple cider vinegar
3 tablespoons unsalted butter, melted
120 g panko bread crumbs
3 cloves garlic, minced
8 g minced flat-leaf parsley, plus
more for garnish
1 teaspoon kosher salt
Pinch of cayenne pepper
680 g prawns, peeled and deveined
Vegetable oil, for spraying
Lemon wedges, for serving

Stir the sherry and melted butter together in a shallow bowl or pie plate and whisk until combined. Set aside. Whisk together the panko, garlic, parsley, salt, and cayenne pepper on a large plate or shallow bowl.

Thread the prawns onto metal skewers designed for the air fryer or bamboo skewers, 3 to 4 per skewer. Dip 1 prawns skewer in the butter mixture, then dredge in the panko mixture until each prawns is lightly coated. Place the skewer on a plate or rimmed baking sheet and repeat the process with the remaining skewers.

Preheat the air fryer to 176ºC. Arrange 4 skewers in the air fryer basket. Spray the skewers with oil and air fry for 8 minutes, until the bread crumbs are golden brown and the prawns are cooked through. Transfer the cooked skewers to a serving plate and keep warm while cooking the remaining 4 skewers in the air fryer.

Sprinkle the cooked skewers with additional fresh parsley and serve with lemon wedges if desired.

chilli Tilapia

Prep time: 5 minutes | Cook time: 20 minutes | Serves 4

4 tilapia fillets, boneless
1 teaspoon chilli flakes
1 teaspoon dried oregano
1 tablespoon avocado oil
1 teaspoon mustard

Rub the tilapia fillets with chilli flakes, dried oregano, avocado oil, and mustard and put in the air fryer.
Cook it for 10 minutes per side at 182ºC.

Friday Night Fish-Fry

Prep time: 10 minutes | Cook time: 10 minutes | Serves 4

1 large egg
45 g powdered Parmesan cheese
1 teaspoon smoked paprika
¼ teaspoon celery salt
¼ teaspoon ground black pepper
4 cod fillets, 110 g each
Chopped fresh oregano or parsley, for garnish (optional)
Lemon slices, for serving (optional)

Spray the air fryer basket with avocado oil. Preheat the air fryer to 204ºC.
Crack the egg in a shallow bowl and beat it lightly with a fork. Combine the Parmesan cheese, paprika, celery salt, and pepper in a separate shallow bowl.
One at a time, dip the fillets into the egg, then dredge them in the Parmesan mixture. Using your hands, press the Parmesan onto the fillets to form a nice crust. As you finish, place the fish in the air fryer basket.

Air fry the fish in the air fryer for 10 minutes, or until it is cooked through and flakes easily with a fork. Garnish with fresh oregano or parsley and serve with lemon slices, if desired.

Store leftovers in an airtight container in the refrigerator for up to 3 days. Reheat in a preheated 204ºC air fryer for 5 minutes, or until warmed through.

Panko Crab Sticks with Mayo Sauce

Prep time: 5 minutes | Cook time: 12 minutes | Serves 4

Crab Sticks:
2 eggs
120 g plain flour
50 g panko bread crumbs
1 tablespoon Old Bay seasoning
455 g crab sticks
Cooking spray
Mayo Sauce:
115 g mayonnaise
1 lime, juiced
2 garlic cloves, minced

Preheat air fryer to 200ºC.
In a bowl, beat the eggs. In a shallow bowl, place the flour. In another shallow bowl, thoroughly combine the panko bread crumbs and old bay seasoning.
Dredge the crab sticks in the flour, shaking off any excess, then in the beaten eggs, finally press them in the bread crumb mixture to coat well.
Arrange the crab sticks in the air fryer basket and spray with cooking spray.
Air fry for 12 minutes until golden brown. Flip the crab sticks halfway through the cooking time.
Meanwhile, make the sauce by whisking together the mayo, lime juice, and garlic in a small bowl.
Serve the crab sticks with the mayo sauce on the side.

Pecan-Crusted Tilapia

Prep time: 10minutes | Cook time: 10 minutes | Serves 4

160 g pecans
45 g panko bread crumbs
70 g plain flour
2 tablespoons Cajun seasoning
2 eggs, beaten with 2
tablespoons water
4 tilapia fillets, 170g each
Vegetable oil, for spraying
Lemon wedges, for serving

Grind the pecans in the food processor until they resemble coarse meal. Combine the ground pecans with the panko on a plate. On a second plate, combine the flour and Cajun seasoning. Dry the tilapia fillets using paper towels and dredge them in the flour mixture, shaking off any excess. Dip the fillets in the egg mixture and then dredge them in the pecan and panko mixture, pressing the coating onto the fillets. Place the breaded fillets on a plate or rack.

Preheat the air fryer to 192ºC. Spray both sides of the breaded fillets with oil. Carefully transfer 2 of the fillets to the air fryer basket and air fry for 9 to 10 minutes, flipping once halfway through, until the flesh is opaque and flaky. Repeat with the remaining fillets.

Serve immediately with lemon wedges.

Roasted Halibut Steaks with Parsley

Prep time: 5 minutes | Cook time: 10 minutes | Serves 4

455 g halibut steaks
60 ml vegetable oil
2½ tablespoons Worcester sauce
2 tablespoons honey
2 tablespoons vermouth or white wine vinegar
1 tablespoon freshly squeezed lemon juice
1 tablespoon fresh parsley leaves, coarsely chopped
Salt and pepper, to taste
1 teaspoon dried basil

Preheat the air fryer to 200ºC.
Put all the ingredients in a large mixing dish and gently stir until the fish is coated evenly.
Transfer the fish to the air fryer basket and roast for 10 minutes, flipping the fish halfway through, or until the fish reaches an internal temperature of at least 64ºC on a meat thermometer.
Let the fish cool for 5 minutes and serve.

Swordfish Skewers with Caponata

Prep time: 15 minutes | Cook time: 20 minutes | Serves 2

280 g small Italian aubergine, cut into 1-inch pieces
170 g cherry tomatoes
3 spring onions, cut into 2 inches long
2 tablespoons extra-virgin olive oil, divided
Salt and pepper, to taste
340 g skinless swordfish steaks, 1¼ inches thick, cut into 1-inch pieces
2 teaspoons honey, divided
2 teaspoons ground coriander, divided
1 teaspoon grated lemon zest, divided
1 teaspoon juice
4 (6-inch) wooden skewers
1 garlic clove, minced
½ teaspoon ground cumin
1 tablespoon chopped fresh basil

Preheat the air fryer to 204ºC.
Toss aubergine, tomatoes, and spring onions with 1 tablespoon oil, ¼ teaspoon salt, and ⅛ teaspoon pepper in bowl; transfer to air fryer basket. Air fry until aubergine is softened and browned and tomatoes have begun to burst, about 14 minutes, tossing halfway through cooking. Transfer vegetables to cutting board and set aside to cool slightly.
Pat swordfish dry with paper towels. Combine 1 teaspoon oil, 1 teaspoon honey, 1 teaspoon coriander, ½ teaspoon lemon zest, ⅛ teaspoon salt, and pinch pepper in a clean bowl. Add swordfish and toss to coat. Thread swordfish onto skewers, leaving about ¼ inch between each piece (3 or 4 pieces per skewer).
Arrange skewers in air fryer basket, spaced evenly apart. (Skewers may overlap slightly.) Return basket to air fryer and air fry until swordfish is browned and registers 140ºF (60ºC), 6 to 8 minutes, flipping and rotating skewers halfway through cooking.
Meanwhile, combine remaining 2 teaspoons oil, remaining 1 teaspoon honey, remaining 1 teaspoon coriander, remaining ½ teaspoon lemon zest, lemon juice, garlic, cumin, ¼ teaspoon salt, and ⅛ teaspoon pepper in large bowl. Microwave, stirring once, until fragrant, about 30 seconds. Coarsely chop the cooked vegetables, transfer to bowl with dressing, along with any accumulated juices, and gently toss to combine. Stir in basil and season with salt and pepper to taste. Serve skewers with caponata.

Coconut Prawns

Prep time: 5 minutes | Cook time: 6 minutes | Serves 2

230 g medium prawns, peeled and deveined
2 tablespoons salted butter, melted
½ teaspoon Old Bay seasoning
25 g desiccated, unsweetened coconut

In a large bowl, toss the prawns in butter and Old Bay seasoning.
Place shredded coconut in bowl. Coat each piece of prawns in the coconut and place into the air fryer basket.
Adjust the temperature to 204ºC and air fry for 6 minutes.
Gently turn the prawns halfway through the cooking time. Serve immediately.

Greek Fish Pitas

Prep time: 10 minutes | Cook time: 15 minutes | Serves 4

455 g pollock, cut into 1-inch pieces
60 ml olive oil
1 teaspoon salt
½ teaspoon dried oregano
½ teaspoon dried thyme
½ teaspoon garlic powder
¼ teaspoon cayenne
4 whole wheat pitas
75 g shredded lettuce
2 plum tomatoes, diced
Nonfat plain Greek yogurt
Lemon, quartered

Preheat the air fryer to 192ºC.
In a medium bowl, combine the pollock with olive oil, salt, oregano, thyme, garlic powder, and cayenne.
Put the pollock into the air fryer basket and roast for 15 minutes.
Serve inside pitas with lettuce, tomato, and Greek yogurt with a lemon wedge on the side.

Cod with Avocado

Prep time: 30 minutes | Cook time: 10 minutes | Serves 2

90 g shredded cabbage
60 ml full-fat sour cream
2 tablespoons full-fat mayonnaise
20 g chopped pickled jalapeños
2 (85 g) cod fillets
1 teaspoon chilli powder
1 teaspoon cumin
½ teaspoon paprika
¼ teaspoon garlic powder
1 medium avocado, peeled, pitted, and sliced
½ medium lime

In a large bowl, place cabbage, sour cream, mayonnaise, and jalapeños. Mix until fully coated. Let sit for 20 minutes in the refrigerator.
Sprinkle cod fillets with chilli powder, cumin, paprika, and garlic powder. Place each fillet into the air fryer basket.
Adjust the temperature to 188ºC and set the timer for 10 minutes.
Flip the fillets halfway through the cooking time. When fully cooked, fish should have an internal temperature of at least 64ºC.
To serve, divide slaw mixture into two serving bowls, break cod fillets into pieces and spread over the bowls, and top with avocado.
Squeeze lime juice over each bowl. Serve immediately.

Fried Catfish Fillets

Prep time: 10 minutes | Cook time: 20 minutes | Serves 4

1 egg	¼ teaspoon garlic powder
100 g finely ground cornmeal	¼ teaspoon freshly ground black
30 g plain flour	pepper
¾ teaspoon salt	4 140 g catfish fillets, halved
1 teaspoon paprika	crosswise
1 teaspoon Old Bay seasoning	Olive oil spray

In a shallow bowl, beat the egg with 2 tablespoons water.

On a plate, stir together the cornmeal, flour, salt, paprika, Old Bay, garlic powder, and pepper.

Dip the fish into the egg mixture and into the cornmeal mixture to coat. Press the cornmeal mixture into the fish and gently shake off any excess.

Insert the crisper plate into the basket and the basket into the unit to 204ºC.

Once the unit is preheated, place a baking paper liner into the basket. Place the coated fish on the liner and spray it with olive oil.. Cook for 10 minutes, remove the basket and spray the fish with olive oil. Flip the fish and spray the other side with olive oil. Reinsert the basket to resume cooking. Check the fish after 7 minutes more. If the fish is golden and crispy and registers at least 64ºC on a food thermometer, it is ready. If not, resume cooking. When the cooking is complete, serve.

Baked Grouper with Tomatoes and Garlic

Prep time: 5 minutes | Cook time: 12 minutes | Serves 4

4 grouper fillets	45 g sliced Kalamata olives
½ teaspoon salt	10 g fresh dill, roughly chopped
3 garlic cloves, minced	Juice of 1 lemon
1 tomato, sliced	¼ cup olive oil

Preheat the air fryer to 192ºC.

Season the grouper fillets on all sides with salt, then place into the air fryer basket and top with the minced garlic, tomato slices, olives, and fresh dill.

Drizzle the lemon juice and olive oil over the top of the grouper, then bake for 10 to 12 minutes, or until the internal temperature reaches 64ºC.

Lemon Mahi-Mahi

Prep time: 5 minutes | Cook time: 14 minutes | Serves 2

Olive or vegetable oil, for spraying	¼ teaspoon salt
2 (170 g) mahi-mahi fillets	¼ teaspoon freshly ground black pepper
1 tablespoon lemon juice	1 tablespoon chopped fresh dill
1 tablespoon olive oil	2 lemon slices

Line the air fryer basket with baking paper and spray lightly with oil.

Place the mahi-mahi in the prepared basket.

In a small bowl, whisk together the lemon juice and olive oil. Brush the mixture evenly over the mahi-mahi.

Sprinkle the mahi-mahi with the salt and black pepper and top with the dill.

Air fry at 204ºC for 12 to 14 minutes, depending on the thickness of the fillets, until they flake easily.

Transfer to plates, top each with a lemon slice, and serve.

Oyster Po'Boy

Prep time: 20 minutes | Cook time: 5 minutes | Serves 4

105 g plain flour	1 (12-inch) French baguette, quartered and sliced horizontally
40 g yellow cornmeal	Tartar Sauce, as needed
1 tablespoon Cajun seasoning	150 g shredded lettuce, divided
1 teaspoon salt	2 tomatoes, cut into slices
2 large eggs, beaten	Cooking spray
1 teaspoon hot sauce	
455 g pre-shucked oysters	

In a shallow bowl, whisk the flour, cornmeal, Cajun seasoning, and salt until blended. In a second shallow bowl, whisk together the eggs and hot sauce.

One at a time, dip the oysters in the cornmeal mixture, the eggs, and again in the cornmeal, coating thoroughly.

Preheat the air fryer to 204ºC. Line the air fryer basket with baking paper.

Place the oysters on the baking paper and spritz with oil.

Air fry for 2 minutes. Shake the basket, spritz the oysters with oil, and air fry for 3 minutes more until lightly browned and crispy.

Spread each sandwich half with Tartar Sauce. Assemble the po'boys by layering each sandwich with fried oysters, ½ cup shredded lettuce, and 2 tomato slices.

Serve immediately.

Prawns Curry

Prep time: 30 minutes | Cook time: 10 minutes | Serves 4

180 ml unsweetened full-fat coconut milk	1 teaspoon ground turmeric
10 g finely chopped yellow onion	1 teaspoon salt
2 teaspoons garam masala	¼ to ½ teaspoon cayenne pepper
1 tablespoon minced fresh ginger	455 g raw prawns (21 to 25 count), peeled and deveined
1 tablespoon minced garlic	2 teaspoons chopped fresh coriander

In a large bowl, stir together the coconut milk, onion, garam masala, ginger, garlic, turmeric, salt and cayenne, until well blended.

Add the prawns and toss until coated with sauce on all sides. Marinate at room temperature for 30 minutes.

Transfer the prawns and marinade to a baking pan. Place the pan in the air fryer basket. Set the air fryer to 192ºC for 10 minutes, stirring halfway through the cooking time.

Transfer the prawns to a serving bowl or platter. Sprinkle with the cilantro and serve.

Seasoned Breaded Prawns

Prep time: 15 minutes | Cook time: 10 to 15 minutes | Serves 4

2 teaspoons Old Bay seasoning, divided
½ teaspoon garlic powder
½ teaspoon onion powder
455 g large prawns, peeled and

deveined, with tails on
2 large eggs
75 g whole-wheat panko bread crumbs
Cooking spray

Preheat the air fryer to 192ºC.
Spray the air fryer basket lightly with cooking spray.
In a medium bowl, mix together 1 teaspoon of Old Bay seasoning, garlic powder, and onion powder. Add the prawns and toss with the seasoning mix to lightly coat.
In a separate small bowl, whisk the eggs with 1 teaspoon water.
In a shallow bowl, mix together the remaining 1 teaspoon Old Bay seasoning and the panko bread crumbs.
Dip each prawns in the egg mixture and dredge in the bread crumb mixture to evenly coat.
Place the prawns in the air fryer basket, in a single layer. Lightly spray the prawns with cooking spray. You many need to cook the prawns in batches.
Air fry for 10 to 15 minutes, or until the prawns is cooked through and crispy, shaking the basket at 5-minute intervals to redistribute and evenly cook.
Serve immediately.

Cod with Jalapeño

Prep time: 5 minutes | Cook time: 14 minutes | Serves 4

4 cod fillets, boneless
1 jalapeño, minced

1 tablespoon avocado oil
½ teaspoon minced garlic

In the shallow bowl, mix minced jalapeño, avocado oil, and minced garlic.
Put the cod fillets in the air fryer basket in one layer and top with minced jalapeño mixture.
Cook the fish at 185ºC for 7 minutes per side.

Coconut Prawns with Spicy Dipping Sauce

Prep time: 15 minutes | Cook time: 8 minutes | Serves 4

70 g pork scratchings
70 g desiccated, unsweetened coconut
85 g coconut flour
1 teaspoon onion powder
1 teaspoon garlic powder
2 eggs
680 g large prawns, peeled and deveined

½ teaspoon salt
¼ teaspoon freshly ground black pepper
Spicy Dipping Sauce:
115 g mayonnaise
2 tablespoons Sriracha
Zest and juice of ½ lime
1 clove garlic, minced

Preheat the air fryer to 200ºC.
In a food processor fitted with a metal blade, combine the pork scratchings and desiccated coconut. Pulse until the mixture resembles coarse crumbs. Transfer to a shallow bowl.
In another shallow bowl, combine the coconut flour, onion powder, and garlic powder; mix until thoroughly combined.
In a third shallow bowl, whisk the eggs until slightly frothy.
In a large bowl, season the prawns with the salt and pepper, tossing gently to coat.
Working a few pieces at a time, dredge the prawns in the flour mixture, followed by the eggs, and finishing with the pork rind crumb mixture. Arrange the prawns on a baking sheet until ready to air fry.
Working in batches if necessary, arrange the prawns in a single layer in the air fryer basket. Pausing halfway through the cooking time to turn the prawns, air fry for 8 minutes until cooked through.
To make the sauce: In a small bowl, combine the mayonnaise, Sriracha, lime zest and juice, and garlic. Whisk until thoroughly combined. Serve alongside the prawns.

Crab and Bell Pepper Cakes

Prep time: 5 minutes | Cook time: 10 minutes | Serves 4

230 g jumbo lump crabmeat
1 tablespoon Old Bay seasoning
40 g bread crumbs
40 g diced red bell pepper
40 g diced green bell pepper

1 egg
60 g mayonnaise
Juice of ½ lemon
1 teaspoon plain flour
Cooking oil spray

Sort through the crabmeat, picking out any bits of shell or cartilage.
In a large bowl, stir together the Old Bay seasoning, bread crumbs, red and green bell peppers, egg, mayonnaise, and lemon juice. Gently stir in the crabmeat.
Insert the crisper plate into the basket and the basket into the unit. Preheat the unit to 192ºC.
Form the mixture into 4 patties. Sprinkle ¼ teaspoon of flour on top of each patty.
Once the unit is preheated, spray the crisper plate with cooking oil. Place the crab cakes into the basket and spray them with cooking oil.
Cook for 10 minutes.
When the cooking is complete, the crab cakes will be golden brown and firm.

Bacon-Wrapped Scallops

Prep time: 5 minutes | Cook time: 10 minutes | Serves 4

8 sea scallops, 30 g each, cleaned and patted dry
8 slices bacon

¼ teaspoon salt
¼ teaspoon ground black pepper

Wrap each scallop in 1 slice bacon and secure with a toothpick. Sprinkle with salt and pepper.
Place scallops into ungreased air fryer basket. Adjust the temperature to 182ºC and air fry for 10 minutes. Scallops will be opaque and firm, and have an internal temperature of 56ºC when done. Serve warm.

Baked Tilapia with Garlic Aioli

Prep time: 5 minutes | Cook time: 15 minutes | Serves 4

Tilapia:
4 tilapia fillets
1 tablespoon extra-virgin olive oil
1 teaspoon garlic powder
1 teaspoon paprika
1 teaspoon dried basil
A pinch of lemon-pepper seasoning
Garlic Aioli:
2 garlic cloves, minced
1 tablespoon mayonnaise
Juice of ½ lemon
1 teaspoon extra-virgin olive oil
Salt and pepper, to taste

Preheat the air fryer to 204°C.
On a clean work surface, brush both sides of each fillet with the olive oil. Sprinkle with the garlic powder, paprika, basil, and lemon-pepper seasoning.
Place the fillets in the air fryer basket and bake for 15 minutes, flipping the fillets halfway through, or until the fish flakes easily and is no longer translucent in the center.
Meanwhile, make the garlic aioli: Whisk together the garlic, mayo, lemon juice, olive oil, salt, and pepper in a small bowl until smooth. Remove the fish from the basket and serve with the garlic aioli on the side.

Apple Cider Mussels

Prep time: 10 minutes | Cook time: 2 minutes | Serves 5

900 g mussels, cleaned and de-bearded
1 teaspoon onion powder
1 teaspoon ground cumin
1 tablespoon avocado oil
60 ml apple cider vinegar

Mix mussels with onion powder, ground cumin, avocado oil, and apple cider vinegar.
Put the mussels in the air fryer and cook at 202°C for 2 minutes.

Mustard-Crusted Fish Fillets

Prep time: 5 minutes | Cook time: 8 to 11 minutes | Serves 4

5 teaspoons yellow mustard
1 tablespoon freshly squeezed lemon juice
4 sole fillets, 100 g each
½ teaspoon dried thyme
½ teaspoon dried marjoram
⅛ teaspoon freshly ground black pepper
1 slice whole-wheat bread, crumbled
2 teaspoons olive oil

In a small bowl, mix the mustard and lemon juice. Spread this evenly over the fillets. Place them in the air fryer basket.
In another small bowl, mix the thyme, marjoram, pepper, bread crumbs, and olive oil. Mix until combined.
Gently but firmly press the spice mixture onto the top of each fish fillet.
Bake at 160°C for 8 to 11 minutes, or until the fish reaches an internal temperature of at least 64°C on a meat thermometer and the topping is browned and crisp. Serve immediately.

Mackerel with Spinach

Prep time: 15 minutes | Cook time: 20 minutes | Serves 5

455 g mackerel, trimmed
1 bell pepper, chopped
15 g spinach, chopped
1 tablespoon avocado oil
1 teaspoon ground black pepper
1 teaspoon tomato paste

In the mixing bowl, mix bell pepper with spinach, ground black pepper, and tomato paste.
Fill the mackerel with spinach mixture.
Then brush the fish with avocado oil and put it in the air fryer.
Cook the fish at 185°C for 20 minutes.

Chapter 6 Poultry

Chapter 6 Poultry

Chicken Paillard

Prep time: 10 minutes | Cook time: 10 minutes | Serves 2

2 large eggs, room temperature
1 tablespoon water
40 g powdered Parmesan cheese or pork dust
2 teaspoons dried thyme leaves
1 teaspoon ground black pepper
2 (140 g) boneless, skinless chicken breasts, pounded to ½ inch thick

Lemon Butter Sauce:
2 tablespoons unsalted butter, melted
2 teaspoons lemon juice
¼ teaspoon finely chopped fresh thyme leaves, plus more for garnish
⅛ teaspoon fine sea salt
Lemon slices, for serving

Spray the air fryer basket with avocado oil. Preheat the air fryer to 200ºC.
Beat the eggs in a shallow dish, then add the water and stir well.
In a separate shallow dish, mix together the Parmesan, thyme, and pepper until well combined.
One at a time, dip the chicken breasts in the eggs and let any excess drip off, then dredge both sides of the chicken in the Parmesan mixture. As you finish, set the coated chicken in the air fryer basket. Roast the chicken in the air fryer for 5 minutes, then flip the chicken and cook for another 5 minutes, or until cooked through and the internal temperature reaches 76ºC.
While the chicken cooks, make the lemon butter sauce: In a small bowl, mix together all the sauce ingredients until well combined.
Plate the chicken and pour the sauce over it. Garnish with chopped fresh thyme and serve with lemon slices.
Store leftovers in an airtight container in the refrigerator for up to 4 days. Reheat in a preheated 200ºC air fryer for 5 minutes, or until heated through.

Curried Orange Honey Chicken

Prep time: 10 minutes | Cook time: 16 to 19 minutes | Serves 4

340 g boneless, skinless chicken thighs, cut into 1-inch pieces
1 yellow bell pepper, cut into 1½-inch pieces
1 small red onion, sliced
Olive oil for misting

60 ml chicken stock
2 tablespoons honey
60 ml orange juice
1 tablespoon cornflour
2 to 3 teaspoons curry powder

Preheat the air fryer to 190ºC.
Put the chicken thighs, pepper, and red onion in the air fryer basket and mist with olive oil.
Roast for 12 to 14 minutes or until the chicken is cooked to 76ºC, shaking the basket halfway through cooking time.
Remove the chicken and vegetables from the air fryer basket and set aside.
In a metal bowl, combine the stock, honey, orange juice, cornflour, and curry powder, and mix well. Add the chicken and vegetables,

stir, and put the bowl in the basket.
Return the basket to the air fryer and roast for 2 minutes. Remove and stir, then roast for 2 to 3 minutes or until the sauce is thickened and bubbly.
Serve warm.

Chicken Manchurian

Prep time: 10 minutes | Cook time: 20 minutes | Serves 2

450 g boneless, skinless chicken breasts, cut into 1-inch pieces
60 g ketchup
1 tablespoon tomato-based chili sauce, such as Heinz
1 tablespoon soy sauce
1 tablespoon rice vinegar

2 teaspoons vegetable oil
1 teaspoon hot sauce, such as Tabasco
½ teaspoon garlic powder
¼ teaspoon cayenne pepper
2 spring onions, thinly sliced
Cooked white rice, for serving

Preheat the air fryer to 180ºC.
In a bowl, combine the chicken, ketchup, chili sauce, soy sauce, vinegar, oil, hot sauce, garlic powder, cayenne, and three-quarters of the spring onions and toss until evenly coated.
Scrape the chicken and sauce into a metal cake pan and place the pan in the air fryer. Bake until the chicken is cooked through and the sauce is reduced to a thick glaze, about 20 minutes, flipping the chicken pieces halfway through.
Remove the pan from the air fryer. Spoon the chicken and sauce over rice and top with the remaining spring onions. Serve immediately.

Hawaiian Chicken Bites

Prep time: 1 hour 15 minutes | Cook time: 15 minutes | Serves 4

120 ml pineapple juice
2 tablespoons apple cider vinegar
½ tablespoon minced ginger
120 g ketchup
2 garlic cloves, minced

110 g brown sugar
2 tablespoons sherry
120 ml soy sauce
4 chicken breasts, cubed
Cooking spray

Combine the pineapple juice, cider vinegar, ginger, ketchup, garlic, and sugar in a saucepan. Stir to mix well. Heat over low heat for 5 minutes or until thickened. Fold in the sherry and soy sauce.
Dunk the chicken cubes in the mixture. Press to submerge. Wrap the bowl in plastic and refrigerate to marinate for at least an hour.
Preheat the air fryer to 180ºC. Spritz the air fryer basket with cooking spray.
Remove the chicken cubes from the marinade. Shake the excess off and put in the preheated air fryer. Spritz with cooking spray.
Air fry for 15 minutes or until the chicken cubes are glazed and well browned. Shake the basket at least three times during the frying.
Serve immediately.

Chicken, Courgette, and Spinach Salad

Prep time: 10 minutes | Cook time: 20 minutes | Serves 4

3 (140 g) boneless, skinless chicken breasts, cut into 1-inch cubes	1 medium red onion, sliced
	1 red bell pepper, sliced
	1 small courgette, cut into strips
5 teaspoons extra-virgin olive oil	3 tablespoons freshly squeezed lemon juice
½ teaspoon dried thyme	85 g fresh baby spinach leaves

Insert the crisper plate into the basket and the basket into the unit. Preheat the unit by selecting AIR ROAST, setting the temperature to 190ºC, and setting the time to 3 minutes. Select START/STOP to begin.

In a large bowl, combine the chicken, olive oil, and thyme. Toss to coat. Transfer to a medium metal bowl that fits into the basket.

Once the unit is preheated, place the bowl into the basket.

Select AIR ROAST, set the temperature to 190ºC, and set the time to 20 minutes. Select START/STOP to begin.

After 8 minutes, add the red onion, red bell pepper, and courgette to the bowl. Resume cooking. After about 6 minutes more, stir the chicken and vegetables. Resume cooking.

When the cooking is complete, a food thermometer inserted into the chicken should register at least 76ºC. Remove the bowl from the unit and stir in the lemon juice.

Put the spinach in a serving bowl and top with the chicken mixture. Toss to combine and serve immediately.

Garlic Parmesan Drumsticks

Prep time: 5 minutes | Cook time: 25 minutes | Serves 4

8 (115 g) chicken drumsticks	2 tablespoons salted butter, melted
½ teaspoon salt	
⅛ teaspoon ground black pepper	45 g grated Parmesan cheese
½ teaspoon garlic powder	1 tablespoon dried parsley

Sprinkle drumsticks with salt, pepper, and garlic powder. Place drumsticks into ungreased air fryer basket.

Adjust the temperature to 200ºC and air fry for 25 minutes, turning drumsticks halfway through cooking. Drumsticks will be golden and have an internal temperature of at least 76ºC when done.

Transfer drumsticks to a large serving dish. Pour butter over drumsticks, and sprinkle with Parmesan and parsley. Serve warm.

Ranch Chicken Wings

Prep time: 10 minutes | Cook time: 40 minutes | Serves 4

2 tablespoons water	1 (30 g) envelope ranch salad dressing mix
2 tablespoons hot pepper sauce	
2 tablespoons unsalted butter, melted	1 teaspoon paprika
	4 1.8 kg chicken wings, tips removed
2 tablespoons apple cider vinegar	Cooking oil spray

In a large bowl, whisk the water, hot pepper sauce, melted butter, vinegar, salad dressing mix, and paprika until combined.

Add the wings and toss to coat. At this point, you can cover the bowl and marinate the wings in the refrigerator for 4 to 24 hours for best results. However, you can just let the wings stand for 30 minutes in the refrigerator.

Insert the crisper plate into the basket and the basket into the unit. Preheat the unit by selecting AIR FRY, setting the temperature to 200ºC, and setting the time to 3 minutes. Select START/STOP to begin.

Once the unit is preheated, spray the crisper plate with cooking oil. Working in batches, put half the wings into the basket; it is okay to stack them. Refrigerate the remaining wings.

Select AIR FRY, set the temperature to 200ºC, and set the time to 20 minutes. Select START/STOP to begin.

After 5 minutes, remove the basket and shake it. Reinsert the basket to resume cooking. Remove and shake the basket every 5 minutes, three more times, until the chicken is browned and glazed and a food thermometer inserted into the wings registers 76ºC.

Repeat steps 4, 5, and 6 with the remaining wings.

When the cooking is complete, serve warm.

Chicken Chimichangas

Prep time: 20 minutes | Cook time: 8 to 10 minutes | Serves 4

280 g cooked chicken, shredded	Oil for misting or cooking spray
2 tablespoons chopped green chilies	Chimichanga Sauce:
	2 tablespoons butter
½ teaspoon oregano	2 tablespoons flour
½ teaspoon cumin	235 ml chicken broth
½ teaspoon onion powder	60 g light sour cream
¼ teaspoon garlic powder	¼ teaspoon salt
Salt and pepper, to taste	60 g Pepper Jack or Monterey Jack cheese, shredded
8 flour tortillas (6- or 7-inch diameter)	

Make the sauce by melting butter in a saucepan over medium-low heat. Stir in flour until smooth and slightly bubbly. Gradually add broth, stirring constantly until smooth. Cook and stir 1 minute, until the mixture slightly thickens. Remove from heat and stir in sour cream and salt. Set aside.

In a medium bowl, mix together the chicken, chilies, oregano, cumin, onion powder, garlic, salt, and pepper. Stir in 3 to 4 tablespoons of the sauce, using just enough to make the filling moist but not soupy.

Divide filling among the 8 tortillas. Place filling down the centre of tortilla, stopping about 1 inch from edges. Fold one side of tortilla over filling, fold the two sides in, and then roll up. Mist all sides with oil or cooking spray.

Place chimichangas in air fryer basket seam side down. To fit more into the basket, you can stand them on their sides with the seams against the sides of the basket.

Air fry at 180ºC for 8 to 10 minutes or until heated through and crispy brown outside.

Add the shredded cheese to the remaining sauce. Stir over low heat, warming just until the cheese melts. Don't boil or sour cream may curdle.

Drizzle the sauce over the chimichangas.

Thanksgiving Turkey Breast

Prep time: 5 minutes | Cook time: 30 minutes | Serves 4

1½ teaspoons fine sea salt
1 teaspoon ground black pepper
1 teaspoon chopped fresh rosemary leaves
1 teaspoon chopped fresh sage
1 teaspoon chopped fresh tarragon
1 teaspoon chopped fresh thyme leaves
1 (900 g) turkey breast
3 tablespoons ghee or unsalted butter, melted
3 tablespoons Dijon mustard

Spray the air fryer with avocado oil. Preheat the air fryer to 200ºC.
In a small bowl, stir together the salt, pepper, and herbs until well combined. Season the turkey breast generously on all sides with the seasoning.
In another small bowl, stir together the ghee and Dijon. Brush the ghee mixture on all sides of the turkey breast.
Place the turkey breast in the air fryer basket and air fry for 30 minutes, or until the internal temperature reaches 76ºC. Transfer the breast to a cutting board and allow it to rest for 10 minutes before cutting it into ½-inch-thick slices.
Store leftovers in an airtight container in the refrigerator for up to 4 days or in the freezer for up to a month. Reheat in a preheated 180ºC air fryer for 4 minutes, or until warmed through.

French Garlic Chicken

Prep time: 30 minutes | Cook time: 27 minutes | Serves 4

2 tablespoon extra-virgin olive oil
1 tablespoon Dijon mustard
1 tablespoon apple cider vinegar
3 cloves garlic, minced
2 teaspoons herbes de Provence
½ teaspoon kosher salt
1 teaspoon black pepper
450 g boneless, skinless chicken thighs, halved crosswise
2 tablespoons butter
8 cloves garlic, chopped
60 g heavy whipping cream

In a small bowl, combine the olive oil, mustard, vinegar, minced garlic, herbes de Provence, salt, and pepper. Use a wire whisk to emulsify the mixture.
Pierce the chicken all over with a fork to allow the marinade to penetrate better. Place the chicken in a resealable plastic bag, pour the marinade over, and seal. Massage until the chicken is well coated. Marinate at room temperature for 30 minutes or in the refrigerator for up to 24 hours.
When you are ready to cook, place the butter and chopped garlic in a baking pan and place it in the air fryer basket. Set the air fryer to 200ºC for 5 minutes, or until the butter has melted and the garlic is sizzling.
Add the chicken and the marinade to the seasoned butter. Set the air fryer to 180ºC for 15 minutes. Use a meat thermometer to ensure the chicken has reached an internal temperature of 76ºC. Transfer the chicken to a plate and cover lightly with foil to keep warm.
Add the cream to the pan, stirring to combine with the garlic, butter, and cooking juices. Place the pan in the air fryer basket. Set the air fryer to 180ºC for 7 minutes.
Pour the thickened sauce over the chicken and serve.

Cheesy Pepperoni and Chicken Pizza

Prep time: 15 minutes | Cook time: 15 minutes | Serves 6

280 g cooked chicken, cubed
240 g pizza sauce
20 slices pepperoni
20 g grated Parmesan cheese
225 g shredded Mozzarella cheese
Cooking spray

Preheat the air fryer to 190ºC. Spritz a baking pan with cooking spray.
Arrange the chicken cubes in the prepared baking pan, then top the cubes with pizza sauce and pepperoni. Stir to coat the cubes and pepperoni with sauce.
Scatter the cheeses on top, then place the baking pan in the preheated air fryer. Air fryer for 15 minutes or until frothy and the cheeses melt.
Serve immediately.

Chicken and Gruyère Cordon Bleu

Prep time: 15 minutes | Cook time: 15 minutes | Serves 4

4 chicken breast filets
75 g chopped ham
75 g grated Swiss cheese, or Gruyère cheese
30 g all-purpose flour
Pinch salt
Freshly ground black pepper, to taste
½ teaspoon dried marjoram
1 egg
120 g panko bread crumbs
Olive oil spray

Put the chicken breast filets on a work surface and gently press them with the palm of your hand to make them a bit thinner. Don't tear the meat.
In a small bowl, combine the ham and cheese. Divide this mixture among the chicken filets. Wrap the chicken around the filling to enclose it, using toothpicks to hold the chicken together.
In a shallow bowl, stir together the flour, salt, pepper, and marjoram.
In another bowl, beat the egg.
Spread the panko on a plate.
Dip the chicken in the flour mixture, in the egg, and in the panko to coat thoroughly. Press the crumbs into the chicken so they stick well.
Insert the crisper plate into the basket and the basket into the unit. Preheat the unit by selecting BAKE, setting the temperature to 190ºC, and setting the time to 3 minutes. Select START/STOP to begin.
Once the unit is preheated, spray the crisper plate with olive oil. Place the chicken into the basket and spray it with olive oil.
Select BAKE, set the temperature to 190ºC, and set the time to 15 minutes. Select START/STOP to begin.
1When the cooking is complete, the chicken should be cooked through and a food thermometer inserted into the chicken should register 76ºC. Carefully remove the toothpicks and serve.

Tex-Mex Chicken Roll-Ups

Prep time: 10 minutes | Cook time: 14 to 17 minutes | Serves 8

900 g boneless, skinless chicken breasts or thighs
1 teaspoon chili powder
½ teaspoon smoked paprika
½ teaspoon ground cumin
Sea salt and freshly ground

black pepper, to taste
170 g Monterey Jack cheese, shredded
115 g canned diced green chilies
Avocado oil spray

Place the chicken in a large zip-top bag or between two pieces of plastic wrap. Using a meat mallet or heavy skillet, pound the chicken until it is about ¼ inch thick.

In a small bowl, combine the chili powder, smoked paprika, cumin, and salt and pepper to taste. Sprinkle both sides of the chicken with the seasonings.

Sprinkle the chicken with the Monterey Jack cheese, then the diced green chilies.

Roll up each piece of chicken from the long side, tucking in the ends as you go. Secure the roll-up with a toothpick.

Set the air fryer to 180ºC. . Spray the outside of the chicken with avocado oil. Place the chicken in a single layer in the basket, working in batches if necessary, and roast for 7 minutes. Flip and cook for another 7 to 10 minutes, until an instant-read thermometer reads 70ºC.

Remove the chicken from the air fryer and allow it to rest for about 5 minutes before serving.

Bacon Lovers' Stuffed Chicken

Prep time: 15 minutes | Cook time: 10 minutes | Serves 4

4 (140 g) boneless, skinless chicken breasts, pounded to ¼ inch thick
2 (150 g) packages Boursin cheese (or Kite Hill brand chive cream cheese style spread,

softened, for dairy-free)
8 slices thin-cut bacon or beef bacon
Sprig of fresh coriander, for garnish (optional)

Spray the air fryer basket with avocado oil. Preheat the air fryer to 200ºC.

Place one of the chicken breasts on a cutting board. With a sharp knife held parallel to the cutting board, make a 1-inch-wide incision at the top of the breast. Carefully cut into the breast to form a large pocket, leaving a ½-inch border along the sides and bottom. Repeat with the other 3 chicken breasts.

Snip the corner of a large resealable plastic bag to form a ¾-inch hole. Place the Boursin cheese in the bag and pipe the cheese into the pockets in the chicken breasts, dividing the cheese evenly among them.

Wrap 2 slices of bacon around each chicken breast and secure the ends with toothpicks. Place the bacon-wrapped chicken in the air fryer basket and air fry until the bacon is crisp and the chicken's internal temperature reaches 76ºC, about 18 to 20 minutes, flipping after 10 minutes. Garnish with a sprig of coriander before serving, if desired.

Store leftovers in an airtight container in the refrigerator for up to 4 days. Reheat in a preheated 200ºC air fryer for 5 minutes, or until warmed through.

Chicken Pesto Pizzas

Prep time: 10 minutes | Cook time: 12 minutes | Serves 4

450 g chicken mince thighs
¼ teaspoon salt
⅛ teaspoon ground black pepper
20 g basil pesto

225 g shredded Mozzarella cheese
4 grape tomatoes, sliced

Cut four squares of parchment paper to fit into your air fryer basket. Place chicken mince in a large bowl and mix with salt and pepper. Divide mixture into four equal sections.

Wet your hands with water to prevent sticking, then press each section into a 6-inch circle onto a piece of ungreased parchment. Place each chicken crust into air fryer basket, working in batches if needed.

Adjust the temperature to 180ºC and air fry for 10 minutes, turning crusts halfway through cooking.

Spread 1 tablespoon pesto across the top of each crust, then sprinkle with ¼ of the Mozzarella and top with 1 sliced tomato. Continue cooking at 180ºC for 2 minutes. Cheese will be melted and brown when done. Serve warm.

Korean Honey Wings

Prep time: 10 minutes | Cook time: 25 minutes per batch | Serves 4

55 g gochujang, or red pepper paste
55 g mayonnaise
2 tablespoons honey
1 tablespoon sesame oil
2 teaspoons minced garlic
1 tablespoon sugar

2 teaspoons ground ginger
1.4 kg whole chicken wings
Olive oil spray
1 teaspoon salt
½ teaspoon freshly ground black pepper

In a large bowl, whisk the gochujang, mayonnaise, honey, sesame oil, garlic, sugar, and ginger. Set aside.

Insert the crisper plate into the basket and the basket into the unit. Preheat the unit by selecting AIR FRY, setting the temperature to 200ºC, and setting the time to 3 minutes. Select START/STOP to begin.

To prepare the chicken wings, cut the wings in half. The meatier part is the drumette. Cut off and discard the wing tip from the flat part (or save the wing tips in the freezer to make chicken stock).

Once the unit is preheated, spray the crisper plate with olive oil. Working in batches, place half the chicken wings into the basket, spray them with olive oil, and sprinkle with the salt and pepper.

Select AIR FRY, set the temperature to 200ºC, and set the time to 20 minutes. Select START/STOP to begin.

After 10 minutes, remove the basket, flip the wings, and spray them with more olive oil. Reinsert the basket to resume cooking.

Cook the wings to an internal temperature of 76ºC, then transfer them to the bowl with the prepared sauce and toss to coat.

Repeat steps 4, 5, 6, and 7 for the remaining chicken wings.

Return the coated wings to the basket and air fry for 4 to 6 minutes more until the sauce has glazed the wings and the chicken is crisp. After 3 minutes, check the wings to make sure they aren't burning. Serve hot.

Classic Chicken Kebab

Prep time: 35 minutes | Cook time: 25 minutes | Serves 4

60 ml olive oil	450 g boneless skinless chicken
1 teaspoon garlic powder	thighs, cut into 1-inch pieces
1 teaspoon onion powder	1 red bell pepper, cut into 1-inch
1 teaspoon ground cumin	pieces
½ teaspoon dried oregano	1 red onion, cut into 1-inch
½ teaspoon dried basil	pieces
60 ml lemon juice	1 courgette, cut into 1-inch
1 tablespoon apple cider vinegar	pieces
Olive oil cooking spray	12 cherry tomatoes

In a large bowl, mix together the olive oil, garlic powder, onion powder, cumin, oregano, basil, lemon juice, and apple cider vinegar.

Spray six skewers with olive oil cooking spray.

On each skewer, slide on a piece of chicken, then a piece of bell pepper, onion, courgette, and finally a tomato and then repeat. Each skewer should have at least two pieces of each item.

Once all of the skewers are prepared, place them in a 9-by-13-inch baking dish and pour the olive oil marinade over the top of the skewers. Turn each skewer so that all sides of the chicken and vegetables are coated.

Cover the dish with plastic wrap and place it in the refrigerator for 30 minutes.

After 30 minutes, preheat the air fryer to 192ºC. (If using a grill attachment, make sure it is inside the air fryer during preheating.)

Remove the skewers from the marinade and lay them in a single layer in the air fryer basket. If the air fryer has a grill attachment, you can also lay them on this instead.

Cook for 10 minutes. Rotate the kebabs, then cook them for 15 minutes more.

Remove the skewers from the air fryer and let them rest for 5 minutes before serving.

Coconut Chicken Wings with Mango Sauce

Prep time: 15 minutes | Cook time: 20 minutes | Serves 4

16 chicken drumettes (party wings)	coconut
	60 g all-purpose flour
60 ml full-fat coconut milk	Cooking oil spray
1 tablespoon sriracha	165 g mango, cut into ½-inch
1 teaspoon onion powder	chunks
1 teaspoon garlic powder	15 g fresh coriander, chopped
Salt and freshly ground black	25 g red onion, chopped
pepper, to taste	2 garlic cloves, minced
25 g shredded unsweetened	Juice of ½ lime

Place the drumettes in a resealable plastic bag.

In a small bowl, whisk the coconut milk and sriracha.

Drizzle the drumettes with the sriracha–coconut milk mixture. Season the drumettes with the onion powder, garlic powder, salt, and pepper. Seal the bag. Shake it thoroughly to combine the seasonings and coat the chicken. Marinate for at least 30 minutes, preferably overnight, in the refrigerator.

When the drumettes are almost done marinating, in a large bowl, stir together the shredded coconut and flour.

Dip the drumettes into the coconut-flour mixture. Press the flour mixture onto the chicken with your hands.

Insert the crisper plate into the basket and the basket into the unit. Preheat the unit by selecting AIR FRY, setting the temperature to 200ºC, and setting the time to 3 minutes. Select START/STOP to begin.

Once the unit is preheated, spray the crisper plate and the basket with cooking oil. Place the drumettes in the air fryer. It is okay to stack them. Spray the drumettes with cooking oil, being sure to cover the bottom layer.

Select AIR FRY, set the temperature to 200ºC, and set the time to 20 minutes. Select START/STOP to begin.

After 5 minutes, remove the basket and shake it to ensure all pieces cook through. Reinsert the basket to resume cooking. Remove and shake the basket every 5 minutes, twice more, until a food thermometer inserted into the drumettes registers 76ºC.

1When the cooking is complete, let the chicken cool for 5 minutes.

1While the chicken cooks and cools, make the salsa. In a small bowl, combine the mango, coriander, red onion, garlic, and lime juice. Mix well until fully combined. Serve with the wings.

Turkey and Cranberry Quesadillas

Prep time: 7 minutes | Cook time: 4 to 8 minutes | Serves 4

6 low-sodium whole-wheat tortillas	2 tablespoons cranberry sauce
	2 tablespoons dried cranberries
75 g shredded low-sodium low-fat Swiss cheese	½ teaspoon dried basil
	Olive oil spray, for spraying the
105 g shredded cooked low-sodium turkey breast	tortillas

Preheat the air fryer to 200ºC.

Put 3 tortillas on a work surface.

Evenly divide the Swiss cheese, turkey, cranberry sauce, and dried cranberries among the tortillas. Sprinkle with the basil and top with the remaining tortillas.

Spray the outsides of the tortillas with olive oil spray.

One at a time, air fry the quesadillas in the air fryer for 4 to 8 minutes, or until crisp and the cheese is melted. Cut into quarters and serve.

Coriander Lime Chicken Thighs

Prep time: 15 minutes | Cook time: 22 minutes | Serves 4

4 bone-in, skin-on chicken thighs	2 teaspoons chili powder
	1 teaspoon cumin
1 teaspoon baking powder	2 medium limes
½ teaspoon garlic powder	5 g chopped fresh coriander

Pat chicken thighs dry and sprinkle with baking powder.

In a small bowl, mix garlic powder, chili powder, and cumin and sprinkle evenly over thighs, gently rubbing on and under chicken skin.

Cut one lime in half and squeeze juice over thighs. Place chicken into the air fryer basket.

Adjust the temperature to 190ºC and roast for 22 minutes.

Cut other lime into four wedges for serving and garnish cooked chicken with wedges and coriander.

Chicken with Lettuce

450 g chicken breast tenders, chopped into bite-size pieces	1 tablespoon olive oil
½ onion, thinly sliced	1 tablespoon fajita seasoning
½ red bell pepper, seeded and thinly sliced	1 teaspoon kosher salt
½ green bell pepper, seeded and thinly sliced	Juice of ½ lime
	8 large lettuce leaves
	230 g prepared guacamole

Preheat the air fryer to 200ºC.

In a large bowl, combine the chicken, onion, and peppers. Drizzle with the olive oil and toss until thoroughly coated. Add the fajita seasoning and salt and toss again.

Working in batches if necessary, arrange the chicken and vegetables in a single layer in the air fryer basket. Pausing halfway through the cooking time to shake the basket, air fry for 14 minutes, or until the vegetables are tender and a thermometer inserted into the thickest piece of chicken registers 76ºC.

Transfer the mixture to a serving platter and drizzle with the fresh lime juice. Serve with the lettuce leaves and top with the guacamole.

Chicken Wellington

2 (140 g) boneless, skinless chicken breasts	2 tablespoons White Worcestershire sauce (or white wine)
120 ml White Worcestershire sauce	Salt and freshly ground black pepper, to taste
3 tablespoons butter	1 tablespoon chopped fresh tarragon
25 g finely diced onion (about ½ onion)	2 sheets puff pastry, thawed
225 g button mushrooms, finely chopped	1 egg, beaten
60 ml chicken stock	Vegetable oil

Place the chicken breasts in a shallow dish. Pour the White Worcestershire sauce over the chicken coating both sides and marinate for 30 minutes.

While the chicken is marinating, melt the butter in a large skillet over medium-high heat on the stovetop. Add the onion and sauté for a few minutes, until it starts to soften. Add the mushrooms and sauté for 3 to 5 minutes until the vegetables are brown and soft. Deglaze the skillet with the chicken stock, scraping up any bits from the bottom of the pan. Add the White Worcestershire sauce and simmer for 2 to 3 minutes until the mixture reduces and starts to thicken. Season with salt and freshly ground black pepper. Remove the mushroom mixture from the heat and stir in the fresh tarragon. Let the mushroom mixture cool.

Preheat the air fryer to 180ºC.

Remove the chicken from the marinade and transfer it to the air fryer basket. Tuck the small end of the chicken breast under the thicker part to shape it into a circle rather than an oval. Pour the marinade over the chicken and air fry for 10 minutes.

Roll out the puff pastry and cut out two 6-inch squares. Brush the perimeter of each square with the egg wash. Place half of the mushroom mixture in the centre of each puff pastry square. Place the chicken breasts, top side down on the mushroom mixture. Starting with one corner of puff pastry and working in one direction, pull the pastry up over the chicken to enclose it and press the ends of the pastry together in the middle. Brush the pastry with the egg wash to seal the edges. Turn the Wellingtons over and set aside.

Make a decorative design with the remaining puff pastry, cut out four 10-inch strips. For each Wellington, twist two of the strips together, place them over the chicken breast wrapped in puff pastry, and tuck the ends underneath to seal it. Brush the entire top and sides of the Wellingtons with the egg wash.

Preheat the air fryer to 180ºC. .

Spray or brush the air fryer basket with vegetable oil. Air fry the chicken Wellingtons for 13 minutes. Carefully turn the Wellingtons over. Air fry for another 8 minutes. Transfer to serving plates, light a candle and enjoy!

Thai Curry Meatballs

450 g chicken mince	1 tablespoon fish sauce
15 g chopped fresh coriander	2 garlic cloves, minced
1 teaspoon chopped fresh mint	2 teaspoons minced fresh ginger
1 tablespoon fresh lime juice	½ teaspoon kosher salt
1 tablespoon Thai red, green, or yellow curry paste	½ teaspoon black pepper
	¼ teaspoon red pepper flakes

Preheat the air fryer to 200ºC.

In a large bowl, gently mix the chicken mince, coriander, mint, lime juice, curry paste, fish sauce, garlic, ginger, salt, black pepper, and red pepper flakes until thoroughly combined.

Form the mixture into 16 meatballs. Place the meatballs in a single layer in the air fryer basket. Air fry for 10 minutes, turning the meatballs halfway through the cooking time. Use a meat thermometer to ensure the meatballs have reached an internal temperature of 76ºC. Serve immediately.

One-Dish Chicken and Rice

190 g long-grain white rice, rinsed and drained	3 cloves garlic, minced
120 g cut frozen green beans (do not thaw)	1 tablespoon toasted sesame oil
1 tablespoon minced fresh ginger	1 teaspoon kosher salt
	1 teaspoon black pepper
	450 g chicken wings, preferably drumettes

In a baking pan, combine the rice, green beans, ginger, garlic, sesame oil, salt, and pepper. Stir to combine. Place the chicken wings on top of the rice mixture.

Cover the pan with foil. Make a long slash in the foil to allow the pan to vent steam. Place the pan in the air fryer basket. Set the air fryer to (190ºC for 30 minutes.

Remove the foil. Set the air fryer to 200ºC for 10 minutes, or until the wings have browned and rendered fat into the rice and vegetables, turning the wings halfway through the cooking time.

Lemon Chicken with Garlic

Prep time: 5 minutes | Cook time: 20 to 25 minutes | Serves 4

8 bone-in chicken thighs, skin on
1 tablespoon olive oil
1½ teaspoons lemon-pepper seasoning
½ teaspoon paprika
½ teaspoon garlic powder
¼ teaspoon freshly ground black pepper
Juice of ½ lemon

Preheat the air fryer to 180ºC.

Place the chicken in a large bowl and drizzle with the olive oil. Top with the lemon-pepper seasoning, paprika, garlic powder, and freshly ground black pepper. Toss until thoroughly coated.

Working in batches if necessary, arrange the chicken in a single layer in the basket of the air fryer. Pausing halfway through the cooking time to turn the chicken, air fry for 20 to 25 minutes, until a thermometer inserted into the thickest piece registers 76ºC.

Transfer the chicken to a serving platter and squeeze the lemon juice over the top.

Garlic Soy Chicken Thighs

Prep time: 10 minutes | Cook time: 30 minutes | Serves 1 to 2

2 tablespoons chicken stock
2 tablespoons reduced-sodium soy sauce
1½ tablespoons sugar
4 garlic cloves, smashed and peeled
2 large spring onions, cut into 2- to 3-inch batons, plus more, thinly sliced, for garnish
2 bone-in, skin-on chicken thighs (198 to 225 g each)

Preheat the air fryer to 190ºC.

In a metal cake pan, combine the chicken stock, soy sauce, and sugar and stir until the sugar dissolves. Add the garlic cloves, spring onions, and chicken thighs, turning the thighs to coat them in the marinade, then resting them skin-side up. Place the pan in the air fryer and bake, flipping the thighs every 5 minutes after the first 10 minutes, until the chicken is cooked through and the marinade is reduced to a sticky glaze over the chicken, about 30 minutes.

Remove the pan from the air fryer and serve the chicken thighs warm, with any remaining glaze spooned over top and sprinkled with more sliced spring onions.

South Indian Pepper Chicken

Prep time: 30 minutes | Cook time: 15 minutes | Serves 4

Spice Mix:
1 dried red chili, or ½ teaspoon dried red pepper flakes
1-inch piece cinnamon or cassia bark
1½ teaspoons coriander seeds
1 teaspoon fennel seeds
1 teaspoon cumin seeds
1 teaspoon black peppercorns
½ teaspoon cardamom seeds
¼ teaspoon ground turmeric
1 teaspoon kosher salt
Chicken:
450 g boneless, skinless chicken thighs, cut crosswise into thirds
2 medium onions, cut into ½-inch-thick slices
60 ml olive oil
Cauliflower rice, steamed rice, or naan bread, for serving

For the spice mix: Combine the dried chili, cinnamon, coriander, fennel, cumin, peppercorns, and cardamom in a clean coffee or spice grinder. Grind, shaking the grinder lightly so all the seeds and bits get into the blades, until the mixture is broken down to a fine powder. Stir in the turmeric and salt.

For the chicken: Place the chicken and onions in resealable plastic bag. Add the oil and 1½ tablespoons of the spice mix. Seal the bag and massage until the chicken is well coated. Marinate at room temperature for 30 minutes or in the refrigerator for up to 24 hours. Place the chicken and onions in the air fryer basket. Set the air fryer to 180ºC for 10 minutes, stirring once halfway through the cooking time. Increase the temperature to 200ºC for 5 minutes. Use a meat thermometer to ensure the chicken has reached an internal temperature of 76ºC.

Serve with steamed rice, cauliflower rice, or naan.

Greek Chicken Stir-Fry

Prep time: 15 minutes | Cook time: 15 minutes | Serves 2

1 (170 g) chicken breast, cut into 1-inch cubes
½ medium courgette, chopped
½ medium red bell pepper, seeded and chopped
¼ medium red onion, peeled
and sliced
1 tablespoon coconut oil
1 teaspoon dried oregano
½ teaspoon garlic powder
¼ teaspoon dried thyme

Place all ingredients into a large mixing bowl and toss until the coconut oil coats the meat and vegetables. Pour the contents of the bowl into the air fryer basket.

Adjust the temperature to (190ºC and air fry for 15 minutes.

Shake the basket halfway through the cooking time to redistribute the food. Serve immediately.

Herbed Roast Chicken Breast

Prep time: 10 minutes | Cook time: 25 minutes | Serves 2 to 4

2 tablespoons salted butter or ghee, at room temperature
1 teaspoon dried Italian seasoning, crushed
½ teaspoon kosher salt
½ teaspoon smoked paprika
¼ teaspoon black pepper
2 bone-in, skin-on chicken breast halves (280 g each)
Lemon wedges, for serving

In a small bowl, stir together the butter, Italian seasoning, salt, paprika, and pepper until thoroughly combined.

Using a small sharp knife, carefully loosen the skin on each chicken breast half, starting at the thin end of each. Very carefully separate the skin from the flesh, leaving the skin attached at the thick end of each breast. Divide the herb butter into quarters. Rub one-quarter of the butter onto the flesh of each breast. Fold and lightly press the skin back onto each breast. Rub the remaining butter onto the skin of each breast.

Place the chicken in the air fryer basket. Set the air fryer to (190ºC for 25 minutes. Use a meat thermometer to ensure the chicken breasts have reached an internal temperature of 76ºC.

Transfer the chicken to a cutting board. Lightly cover with aluminum foil and let rest for 5 to 10 minutes.

Serve with lemon wedges.

Chicken and Ham Meatballs with Dijon Sauce

Prep time: 10 minutes | Cook time: 15 minutes | Serves 4

Meatballs:
230 g ham, diced
230 g chicken mince
110 g grated Swiss cheese
1 large egg, beaten
3 cloves garlic, minced
15 g chopped onions
1½ teaspoons sea salt
1 teaspoon ground black pepper

Cooking spray
Dijon Sauce:
3 tablespoons Dijon mustard
2 tablespoons lemon juice
60 ml chicken broth, warmed
¼ teaspoon sea salt
¼ teaspoon ground black pepper
Chopped fresh thyme leaves, for garnish

Preheat the air fryer to 200°C. Spritz the air fryer basket with cooking spray.

Combine the ingredients for the meatballs in a large bowl. Stir to mix well, then shape the mixture in twelve 1½-inch meatballs.

Arrange the meatballs in a single layer in the air fryer basket. Air fry for 15 minutes or until lightly browned. Flip the balls halfway through. You may need to work in batches to avoid overcrowding.

Meanwhile, combine the ingredients, except for the thyme leaves, for the sauce in a small bowl. Stir to mix well.

Transfer the cooked meatballs on a large plate, then baste the sauce over. Garnish with thyme leaves and serve.

Italian Flavour Chicken Breasts with Roma Tomatoes

Prep time: 10 minutes | Cook time: 60 minutes | Serves 8

1.4 kg chicken breasts, bone-in
1 teaspoon minced fresh basil
1 teaspoon minced fresh rosemary
2 tablespoons minced fresh parsley
1 teaspoon cayenne pepper

½ teaspoon salt
½ teaspoon freshly ground black pepper
4 medium Roma tomatoes, halved
Cooking spray

Preheat the air fryer to 190°C. Spritz the air fryer basket with cooking spray.

Combine all the ingredients, except for the chicken breasts and tomatoes, in a large bowl. Stir to mix well.

Dunk the chicken breasts in the mixture and press to coat well.

Transfer the chicken breasts in the preheated air fryer. You may need to work in batches to avoid overcrowding.

Air fry for 25 minutes or until the internal temperature of the thickest part of the breasts reaches at least 76°C. Flip the breasts halfway through the cooking time.

Remove the cooked chicken breasts from the basket and adjust the temperature to 180°C.

Place the tomatoes in the air fryer and spritz with cooking spray. Sprinkle with a touch of salt and cook for 10 minutes or until tender. Shake the basket halfway through the cooking time.

Serve the tomatoes with chicken breasts on a large serving plate.

Turkey Meatloaf

Prep time: 10 minutes | Cook time: 50 minutes | Serves 4

230 g sliced mushrooms
1 small onion, coarsely chopped
2 cloves garlic
680 g 85% lean turkey mince
2 eggs, lightly beaten
1 tablespoon tomato paste
25 g almond meal

2 tablespoons almond milk
1 tablespoon dried oregano
1 teaspoon salt
½ teaspoon freshly ground black pepper
1 Roma tomato, thinly sliced

Preheat the air fryer to 180°C. . Lightly coat a round pan with olive oil and set aside.

In a food processor fitted with a metal blade, combine the mushrooms, onion, and garlic. Pulse until finely chopped. Transfer the vegetables to a large mixing bowl.

Add the turkey, eggs, tomato paste, almond meal, milk, oregano, salt, and black pepper. Mix gently until thoroughly combined. Transfer the mixture to the prepared pan and shape into a loaf. Arrange the tomato slices on top.

Air fry for 50 minutes or until the meatloaf is nicely browned and a thermometer inserted into the thickest part registers 76°C. Remove from the air fryer and let rest for about 10 minutes before slicing.

African Piri-Piri Chicken Drumsticks

Prep time: 30 minutes | Cook time: 20 minutes | Serves 2

Chicken:
1 tablespoon chopped fresh thyme leaves
1 tablespoon minced fresh ginger
1 small shallot, finely chopped
2 garlic cloves, minced
80 ml piri-piri sauce or hot sauce
3 tablespoons extra-virgin olive oil
Zest and juice of 1 lemon

1 teaspoon smoked paprika
½ teaspoon kosher salt
½ teaspoon black pepper
4 chicken drumsticks
Glaze:
2 tablespoons butter or ghee
1 teaspoon chopped fresh thyme leaves
1 garlic clove, minced
1 tablespoon piri-piri sauce
1 tablespoon fresh lemon juice

For the chicken: In a small bowl, stir together all the ingredients except the chicken. Place the chicken and the marinade in a gallon-size resealable plastic bag. Seal the bag and massage to coat. Refrigerate for at least 2 hours or up to 24 hours, turning the bag occasionally.

Place the chicken legs in the air fryer basket. Set the air fryer to 200°C for 20 minutes, turning the chicken halfway through the cooking time.

Meanwhile, for the glaze: Melt the butter in a small saucepan over medium-high heat. Add the thyme and garlic. Cook, stirring, until the garlic just begins to brown, 1 to 2 minutes. Add the piri-piri sauce and lemon juice. Reduce the heat to medium-low and simmer for 1 to 2 minutes.

Transfer the chicken to a serving platter. Pour the glaze over the chicken. Serve immediately.

Crunchy Chicken Tenders

Prep time: 5 minutes | Cook time: 12 minutes | Serves 4

1 egg
60 ml unsweetened almond milk
30 g whole wheat flour
30 g whole wheat bread crumbs
½ teaspoon salt
½ teaspoon black pepper

½ teaspoon dried thyme
½ teaspoon dried sage
½ teaspoon garlic powder
450 g chicken tenderloins
1 lemon, quartered

Preheat the air fryer to 184°C.
In a shallow bowl, beat together the egg and almond milk until frothy.
In a separate shallow bowl, whisk together the flour, bread crumbs, salt, pepper, thyme, sage, and garlic powder.
Dip each chicken tenderloin into the egg mixture, then into the bread crumb mixture, coating the outside with the crumbs. Place the breaded chicken tenderloins into the bottom of the air fryer basket in an even layer, making sure that they don't touch each other.
Cook for 6 minutes, then turn and cook for an additional 5 to 6 minutes. Serve with lemon slices.

Barbecue Chicken Bites

Prep time: 5 minutes | Cook time: 19 minutes | Serves 4

Oil, for spraying
2 (170 g) boneless, skinless chicken breasts, cut into bite-size pieces

60 g all-purpose flour
1 tablespoon granulated garlic
2 teaspoons seasoned salt
280 g barbecue sauce

Line the air fryer basket with parchment and spray lightly with oil.
Place the chicken, flour, garlic, and seasoned salt in a zip-top plastic bag, seal, and shake well until evenly coated.
Place the chicken in an even layer in the prepared basket and spray liberally with oil. You may need to work in batches, depending on the size of your air fryer.
Roast at 200°C for 8 minutes, flip, spray with more oil, and cook for another 8 minutes, or until the internal temperature reaches 76°C and the juices run clear.
Transfer the chicken to a large bowl and toss with the barbecue sauce.
Line the air fryer basket with fresh parchment, return the chicken to the basket, and cook for another 3 minutes.

Apricot-Glazed Chicken Drumsticks

Prep time: 15 minutes | Cook time: 30 minutes | Makes 6 drumsticks

For the Glaze:
160 g apricot preserves
½ teaspoon tamari
¼ teaspoon chili powder
2 teaspoons Dijon mustard
For the Chicken:

6 chicken drumsticks
½ teaspoon seasoning salt
1 teaspoon salt
½ teaspoon ground black pepper
Cooking spray

Make the glaze: Combine the ingredients for the glaze in a saucepan, then heat over low heat for 10 minutes or until thickened. Turn off the heat and sit until ready to use. Make the Chicken: Preheat the air fryer to 190°C. Spritz the air fryer basket with cooking spray.
Combine the seasoning salt, salt, and pepper in a small bowl. Stir to mix well.
Place the chicken drumsticks in the preheated air fryer. Spritz with cooking spray and sprinkle with the salt mixture on both sides.
Air fry for 20 minutes or until well browned. Flip the chicken halfway through.
Baste the chicken with the glaze and air fryer for 2 more minutes or until the chicken tenderloin is glossy.
Serve immediately.

Chicken Drumsticks with Barbecue-Honey Sauce

Prep time: 5 minutes | Cook time: 40 minutes | Serves 5

1 tablespoon olive oil
10 chicken drumsticks
Chicken seasoning or rub, to taste

Salt and ground black pepper, to taste
240 ml barbecue sauce
85 g honey

Preheat the air fryer to 200°C. Grease the air fryer basket with olive oil.
Rub the chicken drumsticks with chicken seasoning or rub, salt and ground black pepper on a clean work surface.
Arrange the chicken drumsticks in a single layer in the air fryer, then air fry for 18 minutes or until lightly browned. Flip the drumsticks halfway through. You may need to work in batches to avoid overcrowding.
Meanwhile, combine the barbecue sauce and honey in a small bowl. Stir to mix well.
Remove the drumsticks from the air fryer and baste with the sauce mixture to serve.

Easy Chicken Nachos

Prep time: 5 minutes | Cook time: 5 minutes | Serves 8

Oil, for spraying
420 g shredded cooked chicken
1 (30 g) package ranch seasoning
60 g sour cream

55 g corn tortilla chips
75 g bacon bits
235 g shredded Cheddar cheese
1 tablespoon chopped spring onions

Line the air fryer basket with parchment and spray lightly with oil.
In a small bowl, mix together the chicken, ranch seasoning, and sour cream.
Place the tortilla chips in the prepared basket and top with the chicken mixture. Add the bacon bits, Cheddar cheese, and spring onions.
Air fry at 220°C for 3 to 5 minutes, or until heated through and the cheese is melted.

Yakitori

Prep time: 10 minutes | Cook time: 15 minutes | Serves 4

120 ml mirin
60 ml dry white wine
120 ml soy sauce
1 tablespoon light brown sugar
680 g boneless, skinless chicken thighs, cut into 1½-inch pieces, fat

trimmed
4 medium spring onions, trimmed, cut into 1½-inch pieces
Cooking spray
Special Equipment:
4 (4-inch) bamboo skewers, soaked in water for at least 30 minutes

Combine the mirin, dry white wine, soy sauce, and brown sugar in a saucepan. Bring to a boil over medium heat. Keep stirring.
Boil for another 2 minutes or until it has a thick consistency. Turn off the heat.
Preheat the air fryer to 200°C. Spritz the air fryer basket with cooking spray.
Run the bamboo skewers through the chicken pieces and spring onions alternatively.
Arrange the skewers in the preheated air fryer, then brush with mirin mixture on both sides. Spritz with cooking spray.
Air fry for 10 minutes or until the chicken and spring onions are glossy. Flip the skewers halfway through.
Serve immediately.

Cheese-Encrusted Chicken Tenderloins with Peanuts

Prep time: 10 minutes | Cook time: 25 minutes | Serves 4

45 g grated Parmesan cheese
½ teaspoon garlic powder
1 teaspoon red pepper flakes
Sea salt and ground black pepper, to taste

2 tablespoons peanut oil
680 g chicken tenderloins
2 tablespoons peanuts, roasted and roughly chopped
Cooking spray

Preheat the air fryer to 180°C. Spritz the air fryer basket with cooking spray.
Combine the Parmesan cheese, garlic powder, red pepper flakes, salt, black pepper, and peanut oil in a large bowl. Stir to mix well.
Dip the chicken tenderloins in the cheese mixture, then press to coat well. Shake the excess off.
Transfer the chicken tenderloins in the air fryer basket. Air fry for 12 minutes or until well browned. Flip the tenderloin halfway through.
You may need to work in batches to avoid overcrowding.
Transfer the chicken tenderloins on a large plate and top with roasted peanuts before serving.

Chapter 7 Vegetables and Sides

Chapter 7 Vegetables and Sides

Easy Greek Briami (Ratatouille)

Prep time: 15 minutes | Cook time: 40 minutes | Serves 6

2 Maris Piper potatoes, cubed
100 g plum tomatoes, cubed
1 aubergine, cubed
1 courgette, cubed
1 red onion, chopped
1 red pepper, chopped
2 garlic cloves, minced
1 teaspoon dried mint
1 teaspoon dried parsley

1 teaspoon dried oregano
½ teaspoon salt
½ teaspoon black pepper
¼ teaspoon red pepper flakes
80 ml olive oil
1 (230 g) can tomato paste
65 ml vegetable stock
65 ml water

Preheat the air fryer to 160ºC.
In a large bowl, combine the potatoes, tomatoes, aubergine, courgette onion, bell pepper, garlic, mint, parsley, oregano, salt, black pepper, and red pepper flakes.
In a small bowl, mix together the olive oil, tomato paste, stock, and water.
Pour the oil-and-tomato-paste mixture over the vegetables and toss until everything is coated.
Pour the coated vegetables into the air fryer basket in an even layer and roast for 20 minutes. After 20 minutes, stir well and spread out again. Roast for an additional 10 minutes, then repeat the process and cook for another 10 minutes.

Buffalo Cauliflower with Blue Cheese

Prep time: 15 minutes | Cook time: 5 to 7 minutes per batch | Serves 6

1 large head cauliflower, rinsed and separated into small florets
1 tablespoon extra-virgin olive oil
½ teaspoon garlic powder
Cooking oil spray
80 ml hot wing sauce

190 g nonfat Greek yogurt
60 g buttermilk
½ teaspoon hot sauce
1 celery stalk, chopped
2 tablespoons crumbled blue cheese

Insert the crisper plate into the basket and the basket into the unit. Preheat the unit by selecting AIR FRY, setting the temperature to192ºC, and setting the time to 3 minutes. Select START/STOP to begin.
In a large bowl, toss together the cauliflower florets and olive oil. Sprinkle with the garlic powder and toss again to coat.
Once the unit is preheated, spray the crisper plate with cooking oil. Put half the cauliflower into the basket.
Select AIR FRY, set the temperature to192ºC, and set the time to 7 minutes. Select START/STOP to begin.
After 3 minutes, remove the basket and shake the cauliflower. Reinsert the basket to resume cooking. After 2 minutes, check the cauliflower. It is done when it is browned. If not, resume cooking.
When the cooking is complete, transfer the cauliflower to a serving bowl and toss with half the hot wing sauce.
Repeat steps 4, 5, and 6 with the remaining cauliflower and hot wing sauce.
In a small bowl, stir together the yogurt, buttermilk, hot sauce, celery, and blue cheese. Drizzle the sauce over the finished cauliflower and serve.

Tofu Bites

Prep time: 15 minutes | Cook time: 30 minutes | Serves 4

1 packaged firm tofu, cubed and pressed to remove excess water
1 tablespoon soy sauce
1 tablespoon ketchup
1 tablespoon maple syrup
½ teaspoon vinegar
1 teaspoon liquid smoke

1 teaspoon hot sauce
2 tablespoons sesame seeds
1 teaspoon garlic powder
Salt and ground black pepper, to taste
Cooking spray

Preheat the air fryer to 192ºC.
Spritz a baking dish with cooking spray.
Combine all the ingredients to coat the tofu completely and allow the marinade to absorb for half an hour.
Transfer the tofu to the baking dish, then air fry for 15 minutes. Flip the tofu over and air fry for another 15 minutes on the other side. Serve immediately.

Garlic-Parmesan Crispy Baby Potatoes

Prep time: 10 minutes | Cook time: 15 minutes | Serves 4

Oil, for spraying
450 g baby potatoes
45 g grated Parmesan cheese, divided
3 tablespoons olive oil
2 teaspoons garlic powder
½ teaspoon onion powder

½ teaspoon salt
¼ teaspoon freshly ground black pepper
¼ teaspoon paprika
2 tablespoons chopped fresh parsley, for garnish

Line the air fryer basket with parchment and spray lightly with oil. Rinse the potatoes, pat dry with paper towels, and place in a large bowl.
In a small bowl, mix together 45 g of Parmesan cheese, the olive oil, garlic, onion powder, salt, black pepper, and paprika. Pour the mixture over the potatoes and toss to coat.
Transfer the potatoes to the prepared basket and spread them out in an even layer, taking care to keep them from touching. You may need to work in batches, depending on the size of your air fryer.
Air fry at 200ºC for 15 minutes, stirring after 7 to 8 minutes, or until easily pierced with a fork. Continue to cook for another 1 to 2 minutes, if needed.
Sprinkle with the parsley and the remaining Parmesan cheese and serve.

Sesame Taj Tofu

Prep time: 5 minutes | Cook time: 25 minutes | Serves 4

1 block firm tofu, pressed and cut into 1-inch thick cubes
2 tablespoons soy sauce
2 teaspoons toasted sesame

seeds
1 teaspoon rice vinegar
1 tablespoon cornflour

Preheat the air fryer to 200°C.
Add the tofu, soy sauce, sesame seeds, and rice vinegar in a bowl together and mix well to coat the tofu cubes. Then cover the tofu in cornflour and put it in the air fryer basket.
Air fry for 25 minutes, giving the basket a shake at five-minute intervals to ensure the tofu cooks evenly.
Serve immediately.

Balsamic Brussels Sprouts

Prep time: 5 minutes | Cook time: 12 minutes | Serves 4

180 g trimmed and halved fresh Brussels sprouts
2 tablespoons olive oil
¼ teaspoon salt

¼ teaspoon ground black pepper
2 tablespoons balsamic vinegar
2 slices cooked sugar-free bacon, crumbled

In a large bowl, toss Brussels sprouts in olive oil, then sprinkle with salt and pepper. Place into ungreased air fryer basket. Adjust the temperature to 192°C and set the timer for 12 minutes, shaking the basket halfway through cooking. Brussels sprouts will be tender and browned when done.
Place sprouts in a large serving dish and drizzle with balsamic vinegar. Sprinkle bacon over top. Serve warm.

Fried Courgette Salad

Prep time: 10 minutes | Cook time: 5 to 7 minutes | Serves 4

2 medium courgette, thinly sliced
5 tablespoons olive oil, divided
15 g chopped fresh parsley
2 tablespoons chopped fresh mint

Zest and juice of ½ lemon
1 clove garlic, minced
65 g crumbled feta cheese
Freshly ground black pepper, to taste

Preheat the air fryer to 200°C.
In a large bowl, toss the courgette slices with 1 tablespoon of the olive oil.
Working in batches if necessary, arrange the courgette slices in an even layer in the air fryer basket. Pausing halfway through the cooking time to shake the basket, air fry for 5 to 7 minutes until soft and lightly browned on each side.
Meanwhile, in a small bowl, combine the remaining 4 tablespoons olive oil, parsley, mint, lemon zest, lemon juice, and garlic.
Arrange the courgette on a plate and drizzle with the dressing. Sprinkle the feta and black pepper on top. Serve warm or at room temperature.

Indian Aubergine Bharta

Prep time: 15 minutes | Cook time: 20 minutes | Serves 4

1 medium aubergine
2 tablespoons vegetable oil
25 g finely minced onion
100 g finely chopped fresh tomato

2 tablespoons fresh lemon juice
2 tablespoons chopped fresh coriander
½ teaspoon coarse sea salt
⅛ teaspoon cayenne pepper

Rub the aubergine all over with the vegetable oil. Place the aubergine in the air fryer basket. Set the air fryer to 200°C for 20 minutes, or until the aubergine skin is blistered and charred.
Transfer the aubergine to a re-sealable plastic bag, seal, and set aside for 15 to 20 minutes (the aubergine will finish cooking in the residual heat trapped in the bag).
Transfer the aubergine to a large bowl. Peel off and discard the charred skin. Roughly mash the aubergine flesh. Add the onion, tomato, lemon juice, coriander, salt, and cayenne. Stir to combine.

Rosemary-Roasted Red Potatoes

Prep time: 5 minutes | Cook time: 20 minutes | Serves 6

450 g red potatoes, quartered
65 ml olive oil
½ teaspoon coarse sea salt

¼ teaspoon black pepper
1 garlic clove, minced
4 rosemary sprigs

Preheat the air fryer to 180°C.
In a large bowl, toss the potatoes with the olive oil, salt, pepper, and garlic until well coated.
Pour the potatoes into the air fryer basket and top with the sprigs of rosemary.
Roast for 10 minutes, then stir or toss the potatoes and roast for 10 minutes more.
Remove the rosemary sprigs and serve the potatoes. Season with additional salt and pepper, if needed.

Garlic Roasted Broccoli

Prep time: 8 minutes | Cook time: 10 to 14 minutes | Serves 6

1 head broccoli, cut into bite-size florets
1 tablespoon avocado oil
2 teaspoons minced garlic
⅛ teaspoon red pepper flakes

Sea salt and freshly ground black pepper, to taste
1 tablespoon freshly squeezed lemon juice
½ teaspoon lemon zest

In a large bowl, toss together the broccoli, avocado oil, garlic, red pepper flakes, salt, and pepper.
Set the air fryer to 192°C. Arrange the broccoli in a single layer in the air fryer basket, working in batches if necessary. Roast for 10 to 14 minutes, until the broccoli is lightly charred.
Place the florets in a medium bowl and toss with the lemon juice and lemon zest. Serve.

Parsnip Fries with Romesco Sauce

Prep time: 20 minutes | Cook time: 24 minutes | Serves 4

Romesco Sauce:
1 red pepper, halved and seeded
1 (1-inch) thick slice of Italian bread, torn into pieces
130 g almonds, toasted
Olive oil
½ Jalapeño pepper, seeded
1 tablespoon fresh parsley leaves
1 clove garlic
2 plum tomatoes, peeled and

seeded
1 tablespoon red wine vinegar
¼ teaspoon smoked paprika
½ teaspoon salt
180 ml olive oil
3 parsnips, peeled and cut into long strips
2 teaspoons olive oil
Salt and freshly ground black pepper, to taste

Preheat the air fryer to 200°C.

Place the red pepper halves, cut side down, in the air fryer basket and air fry for 8 to 10 minutes, or until the skin turns black all over. Remove the pepper from the air fryer and let it cool. When it is cool enough to handle, peel the pepper.

Toss the torn bread and almonds with a little olive oil and air fry for 4 minutes, shaking the basket a couple times throughout the cooking time. When the bread and almonds are nicely toasted, remove them from the air fryer and let them cool for just a minute or two.

Combine the toasted bread, almonds, roasted red pepper, Jalapeño pepper, parsley, garlic, tomatoes, vinegar, smoked paprika and salt in a food processor or blender. Process until smooth. With the processor running, add the olive oil through the feed tube until the sauce comes together in a smooth paste that is barely pourable.

Toss the parsnip strips with the olive oil, salt and freshly ground black pepper and air fry at 200°C for 10 minutes, shaking the basket a couple times during the cooking process so they brown and cook evenly. Serve the parsnip fries warm with the Romesco sauce to dip into.

Brussels Sprouts with Pecans and Gorgonzola

Prep time: 10 minutes | Cook time: 25 minutes | Serves 4

65 g pecans
680 g fresh Brussels sprouts, trimmed and quartered
2 tablespoons olive oil

Salt and freshly ground black pepper, to taste
30 g crumbled Gorgonzola cheese

Spread the pecans in a single layer of the air fryer and set the heat to 180°C. Air fry for 3 to 5 minutes until the pecans are lightly browned and fragrant. Transfer the pecans to a plate and continue preheating the air fryer, increasing the heat to 200°C.

In a large bowl, toss the Brussels sprouts with the olive oil and season with salt and black pepper to taste.

Working in batches if necessary, arrange the Brussels sprouts in a single layer in the air fryer basket. Pausing halfway through the baking time to shake the basket, air fry for 20 to 25 minutes until the sprouts are tender and starting to brown on the edges.

Transfer the sprouts to a serving bowl and top with the toasted pecans and Gorgonzola. Serve warm or at room temperature.

Lemon-Garlic Mushrooms

Prep time: 10 minutes | Cook time: 10 to 15 minutes | Serves 6

340 g sliced mushrooms
1 tablespoon avocado oil
Sea salt and freshly ground black pepper, to taste
3 tablespoons unsalted butter
1 teaspoon minced garlic

1 teaspoon freshly squeezed lemon juice
½ teaspoon red pepper flakes
2 tablespoons chopped fresh parsley

Place the mushrooms in a medium bowl and toss with the oil. Season to taste with salt and pepper.

Place the mushrooms in a single layer in the air fryer basket. Set your air fryer to 192°C and roast for 10 to 15 minutes, until the mushrooms are tender.

While the mushrooms cook, melt the butter in a small pot or skillet over medium-low heat. Stir in the garlic and cook for 30 seconds. Remove the pot from the heat and stir in the lemon juice and red pepper flakes.

Toss the mushrooms with the lemon-garlic butter and garnish with the parsley before serving.

Spinach and Sweet Pepper Poppers

Prep time: 10 minutes | Cook time: 8 minutes | Makes 16 poppers

110 g cream cheese, softened
20 g chopped fresh spinach leaves
½ teaspoon garlic powder

8 mini sweet bell peppers, tops removed, seeded, and halved lengthwise

In a medium bowl, mix cream cheese, spinach, and garlic powder. Place 1 tablespoon mixture into each sweet pepper half and press down to smooth.

Place poppers into ungreased air fryer basket. Adjust the temperature to 200°C and air fry for 8 minutes. Poppers will be done when cheese is browned on top and peppers are tender-crisp. Serve warm.

Simple Cougette Crisps

Prep time: 5 minutes | Cook time: 14 minutes | Serves 4

2 courgette, sliced into ¼- to ½-inch-thick rounds
¼ teaspoon garlic granules
⅛ teaspoon sea salt

Freshly ground black pepper, to taste (optional)
Cooking spray

Preheat the air fryer to 200°C. Spritz the air fryer basket with cooking spray.

Put the courgette rounds in the air fryer basket, spreading them out as much as possible. Top with a sprinkle of garlic granules, sea salt, and black pepper (if desired). Spritz the courgette rounds with cooking spray.

Roast for 14 minutes, flipping the courgette rounds halfway through, or until the courgette rounds are crisp-tender.

Let them rest for 5 minutes and serve.

Courgette Balls

Prep time: 5 minutes | Cook time: 10 minutes | Serves 4

4 courgettes
1 egg
45 g grated Parmesan cheese

1 tablespoon Italian herbs
75 g grated coconut

Thinly grate the courgettes and dry with a cheesecloth, ensuring to remove all the moisture.
In a bowl, combine the courgettes with the egg, Parmesan, Italian herbs, and grated coconut, mixing well to incorporate everything. Using the hands, mold the mixture into balls.
Preheat the air fryer to 200°C.
Lay the courgette balls in the air fryer basket and air fry for 10 minutes.
Serve hot.

Cauliflower with Lime Juice

Prep time: 10 minutes | Cook time: 7 minutes | Serves 4

215 g chopped cauliflower florets
2 tablespoons coconut oil, melted

2 teaspoons chili powder
½ teaspoon garlic powder
1 medium lime
2 tablespoons chopped coriander

In a large bowl, toss cauliflower with coconut oil. Sprinkle with chili powder and garlic powder. Place seasoned cauliflower into the air fryer basket.
Adjust the temperature to 180°C and set the timer for 7 minutes. Cauliflower will be tender and begin to turn golden at the edges. Place into a serving bowl.
Cut the lime into quarters and squeeze juice over cauliflower. Garnish with coriander.

Fig, Chickpea, and Rocket Salad

Prep time: 15 minutes | Cook time: 20 minutes | Serves 4

8 fresh figs, halved
250 g cooked chickpeas
1 teaspoon crushed roasted cumin seeds
4 tablespoons balsamic vinegar

2 tablespoons extra-virgin olive oil, plus more for greasing
Salt and ground black pepper, to taste
40 g rocket, washed and dried

Preheat the air fryer to 192°C.
Cover the air fryer basket with aluminum foil and grease lightly with oil. Put the figs in the air fryer basket and air fry for 10 minutes.
In a bowl, combine the chickpeas and cumin seeds.
Remove the air fried figs from the air fryer and replace with the chickpeas. Air fry for 10 minutes. Leave to cool.
In the meantime, prepare the dressing. Mix the balsamic vinegar, olive oil, salt and pepper.
In a salad bowl, combine the rocket with the cooled figs and chickpeas.
Toss with the sauce and serve.

Mushrooms with Goat Cheese

Prep time: 10 minutes | Cook time: 10 minutes | Serves 4

3 tablespoons vegetable oil
450 g mixed mushrooms, trimmed and sliced
1 clove garlic, minced
¼ teaspoon dried thyme

½ teaspoon black pepper
110 g goat cheese, diced
2 teaspoons chopped fresh thyme leaves (optional)

In a baking pan, combine the oil, mushrooms, garlic, dried thyme, and pepper. Stir in the goat cheese. Place the pan in the air fryer basket. Set the air fryer to 200°C for 10 minutes, stirring halfway through the cooking time.
Sprinkle with fresh thyme, if desired.

Polenta Casserole

Prep time: 5 minutes | Cook time: 28 to 30 minutes | Serves 4

10 fresh asparagus spears, cut into 1-inch pieces
320 g cooked polenta, cooled to room temperature
1 egg, beaten
2 teaspoons Worcestershire

sauce
½ teaspoon garlic powder
¼ teaspoon salt
2 slices emmental cheese (about 40 g)
Oil for misting or cooking spray

Mist asparagus spears with oil and air fry at 200°C for 5 minutes, until crisp-tender.
In a medium bowl, mix together the grits, egg, Worcestershire, garlic powder, and salt.
Spoon half of polenta mixture into a baking pan and top with asparagus.
Tear cheese slices into pieces and layer evenly on top of asparagus.
Top with remaining polenta.
Bake at 180°C for 23 to 25 minutes. The casserole will rise a little as it cooks. When done, the top will have browned lightly with just a hint of crispiness.

Fried Asparagus

Prep time: 5 minutes | Cook time: 12 minutes | Serves 4

1 tablespoon olive oil
450 g asparagus spears, ends trimmed
¼ teaspoon salt

¼ teaspoon ground black pepper
1 tablespoon salted butter, melted

In a large bowl, drizzle olive oil over asparagus spears and sprinkle with salt and pepper.
Place spears into ungreased air fryer basket. Adjust the temperature to 192°C and set the timer for 12 minutes, shaking the basket halfway through cooking. Asparagus will be lightly browned and tender when done.
Transfer to a large dish and drizzle with butter. Serve warm.

Garlic Courgette and Red Peppers

Prep time: 5 minutes | Cook time: 15 minutes | Serves 6

2 medium courgette, cubed
1 red pepper, diced
2 garlic cloves, sliced

2 tablespoons olive oil
½ teaspoon salt

Preheat the air fryer to 193ºC.
In a large bowl, mix together the courgette, bell pepper, and garlic with the olive oil and salt.
Pour the mixture into the air fryer basket, and roast for 7 minutes.
Shake or stir, then roast for 7 to 8 minutes more.

Parmesan Herb Focaccia Bread

Prep time: 10 minutes | Cook time: 10 minutes | Serves 6

225 g shredded Mozzarella cheese
30 g) full-fat cream cheese
95 g blanched finely ground almond flour
40 g ground golden flaxseed
20 g grated Parmesan cheese

½ teaspoon bicarbonate of soda
2 large eggs
½ teaspoon garlic powder
¼ teaspoon dried basil
¼ teaspoon dried rosemary
2 tablespoons salted butter, melted and divided

Place Mozzarella, cream cheese, and almond flour into a large microwave-safe bowl and microwave for 1 minute. Add the flaxseed, Parmesan, and bicarbonate of soda and stir until smooth ball forms. If the mixture cools too much, it will be hard to mix. Return to microwave for 10 to 15 seconds to rewarm if necessary.
Stir in eggs. You may need to use your hands to get them fully incorporated. Just keep stirring and they will absorb into the dough. Sprinkle dough with garlic powder, basil, and rosemary and knead into dough. Grease a baking pan with 1 tablespoon melted butter. Press the dough evenly into the pan. Place pan into the air fryer basket.
Adjust the temperature to 200ºC and bake for 10 minutes.
At 7 minutes, cover with foil if bread begins to get too dark.
Remove and let cool at least 30 minutes. Drizzle with remaining butter and serve.

Super Cheesy Gold Aubergine

Prep time: 15 minutes | Cook time: 30 minutes | Serves 4

1 medium aubergine, peeled and cut into ½-inch-thick rounds
1 teaspoon salt, plus more for seasoning
60 g plain flour
2 eggs
90 g Italian bread crumbs
2 tablespoons grated Parmesan cheese

Freshly ground black pepper, to taste
Cooking oil spray
180 g marinara sauce
45 g shredded Parmesan cheese, divided
110 g shredded Mozzarella cheese, divided

Blot the aubergine with paper towels to dry completely. You can also sprinkle with 1 teaspoon of salt to sweat out the moisture; if you do this, rinse the aubergine slices and blot dry again.
Place the flour in a shallow bowl.
In another shallow bowl, beat the eggs.
In a third shallow bowl, stir together the bread crumbs and grated Parmesan cheese and season with salt and pepper.
Dip each aubergine round in the flour, in the eggs, and into the bread crumbs to coat.
Insert the crisper plate into the basket and the basket into the unit. Preheat the unit by selecting AIR FRY, setting the temperature to 200ºC, and setting the time to 3 minutes. Select START/STOP to begin.
Once the unit is preheated, spray the crisper plate and the basket with cooking oil. Working in batches, place the aubergine rounds into the basket. Do not stack them. Spray the aubergine with the cooking oil.
Select AIR FRY, set the temperature to 200ºC, and set the time to 10 minutes. Select START/STOP to begin.
After 7 minutes, open the unit and top each round with 1 teaspoon of marinara sauce and ½ tablespoon each of shredded Parmesan and Mozzarella cheese. Resume cooking for 2 to 3 minutes until the cheese melts.
1Repeat steps 5, 6, 7, 8, and 9 with the remaining aubergine.
1When the cooking is complete, serve immediately.

Spiced Honey-Walnut Carrots

Prep time: 5 minutes | Cook time: 12 minutes | Serves 6

450 g baby carrots
2 tablespoons olive oil
80 g raw honey

¼ teaspoon ground cinnamon
25 g black walnuts, chopped

Preheat the air fryer to 180ºC.
In a large bowl, toss the baby carrots with olive oil, honey, and cinnamon until well coated.
Pour into the air fryer and roast for 6 minutes. Shake the basket, sprinkle the walnuts on top, and roast for 6 minutes more.
Remove the carrots from the air fryer and serve.

Five-Spice Roasted Sweet Potatoes

Prep time: 10 minutes | Cook time: 12 minutes | Serves 4

½ teaspoon ground cinnamon
¼ teaspoon ground cumin
¼ teaspoon paprika
1 teaspoon chili powder
⅛ teaspoon turmeric
½ teaspoon salt (optional)

Freshly ground black pepper, to taste
2 large sweet potatoes, peeled and cut into ¾-inch cubes
1 tablespoon olive oil

In a large bowl, mix together cinnamon, cumin, paprika, chili powder, turmeric, salt, and pepper to taste.
Add potatoes and stir well.
Drizzle the seasoned potatoes with the olive oil and stir until evenly coated.
Place seasoned potatoes in a baking pan or an ovenproof dish that fits inside your air fryer basket.
Cook for 6 minutes at 200ºC, stop, and stir well.
Cook for an additional 6 minutes.

Crispy Green Beans

Prep time: 5 minutes | Cook time: 8 minutes | Serves 4

2 teaspoons olive oil
230 g fresh green beans, ends trimmed

¼ teaspoon salt
¼ teaspoon ground black pepper

In a large bowl, drizzle olive oil over green beans and sprinkle with salt and pepper.
Place green beans into ungreased air fryer basket. Adjust the temperature to 180°C and set the timer for 8 minutes, shaking the basket two times during cooking. Green beans will be dark golden and crispy at the edges when done. Serve warm.

Sweet-and-Sour Brussels Sprouts

Prep time: 10 minutes | Cook time: 20 minutes | Serves 2

70 g Thai sweet chili sauce
2 tablespoons black vinegar or balsamic vinegar
½ teaspoon hot sauce, such as Tabasco
230 g Brussels sprouts, trimmed (large sprouts halved)

2 small shallots, cut into ¼-inch-thick slices
coarse sea salt and freshly ground black pepper, to taste
2 teaspoons lightly packed fresh coriander leaves

In a large bowl, whisk together the chili sauce, vinegar, and hot sauce. Add the Brussels sprouts and shallots, season with salt and pepper, and toss to combine. Scrape the Brussels sprouts and sauce into a cake pan.
Place the pan in the air fryer and roast at 192°C, stirring every 5 minutes, until the Brussels sprouts are tender and the sauce is reduced to a sticky glaze, about 20 minutes.
Remove the pan from the air fryer and transfer the Brussels sprouts to plates. Sprinkle with the coriander and serve warm.

Green Tomato Salad

Prep time: 10 minutes | Cook time: 8 to 10 minutes | Serves 4

4 green tomatoes
½ teaspoon salt
1 large egg, lightly beaten
50 g peanut flour
1 tablespoon Creole seasoning
1 (140 g) bag rocket
Buttermilk Dressing:
230 g mayonnaise
120 g sour cream

2 teaspoons fresh lemon juice
2 tablespoons finely chopped fresh parsley
1 teaspoon dried dill
1 teaspoon dried chives
½ teaspoon salt
½ teaspoon garlic powder
½ teaspoon onion powder

Preheat the air fryer to 200°C.
Slice the tomatoes into ½-inch slices and sprinkle with the salt. Let sit for 5 to 10 minutes.
Place the egg in a small shallow bowl. In another small shallow bowl, combine the peanut flour and Creole seasoning. Dip each tomato slice into the egg wash, then dip into the peanut flour mixture, turning to coat evenly.

Working in batches if necessary, arrange the tomato slices in a single layer in the air fryer basket and spray both sides lightly with olive oil. Air fry until browned and crisp, 8 to 10 minutes.
To make the buttermilk dressing: In a small bowl, whisk together the mayonnaise, sour cream, lemon juice, parsley, dill, chives, salt, garlic powder, and onion powder.
Serve the tomato slices on top of a bed of the rocket with the dressing on the side.

Roasted Aubergine

Prep time: 15 minutes | Cook time: 15 minutes | Serves 4

1 large aubergine
2 tablespoons olive oil

¼ teaspoon salt
½ teaspoon garlic powder

Remove top and bottom from aubergine. Slice aubergine into ¼-inch-thick round slices.
Brush slices with olive oil. Sprinkle with salt and garlic powder. Place aubergine slices into the air fryer basket.
Adjust the temperature to 200°C and set the timer for 15 minutes. Serve immediately.

Roasted Radishes with Sea Salt

Prep time: 5 minutes | Cook time: 18 minutes | Serves 4

450 g radishes, ends trimmed if needed

2 tablespoons olive oil
½ teaspoon sea salt

Preheat the air fryer to 180°C.
In a large bowl, combine the radishes with olive oil and sea salt.
Pour the radishes into the air fryer and roast for 10 minutes. Stir or turn the radishes over and roast for 8 minutes more, then serve.

Golden Pickles

Prep time: 10 minutes | Cook time: 15 minutes | Serves 4

14 dill pickles, sliced
30 g flour
⅛ teaspoon baking powder
Pinch of salt
2 tablespoons cornflour plus 3

tablespoons water
6 tablespoons panko bread crumbs
½ teaspoon paprika
Cooking spray

Preheat the air fryer to 200°C.
Drain any excess moisture out of the dill pickles on a paper towel.
In a bowl, combine the flour, baking powder and salt.
Throw in the cornflour and water mixture and combine well with a whisk.
Put the panko bread crumbs in a shallow dish along with the paprika. Mix thoroughly.
Dip the pickles in the flour batter, before coating in the bread crumbs. Spritz all the pickles with the cooking spray.
Transfer to the air fryer basket and air fry for 15 minutes, or until golden brown.
Serve immediately.

Shishito Pepper Roast

Prep time: 4 minutes | Cook time: 9 minutes | Serves 4

Cooking oil spray (sunflower, safflower, or refined coconut)
450 g shishito, Anaheim, or bell peppers, rinsed

1 tablespoon soy sauce
2 teaspoons freshly squeezed lime juice
2 large garlic cloves, pressed

Insert the crisper plate into the basket and the basket into the unit. Preheat the unit by selecting AIR ROAST, setting the temperature to 200ºC, and setting the time to 3 minutes. Select START/STOP to begin.

Once the unit is preheated, spray the crisper plate and the basket with cooking oil. Place the peppers into the basket and spray them with oil.

Select AIR ROAST, set the temperature to 200ºC, and set the time to 9 minutes. Select START/STOP to begin.

After 3 minutes, remove the basket and shake the peppers. Spray the peppers with more oil. Reinsert the basket to resume cooking. Repeat this step again after 3 minutes.

While the peppers roast, in a medium bowl, whisk the soy sauce, lime juice, and garlic until combined. Set aside.

When the cooking is complete, several of the peppers should have lots of nice browned spots on them. If using Anaheim or bell peppers, cut a slit in the side of each pepper and remove the seeds, which can be bitter.

Place the roasted peppers in the bowl with the sauce. Toss to coat the peppers evenly and serve.

Lemony Broccoli

Prep time: 10 minutes | Cook time: 9 to 14 minutes per batch | Serves 4

1 large head broccoli, rinsed and patted dry
2 teaspoons extra-virgin olive oil

1 tablespoon freshly squeezed lemon juice
Olive oil spray

Cut off the broccoli florets and separate them. You can use the stems, too; peel the stems and cut them into 1-inch chunks.

Insert the crisper plate into the basket and the basket into the unit. Preheat the unit by selecting AIR ROAST, setting the temperature to 200ºC, and setting the time to 3 minutes. Select START/STOP to begin.

In a large bowl, toss together the broccoli, olive oil, and lemon juice until coated.

Once the unit is preheated, spray the crisper plate with olive oil. Working in batches, place half the broccoli into the basket.

Select AIR ROAST, set the temperature to 200ºC, and set the time to 14 minutes. Select START/STOP to begin.

After 5 minutes, remove the basket and shake the broccoli. Reinsert the basket to resume cooking. Check the broccoli after 5 minutes. If it is crisp-tender and slightly brown around the edges, it is done. If not, resume cooking.

When the cooking is complete, transfer the broccoli to a serving bowl. Repeat steps 5 and 6 with the remaining broccoli. Serve immediately.

Burger Bun for One

Prep time: 2 minutes | Cook time: 5 minutes | Serves 1

2 tablespoons salted butter, melted
25 g blanched finely ground almond flour

¼ teaspoon baking powder
⅛ teaspoon apple cider vinegar
1 large egg, whisked

Pour butter into an ungreased ramekin. Add flour, baking powder, and vinegar to ramekin and stir until combined. Add egg and stir until batter is mostly smooth.

Place ramekin into air fryer basket. Adjust the temperature to 180ºC and bake for 5 minutes. When done, the centre will be firm and the top slightly browned. Let cool, about 5 minutes, then remove from ramekin and slice in half. Serve.

Turnip Fries

Prep time: 10 minutes | Cook time: 20 to 30 minutes | Serves 4

900 g turnip, peeled and cut into ¼ to ½-inch fries
2 tablespoons olive oil

Salt and freshly ground black pepper, to taste

Preheat the air fryer to 200ºC.

In a large bowl, combine the turnip and olive oil. Season to taste with salt and black pepper. Toss gently until thoroughly coated.

Working in batches if necessary, spread the turnip in a single layer in the air fryer basket. Pausing halfway through the cooking time to shake the basket, air fry for 20 to 30 minutes until the fries are lightly browned and crunchy.

Mexican Corn in a Cup

Prep time: 5 minutes | Cook time: 10 minutes | Serves 4

650 g frozen corn kernels (do not thaw)
Vegetable oil spray
2 tablespoons butter
60 g sour cream
60 g mayonnaise
20 g grated Parmesan cheese (or feta, cotija, or queso fresco)

2 tablespoons fresh lemon or lime juice
1 teaspoon chili powder
Chopped fresh green onion (optional)
Chopped fresh coriander (optional)

Place the corn in the bottom of the air fryer basket and spray with vegetable oil spray. Set the air fryer to 180ºC for 10 minutes.

Transfer the corn to a serving bowl. Add the butter and stir until melted. Add the sour cream, mayonnaise, cheese, lemon juice, and chili powder; stir until well combined. Serve immediately with green onion and coriander (if using).

Parmesan-Rosemary Radishes

Prep time: 5 minutes | Cook time: 15 to 20 minutes | Serves 4

1 bunch radishes, stemmed, trimmed, and quartered
1 tablespoon avocado oil
2 tablespoons finely grated fresh Parmesan cheese

1 tablespoon chopped fresh rosemary
Sea salt and freshly ground black pepper, to taste

Place the radishes in a medium bowl and toss them with the avocado oil, Parmesan cheese, rosemary, salt, and pepper.
Set the air fryer to192°C. Arrange the radishes in a single layer in the air fryer basket. Roast for 15 to 20 minutes, until golden brown and tender. Let cool for 5 minutes before serving.

Gorgonzola Mushrooms with Horseradish Mayo

Prep time: 15 minutes | Cook time: 10 minutes | Serves 5

60 g bread crumbs
2 cloves garlic, pressed
2 tablespoons chopped fresh coriander
⅓ teaspoon coarse sea salt
½ teaspoon crushed red pepper flakes
1½ tablespoons olive oil

20 medium mushrooms, stems removed
55 g grated Gorgonzola cheese
55 g low-fat mayonnaise
1 teaspoon prepared horseradish, well-drained
1 tablespoon finely chopped fresh parsley

Preheat the air fryer to 192°C.
Combine the bread crumbs together with the garlic, coriander, salt, red pepper, and olive oil.
Take equal-sized amounts of the bread crumb mixture and use them to stuff the mushroom caps. Add the grated Gorgonzola on top of each.
Put the mushrooms in a baking pan and transfer to the air fryer.
Air fry for 10 minutes, ensuring the stuffing is warm throughout.
In the meantime, prepare the horseradish mayo. Mix the mayonnaise, horseradish and parsley.
When the mushrooms are ready, serve with the mayo.

Cabbage Wedges with Caraway Butter

Prep time: 30 minutes | Cook time: 35 to 40 minutes | Serves 6

1 tablespoon caraway seeds
110 g unsalted butter, at room temperature
½ teaspoon grated lemon zest
1 small head green or red cabbage, cut into 6 wedges

1 tablespoon avocado oil
½ teaspoon sea salt
¼ teaspoon freshly ground black pepper

Place the caraway seeds in a small dry skillet over medium-high heat. Toast the seeds for 2 to 3 minutes, then remove them from the heat and let cool. Lightly crush the seeds using a mortar and pestle or with the back of a knife.
Place the butter in a small bowl and stir in the crushed caraway seeds and lemon zest. Form the butter into a log and wrap it in parchment paper or plastic wrap. Refrigerate for at least 1 hour or freeze for 20 minutes.
Brush or spray the cabbage wedges with the avocado oil, and sprinkle with the salt and pepper.
Set the air fryer to192°C. Place the cabbage in a single layer in the air fryer basket and roast for 20 minutes. Flip and cook for 15 to 20 minutes more, until the cabbage is tender and lightly charred. Plate the cabbage and dot with caraway butter. Tent with foil for 5 minutes to melt the butter, and serve.

Chapter 8 Pizzas, Wraps, and Sandwiches

Chapter 8 Pizzas, Wraps, and Sandwiches

Beef and Pepper Fajitas

Prep time: 15 minutes | Cook time: 10 minutes | Serves 4

450 g beef sirloin steak, cut into strips
2 shallots, sliced
1 orange pepper, sliced
1 red pepper, sliced
2 garlic cloves, minced
2 tablespoons Cajun seasoning
1 tablespoon paprika
Salt and ground black pepper, to taste
4 corn tortillas
120 ml shredded Cheddar cheese
Cooking spray

Preheat the air fryer to 182°C and spritz with cooking spray.
Combine all the ingredients, except for the tortillas and cheese, in a large bowl. Toss to coat well.
Pour the beef and vegetables in the preheated air fryer and spritz with cooking spray.
Air fry for 10 minutes or until the meat is browned and the vegetables are soft and lightly wilted. Shake the basket halfway through.
Unfold the tortillas on a clean work surface and spread the cooked beef and vegetables on top.
Scatter with cheese and fold to serve.

Cheesy Spring Chicken Wraps

Prep time: 30 minutes | Cook time: 5 minutes per batch | Serves 12

2 large-sized chicken breasts, cooked and shredded
2 spring onions, chopped
284 g Ricotta cheese
1 tablespoon rice vinegar
1 tablespoon molasses
1 teaspoon grated fresh ginger
60 ml soy sauce
⅓ teaspoon sea salt
¼ teaspoon ground black pepper, or more to taste
48 wonton wrappers or egg roll wrappers
Cooking spray

Preheat the air fryer to 192°C and spritz with cooking spray.
Combine all the ingredients, except for the wrappers in a large bowl. Toss to mix well.
Unfold the wrappers on a clean work surface, then divide and spoon the mixture in the middle of the wrappers.
Dab a little water on the edges of the wrappers, then fold the edge close to you over the filling.
Tuck the edge under the filling and roll up to seal.
Arrange the wraps in the preheated air fryer and air fry in batches for 5 minutes or until lightly browned. Flip the wraps halfway through.
Serve immediately.

Crispy Chicken Egg Rolls

Prep time: 10 minutes | Cook time: 23 to 24 minutes | Serves 4

450 g minced chicken
2 teaspoons olive oil
2 garlic cloves, minced
1 teaspoon grated fresh ginger
475 ml white cabbage, shredded
1 onion, chopped
60 ml soy sauce
8 egg roll wrappers
1 egg, beaten
Cooking spray

Preheat the air fryer to 188°C. Spritz the air fryer basket with cooking spray.
Heat olive oil in a saucepan over medium heat.
Sauté the garlic and ginger in the olive oil for 1 minute, or until fragrant.
Add the minced chicken to the saucepan.
Sauté for 5 minutes, or until the chicken is cooked through.
Add the cabbage, onion and soy sauce and sauté for 5 to 6 minutes, or until the vegetables become soft.
Remove the saucepan from the heat.
Unfold the egg roll wrappers on a clean work surface.
Divide the chicken mixture among the wrappers and brush the edges of the wrappers with the beaten egg.
Tightly roll up the egg rolls, enclosing the filling.
Arrange the rolls in the prepared air fryer basket and air fry for 12 minutes, or until crispy and golden brown. Turn halfway through the cooking time to ensure even cooking.
Transfer to a platter and let cool for 5 minutes before serving.

Bacon and Pepper Sandwiches

Prep time: 15 minutes | Cook time: 7 minutes | Serves 4

80 ml spicy barbecue sauce
2 tablespoons honey
8 slices precooked bacon, cut into thirds
1 red pepper, sliced
1 yellow pepper, sliced
3 pitta pockets, cut in half
300 ml torn butterhead lettuce leaves
2 tomatoes, sliced

In a small bowl, combine the barbecue sauce and the honey.
Brush this mixture lightly onto the bacon slices and the red and yellow pepper slices.
Put the peppers into the air fryer basket and air fry at 176°C for 4 minutes.
Then shake the basket, add the bacon, and air fry for 2 minutes or until the bacon is browned and the peppers are tender.
Fill the pitta halves with the bacon, peppers, any remaining barbecue sauce, lettuce, and tomatoes, and serve immediately.

Golden Cod Tacos with Salsa

Prep time: 5 minutes | Cook time: 15 minutes | Serves 4

2 eggs
300 ml Mexican beer
350 ml coconut flour
350 ml almond flour
½ tablespoon chilli powder
1 tablespoon cumin
Salt, to taste

450 g cod fillet, sliced into large pieces
4 toasted corn tortillas
4 large lettuce leaves, chopped
60 ml salsa
Cooking spray

Preheat the air fryer to 192°C.
Spritz the air fryer basket with cooking spray.
Break the eggs in a bowl, then pour in the beer. Whisk to combine well.
Combine the coconut flour, almond flour, chilli powder, cumin, and salt in a separate bowl. Stir to mix well.
Dunk the cod pieces in the egg mixture, then shake the excess off and dredge into the flour mixture to coat well.
Arrange the cod in the preheated air fryer.
Air fry for 15 minutes or until golden brown. Flip the cod halfway through the cooking time.
Unwrap the toasted tortillas on a large plate, then divide the cod and lettuce leaves on top.
Baste with salsa and wrap to serve.

Air Fried Philly Cheesesteaks

Prep time: 20 minutes | Cook time: 20 minutes | Serves 2

340 g boneless rib-eye steak, sliced thinly
½ teaspoon Worcestershire sauce
½ teaspoon soy sauce
Rock salt and ground black pepper, to taste
½ green pepper, stemmed, deseeded, and thinly sliced

½ small onion, halved and thinly sliced
1 tablespoon vegetable oil
2 soft sub rolls, split three-fourths of the way through
1 tablespoon butter, softened
2 slices provolone cheese, halved

Preheat the air fryer to 204°C.
Combine the steak, Worcestershire sauce, soy sauce, salt, and ground black pepper in a large bowl. Toss to coat well. Set aside.
Combine the pepper, onion, salt, ground black pepper, and vegetable oil in a separate bowl. Toss to coat the vegetables well.
Pour the steak and vegetables in the preheated air fryer.
Air fry for 15 minutes or until the steak is browned and vegetables are tender.
Transfer them on a plate. Set aside.
Brush the sub rolls with butter, then place in the air fryer to toast for 3 minutes or until lightly browned.
Transfer the rolls on a clean work surface and divide the steak and vegetable mix in between the rolls. Spread with cheese.
Arrange the rolls in the air fryer and air fry for 2 minutes or until the cheese melts.
Serve immediately.

Nugget and Veggie Taco Wraps

Prep time: 5 minutes | Cook time: 15 minutes | Serves 4

1 tablespoon water
4 pieces commercial vegan nuggets, chopped
1 small brown onion, diced

1 small red pepper, chopped
2 cobs grilled corn kernels
4 large corn tortillas
Mixed greens, for garnish

Preheat the air fryer to 204°C.
Over a medium heat, sauté the nuggets in the water with the onion, corn kernels and pepper in a skillet, then remove from the heat.
Fill the tortillas with the nuggets and vegetables and fold them up.
Transfer to the inside of the fryer and air fry for 15 minutes.
Once crispy, serve immediately, garnished with the mixed greens.

Cabbage and Mushroom Spring Rolls

Prep time: 20 minutes | Cook time: 35 minutes | Makes 14 spring rolls

2 tablespoons vegetable oil
1 L sliced Chinese leaf
142 g shiitake mushrooms, diced
3 carrots, cut into thin matchsticks
1 tablespoon minced fresh ginger
1 tablespoon minced garlic

1 bunch spring onions, white and light green parts only, sliced
2 tablespoons soy sauce
1 (113 g) package cellophane noodles or vermicelli
¼ teaspoon cornflour
1 (340 g) package frozen spring roll wrappers, thawed
Cooking spray

Heat the olive oil in a non-stick skillet over medium-high heat until shimmering. Add the Chinese leaf, mushrooms, and carrots and sauté for 3 minutes or until tender. Add the ginger, garlic, and spring onions and sauté for 1 minutes or until fragrant.
Mix in the soy sauce and turn off the heat. Discard any liquid remains in the skillet and allow to cool for a few minutes.
Bring a pot of water to a boil, then turn off the heat and pour in the noodles. Let sit for 10 minutes or until the noodles are al dente.
Transfer 235 ml of the noodles in the skillet and toss with the cooked vegetables.
Reserve the remaining noodles for other use.
Dissolve the cornflour in a small dish of water, then place the wrappers on a clean work surface.
Dab the edges of the wrappers with cornflour.
Scoop up 3 tablespoons of filling in the centre of each wrapper, then fold the corner in front of you over the filling.
Tuck the wrapper under the filling, then fold the corners on both sides into the centre. Keep rolling to seal the wrapper.
Repeat with remaining wrappers.
Preheat the air fryer to 204°C and spritz with cooking spray.
Arrange the wrappers in the preheated air fryer and spritz with cooking spray.
Air fry in batches for 10 minutes or until golden brown. Flip the wrappers halfway through.
Serve immediately.

Mexican Flavour Chicken Burgers

Prep time: 15 minutes | Cook time: 20 minutes | Serves 6 to 8

4 skinless and boneless chicken breasts	1 egg
1 small head of cauliflower, sliced into florets	Salt and ground black pepper, to taste
1 jalapeño pepper	2 tomatoes, sliced
3 tablespoons smoked paprika	2 lettuce leaves, chopped
1 tablespoon thyme	6 to 8 brioche buns, sliced lengthwise
1 tablespoon oregano	180 ml taco sauce
1 tablespoon mustard powder	Cooking spray
1 teaspoon cayenne pepper	

Preheat the air fryer to 176ºC and spritz with cooking spray.

In a blender, add the cauliflower florets, jalapeño pepper, paprika, thyme, oregano, mustard powder and cayenne pepper and blend until the mixture has a texture similar to breadcrumbs.

Transfer ¾ of the cauliflower mixture to a medium bowl and set aside.

Beat the egg in a different bowl and set aside.

Add the chicken breasts to the blender with remaining cauliflower mixture. Sprinkle with salt and pepper. Blend until finely chopped and well mixed.

Remove the mixture from the blender and form into 6 to 8 patties.

One by one, dredge each patty in the reserved cauliflower mixture, then into the egg. Dip them in the cauliflower mixture again for additional coating.

Place the coated patties into the air fryer basket and spritz with cooking spray.

Air fry for 20 minutes or until golden and crispy. Flip halfway through to ensure even cooking.

Transfer the patties to a clean work surface and assemble with the buns, tomato slices, chopped lettuce leaves and taco sauce to make burgers.

Serve and enjoy.

Smoky Chicken Parm Sandwiches

Prep time: 10 minutes | Cook time: 11 minutes | Serves 2

2 boneless, skinless chicken breasts (227 g each), sliced horizontally in half and separated into 4 thinner cutlets	1 tablespoon smoked paprika
	Cooking spray
	120 ml marinara sauce, homemade or store-bought
Rock salt and freshly ground black pepper, to taste	170 g smoked Mozzarella cheese, grated
120 ml plain flour	2 store-bought soft, sesame-seed
3 large eggs, lightly beaten	hamburger or Italian buns, split
120 ml dried breadcrumbs	

Season the chicken cutlets all over with salt and pepper.

Set up three shallow bowls: Place the flour in the first bowl, the eggs in the second, and stir together the breadcrumbs and smoked paprika in the third.

Coat the chicken pieces in the flour, then dip fully in the egg.

Dredge in the paprika breadcrumbs, then transfer to a wire rack set over a baking sheet and spray both sides liberally with cooking spray.

Transfer 2 of the chicken cutlets to the air fryer and air fry at 176ºC until beginning to brown, about 6 minutes.

Spread each cutlet with 2 tablespoons of the marinara sauce and sprinkle with one-quarter of the smoked Mozzarella.

Increase the heat to 204ºC and cook until the chicken is cooked through and crisp and the cheese is melted and golden brown, about 5 minutes more.

Transfer the cutlets to a plate, stack on top of each other, and place inside a bun.

Repeat with the remaining chicken cutlets, marinara, smoked Mozzarella, and bun.

Serve the sandwiches warm.

Portobello Pizzas

Prep time: 10 minutes | Cook time: 10 minutes | Serves 4

Olive oil	8 tablespoons pizza sauce
4 large portobello mushroom caps, cleaned and stems removed	16 slices turkey pepperoni
	8 tablespoons Mozzarella cheese
Garlic powder	

Spray the air fryer basket lightly with olive oil.

Lightly spray the outside of the mushrooms with olive oil and sprinkle with a little garlic powder, to taste.

Turn the mushroom over and lightly spray the sides and top edges of the mushroom with olive oil and sprinkle with garlic powder, to taste.

Place the mushrooms in the air fryer basket in a single layer with the top side down.

Leave room between the mushrooms.

You may need to cook them in batches. Air fry at 176ºC for 5 minutes.

Spoon 2 tablespoons of pizza sauce on each mushroom.

Top each with 4 slices of turkey pepperoni and sprinkle with 2 tablespoons of Mozzarella cheese.

Press the pepperoni and cheese down into the pizza sauce to help prevent it from flying around inside the air fryer.

Air fry until the cheese is melted and lightly browned on top, another 3 to 5 minutes.

Pesto Chicken Mini Pizzas

Prep time: 5 minutes | Cook time: 10 minutes | Serves 4

475 ml shredded cooked chicken	4 English muffins, split
	475 ml shredded Mozzarella cheese
180 ml pesto	

In a medium bowl, toss the chicken with the pesto.

Place one-eighth of the chicken on each English muffin half.

Top each English muffin with 60 ml Mozzarella cheese.

Put four pizzas at a time in the air fryer and air fry at 176ºC for 5 minutes.

Repeat this process with the other four pizzas.

Turkey-Hummus Wraps

Prep time: 10 minutes | Cook time: 3 to 7 minutes per batch | Serves 4

4 large wholemeal wraps
120 ml hummus
16 thin slices deli turkey

8 slices provolone cheese
235 ml fresh baby spinach (or more to taste)

To assemble, place 2 tablespoons of hummus on each wrap and spread to within about a half inch from edges.
Top with 4 slices of turkey and 2 slices of provolone.
Finish with 60 ml baby spinach or pile on as much as you like.
Roll up each wrap. You don't need to fold or seal the ends.
Place 2 wraps in air fryer basket, seam side down.
Air fry at 182°C for 3 to 4 minutes to warm filling and melt cheese.
If you like, you can continue cooking for 2 or 3 more minutes, until the wrap is slightly crispy.
Repeat the last step to cook remaining wraps.

Shrimp and Grilled Cheese Sandwiches

Prep time: 10 minutes | Cook time: 5 minutes | Serves 4

300 ml shredded Colby, Cheddar, or Havarti cheese
1 (170 g) can tiny shrimp, drained
3 tablespoons mayonnaise

2 tablespoons minced spring onion
4 slices wholemeal or wholemeal bread
2 tablespoons softened butter

In a medium bowl, combine the cheese, shrimp, mayonnaise, and spring onion, and mix well.
Spread this mixture on two of the slices of bread.
Top with the other slices of bread to make two sandwiches.
Spread the sandwiches lightly with butter.
Air fry at 204°C for 5 to 7 minutes or until the bread is browned and crisp and the cheese is melted.
Cut in half and serve warm.

Chicken-Lettuce Wraps

Prep time: 15 minutes | Cook time: 12 to 16 minutes | Serves 2 to 4

450 g boneless, skinless chicken thighs, trimmed
1 teaspoon vegetable oil
2 tablespoons lime juice
1 shallot, minced
1 tablespoon fish sauce, plus extra for serving
2 teaspoons packed brown sugar
1 garlic clove, minced
⅛ teaspoon red pepper flakes
1 mango, peeled, pitted, and cut

into ¼-inch pieces
80 ml chopped fresh mint
80 ml chopped fresh coriander
80 ml chopped fresh Thai basil
1 head Bibb or butterhead lettuce, leaves separated (227 g)
60 ml chopped dry-roasted peanuts
2 Bird's eye chillies, stemmed and sliced thin

Preheat the air fryer to 204°C.
Pat the chicken dry with paper towels and rub with oil.
Place the chicken in air fryer basket and air fry for 12 to 16 minutes, or until the chicken registers 80°C, flipping and rotating

chicken halfway through cooking.
Meanwhile, whisk lime juice, shallot, fish sauce, sugar, garlic, and pepper flakes together in large bowl; set aside.
Transfer chicken to cutting board, let cool slightly, then shred into bite-size pieces using 2 forks.
Add the shredded chicken, mango, mint, coriander, and basil to bowl with dressing and toss to coat.
Serve the chicken in the lettuce leaves, passing peanuts, chillies, and extra fish sauce separately.

Grilled Cheese Sandwich

Prep time: 5 minutes | Cook time: 5 minutes | Makes 2 sandwiches

4 slices bread
110 g Cheddar cheese slices

2 teaspoons butter or oil

Lay the four cheese slices on two of the bread slices and top with the remaining two slices of bread.
Brush both sides with butter or oil and cut the sandwiches in rectangular halves.
Place in air fryer basket and air fry at 200°C for 5 minutes until the outside is crisp and the cheese melts.

Mediterranean-Pitta Wraps

Prep time: 5 minutes | Cook time: 14 minutes | Serves 4

450 g mackerel fish fillets
2 tablespoons olive oil
1 tablespoon Mediterranean seasoning mix
½ teaspoon chilli powder

Sea salt and freshly ground black pepper, to taste
60 g feta cheese, crumbled
4 tortillas

Toss the fish fillets with the olive oil; place them in the lightly oiled air fryer basket.
Air fry the fish fillets at 204°C for about 14 minutes, turning them over halfway through the cooking time.
Assemble your pittas with the chopped fish and remaining ingredients and serve warm.

Tuna Wraps

Prep time: 10 minutes | Cook time: 4 to 7 minutes | Serves 4

450 g fresh tuna steak, cut into 1-inch cubes
1 tablespoon grated fresh ginger
2 garlic cloves, minced
½ teaspoon toasted sesame oil

4 low-salt wholemeal tortillas
60 ml low-fat mayonnaise
475 ml shredded romaine lettuce
1 red pepper, thinly sliced

In a medium bowl, mix the tuna, ginger, garlic, and sesame oil.
Let it stand for 10 minutes.
Air fry the tuna in the air fryer at 200°C for 4 to 7 minutes, or until done to your liking and lightly browned.
Make wraps with the tuna, tortillas, mayonnaise, lettuce, and pepper.
Serve immediately.

Prawn and Cabbage Egg Rolls Wraps

Prep time: 20 minutes | Cook time: 24 minutes | Serves 4

2 tablespoons olive oil
1 carrot, cut into strips
1-inch piece fresh ginger, grated
1 tablespoon minced garlic
2 tablespoons soy sauce
60 ml chicken broth
1 tablespoon sugar

235 ml shredded Chinese leaf
1 tablespoon sesame oil
8 cooked prawns, minced
8 egg roll wrappers
1 egg, beaten
Cooking spray

Heat the olive oil in a non-stick skillet over medium heat until shimmering.

Add the carrot, ginger, and garlic and sauté for 2 minutes or until fragrant.

Pour in the soy sauce, broth, and sugar.

Bring to a boil. Keep stirring.

Add the Chinese leaf and simmer for 4 minutes or until the it is tender.

Turn off the heat and mix in the sesame oil.

Let sit for 15 minutes.

Meanwhile, preheat the air fryer to 188°C and spritz with cooking spray.

Use a strainer to remove the vegetables from the liquid, then combine with the minced prawns.

Unfold the egg roll wrappers on a clean work surface, then divide the prawn mixture in the centre of wrappers.

Dab the edges of a wrapper with the beaten egg, then fold a corner over the filling and tuck the corner under the filling.

Fold the left and right corner into the centre.

Roll the wrapper up and press to seal.

Repeat with remaining wrappers.

Arrange the wrapper in the preheated air fryer and spritz with cooking spray.

Air fry for 12 minutes or until golden. Flip the wrappers halfway through.

Work in batches to avoid overcrowding.

Serve immediately.

Avocado and Slaw Tacos

Prep time: 15 minutes | Cook time: 6 minutes | Serves 4

60 ml plain flour
¼ teaspoon salt, plus more as needed
¼ teaspoon ground black pepper
2 large egg whites
300 ml panko breadcrumbs
2 tablespoons olive oil
2 avocados, peeled and halved, cut into ½-inch-thick slices
½ small red cabbage, thinly

sliced
1 deseeded jalapeño, thinly sliced
2 spring onions, thinly sliced
120 ml coriander leaves
60 ml mayonnaise
Juice and zest of 1 lime
4 corn tortillas, warmed
120 ml sour cream
Cooking spray

Preheat the air fryer to 204°C.

Spritz the air fryer basket with cooking spray.

Pour the flour in a large bowl and sprinkle with salt and black pepper, then stir to mix well.

Whisk the egg whites in a separate bowl.

Combine the panko with olive oil on a shallow dish.

Dredge the avocado slices in the bowl of flour, then into the egg to coat. Shake the excess off, then roll the slices over the panko.

Arrange the avocado slices in a single layer in the basket and spritz the cooking spray.

Air fry for 6 minutes or until tender and lightly browned. Flip the slices halfway through with tongs.

Combine the cabbage, jalapeño, onions, coriander leaves, mayo, lime juice and zest, and a touch of salt in a separate large bowl. Toss to mix well.

Unfold the tortillas on a clean work surface, then spread with cabbage slaw and air fried avocados.

Top with sour cream and serve.

Chapter 9 Snacks and Appetisers

Chapter 9 Snacks and Appetisers

Ranch Oyster Snack Crackers

Prep time: 3 minutes | Cook time: 12 minutes | Serves 6

Oil, for spraying
60 ml olive oil
2 teaspoons dry ranch seasoning
1 teaspoon chilli powder
½ teaspoon dried dill
½ teaspoon granulated garlic
½ teaspoon salt
1 (255 g) bag oyster crackers or low-salt crackers

Preheat the air fryer to 164°C. Line the air fryer basket with parchment and spray lightly with oil.
In a large bowl, mix together the olive oil, ranch seasoning, chilli powder, dill, garlic, and salt. Add the crackers and toss until evenly coated.
Place the mixture in the prepared basket.
Cook for 10 to 12 minutes, shaking or stirring every 3 to 4 minutes, or until crisp and golden brown.

Air Fried Pot Stickers

Prep time: 10 minutes | Cook time: 18 to 20 minutes | Makes 30 pot stickers

120 ml finely chopped cabbage
60 ml finely chopped red pepper
2 spring onions, finely chopped
1 egg, beaten
2 tablespoons cocktail sauce
2 teaspoons low-salt soy sauce
30 wonton wrappers
1 tablespoon water, for brushing the wrappers

Preheat the air fryer to 182°C.
In a small bowl, combine the cabbage, pepper, spring onions, egg, cocktail sauce, and soy sauce, and mix well.
Put about 1 teaspoon of the mixture in the centre of each wonton wrapper. Fold the wrapper in half, covering the filling; dampen the edges with water, and seal. You can crimp the edges of the wrapper with your fingers, so they look like the pot stickers you get in restaurants. Brush them with water.
Place the pot stickers in the air fryer basket and air fry in 2 batches for 9 to 10 minutes, or until the pot stickers are hot and the bottoms are lightly browned.
Serve hot.

Bruschetta with Basil Pesto

Prep time: 10 minutes | Cook time: 5 to 11 minutes | Serves 4

8 slices French bread, ½ inch thick
2 tablespoons softened butter
240 ml shredded Mozzarella
cheese
120 ml basil pesto
240 ml chopped grape tomatoes
2 spring onions, thinly sliced

Preheat the air fryer to 176°C.

Spread the bread with the butter and place butter-side up in the air fryer basket. Bake for 3 to 5 minutes, or until the bread is light golden brown.
Remove the bread from the basket and top each piece with some of the cheese. Return to the basket in 2 batches and bake for 1 to 3 minutes, or until the cheese melts.
Meanwhile, combine the pesto, tomatoes, and spring onions in a small bowl.
When the cheese has melted, remove the bread from the air fryer and place on a serving plate. Top each slice with some of the pesto mixture and serve.

Rosemary-Garlic Shoestring Fries

Prep time: 5 minutes | Cook time: 18 minutes | Serves 2

1 large russet or Maris Piper potato (about 340 g), scrubbed clean, and julienned
1 tablespoon vegetable oil
Leaves from 1 sprig fresh
rosemary
Rock salt and freshly ground black pepper, to taste
1 garlic clove, thinly sliced
Flaky sea salt, for serving

Preheat the air fryer to 204°C.
Place the julienned potatoes in a large colander and rinse under cold running water until the water runs clear. Spread the potatoes out on a double-thick layer of paper towels and pat dry.
In a large bowl, combine the potatoes, oil, and rosemary. Season with rock salt and pepper and toss to coat evenly. Place the potatoes in the air fryer and air fry for 18 minutes, shaking the basket every 5 minutes and adding the garlic in the last 5 minutes of cooking, or until the fries are golden brown and crisp.
Transfer the fries to a plate and sprinkle with flaky sea salt while they're hot. Serve immediately.

Lemony Pear Chips

Prep time: 15 minutes | Cook time: 9 to 13 minutes | Serves 4

2 firm Bosc or Anjou pears, cut crosswise into ⅛-inch-thick slices
1 tablespoon freshly squeezed
lemon juice
½ teaspoon ground cinnamon
⅛ teaspoon ground cardamom

Preheat the air fryer to 192°C.
Separate the smaller stem-end pear rounds from the larger rounds with seeds. Remove the core and seeds from the larger slices. Sprinkle all slices with lemon juice, cinnamon, and cardamom.
Put the smaller chips into the air fryer basket. Air fry for 3 to 5 minutes, or until light golden brown, shaking the basket once during cooking. Remove from the air fryer.
Repeat with the larger slices, air frying for 6 to 8 minutes, or until light golden brown, shaking the basket once during cooking.
Remove the chips from the air fryer. Cool and serve or store in an airtight container at room temperature up for to 2 days.

Greens Chips with Curried Yoghurt Sauce

Prep time: 10 minutes | Cook time: 5 to 6 minutes | Serves 4

240 ml low-fat Greek yoghurt
1 tablespoon freshly squeezed lemon juice
1 tablespoon curry powder
½ bunch curly kale, stemmed, ribs removed and discarded,

leaves cut into 2- to 3-inch pieces
½ bunch chard, stemmed, ribs removed and discarded, leaves cut into 2- to 3-inch pieces
1½ teaspoons olive oil

In a small bowl, stir together the yoghurt, lemon juice, and curry powder. Set aside.

In a large bowl, toss the kale and chard with the olive oil, working the oil into the leaves with your hands. This helps break up the fibres in the leaves so the chips are tender.

Air fry the greens in batches at 200°C for 5 to 6 minutes, until crisp, shaking the basket once during cooking. Serve with the yoghurt sauce.

Spicy Chicken Bites

Prep time: 10 minutes | Cook time: 10 to 12 minutes | Makes 30 bites

227 g boneless and skinless chicken thighs, cut into 30 pieces

¼ teaspoon rock salt
2 tablespoons hot sauce
Cooking spray

Preheat the air fryer to 200°C.

Spray the air fryer basket with cooking spray and season the chicken bites with the rock salt, then place in the basket and air fry for 10 to 12 minutes or until crispy.

While the chicken bites cook, pour the hot sauce into a large bowl. Remove the bites and add to the sauce bowl, tossing to coat. Serve warm.

Courgette Fries with Roasted Garlic Aioli

Prep time: 20 minutes | Cook time: 12 minutes | Serves 4

1 tablespoon vegetable oil
½ head green or savoy cabbage, finely shredded
Roasted Garlic Aioli:
1 teaspoon roasted garlic
120 ml mayonnaise
2 tablespoons olive oil
Juice of ½ lemon
Salt and pepper, to taste

Courgette Fries:
120 ml flour
2 eggs, beaten
240 ml seasoned breadcrumbs
Salt and pepper, to taste
1 large courgette, cut into ½-inch sticks
Olive oil

Make the aioli: Combine the roasted garlic, mayonnaise, olive oil and lemon juice in a bowl and whisk well. Season the aioli with salt and pepper to taste.

Prepare the courgette fries. Create a dredging station with three shallow dishes. Place the flour in the first shallow dish and season well with salt and freshly ground black pepper. Put the beaten eggs in the second shallow dish. In the third shallow dish, combine the breadcrumbs, salt and pepper. Dredge the courgette sticks, coating

with flour first, then dipping them into the eggs to coat, and finally tossing in breadcrumbs. Shake the dish with the breadcrumbs and pat the crumbs onto the courgette sticks gently with your hands, so they stick evenly.

Place the courgette fries on a flat surface and let them sit at least 10 minutes before air frying to let them dry out a little. Preheat the air fryer to 204°C.

Spray the courgette sticks with olive oil and place them into the air fryer basket. You can air fry the courgette in two layers, placing the second layer in the opposite direction to the first. Air fry for 12 minutes turning and rotating the fries halfway through the cooking time. Spray with additional oil when you turn them over.

Serve courgette fries warm with the roasted garlic aioli.

Tortellini with Spicy Dipping Sauce

Prep time: 5 minutes | Cook time: 20 minutes | Serves 4

177 ml mayonnaise
2 tablespoons mustard
1 egg
120 ml flour

½ teaspoon dried oregano
355 ml breadcrumbs
2 tablespoons olive oil
475 ml frozen cheese tortellini

Preheat the air fryer to 192°C.

In a small bowl, combine the mayonnaise and mustard and mix well. Set aside.

In a shallow bowl, beat the egg. In a separate bowl, combine the flour and oregano. In another bowl, combine the breadcrumbs and olive oil, and mix well.

Drop the tortellini, a few at a time, into the egg, then into the flour, then into the egg again, and then into the breadcrumbs to coat. Put into the air fryer basket, cooking in batches.

Air fry for about 10 minutes, shaking halfway through the cooking time, or until the tortellini are crisp and golden brown on the outside. Serve with the mayonnaise mixture.

Tangy Fried Pickle Spears

Prep time: 5 minutes | Cook time: 15 minutes | Serves 6

2 jars sweet and sour pickle spears, patted dry
2 medium-sized eggs
80 ml milk
1 teaspoon garlic powder

1 teaspoon sea salt
½ teaspoon shallot powder
⅓ teaspoon chilli powder
80 ml plain flour
Cooking spray

Preheat the air fryer to 196°C. Spritz the air fryer basket with cooking spray.

In a bowl, beat together the eggs with milk. In another bowl, combine garlic powder, sea salt, shallot powder, chilli powder and plain flour until well blended.

One by one, roll the pickle spears in the powder mixture, then dredge them in the egg mixture. Dip them in the powder mixture a second time for additional coating.

Arrange the coated pickles in the prepared basket. Air fry for 15 minutes until golden and crispy, shaking the basket halfway through to ensure even cooking.

Transfer to a plate and let cool for 5 minutes before serving.

Roasted Grape Dip

Prep time: 10 minutes | Cook time: 8 to 12 minutes | Serves 6

475 ml seedless red grapes, rinsed and patted dry
1 tablespoon apple cider vinegar
1 tablespoon honey
240 ml low-fat Greek yoghurt
2 tablespoons semi-skimmed milk
2 tablespoons minced fresh basil

In the air fryer basket, sprinkle the grapes with the cider vinegar and drizzle with the honey. Toss to coat. Roast the grapes at 192ºC for 8 to 12 minutes, or until shrivelled but still soft. Remove from the air fryer.
In a medium bowl, stir together the yoghurt and milk.
Gently blend in the grapes and basil. Serve immediately or cover and chill for 1 to 2 hours.

Spinach and Crab Meat Cups

Prep time: 10 minutes | Cook time: 10 minutes | Makes 30 cups

1 (170 g) can crab meat, drained to yield 80 ml meat
60 ml frozen spinach, thawed, drained, and chopped
1 clove garlic, minced
120 ml grated Parmesan cheese
3 tablespoons plain yoghurt
¼ teaspoon lemon juice
½ teaspoon Worcestershire sauce
30 mini frozen filo shells, thawed
Cooking spray

Preheat the air fryer to 200ºC.
Remove any bits of shell that might remain in the crab meat.
Mix the crab meat, spinach, garlic, and cheese together.
Stir in the yoghurt, lemon juice, and Worcestershire sauce and mix well.
Spoon a teaspoon of filling into each filo shell.
Spray the air fryer basket with cooking spray and arrange half the shells in the basket. Air fry for 5 minutes. Repeat with the remaining shells.
Serve immediately.

Easy Roasted Chickpeas

Prep time: 5 minutes | Cook time: 15 minutes | Makes about 240 ml

1 (425 g) can chickpeas, drained
2 teaspoons curry powder
¼ teaspoon salt
1 tablespoon olive oil

Drain chickpeas thoroughly and spread in a single layer on paper towels. Cover with another paper towel and press gently to remove extra moisture. Don't press too hard or you'll crush the chickpeas.
Mix curry powder and salt together.
Place chickpeas in a medium bowl and sprinkle with seasonings. Stir well to coat.
Add olive oil and stir again to distribute oil.
Air fry at 200ºC for 15 minutes, stopping to shake basket about halfway through cooking time.
Cool completely and store in airtight container.

Courgette Feta Roulades

Prep time: 10 minutes | Cook time: 10 minutes | Serves 6

120 ml feta
1 garlic clove, minced
2 tablespoons fresh basil, minced
1 tablespoon capers, minced
⅛ teaspoon salt
⅛ teaspoon red pepper flakes
1 tablespoon lemon juice
2 medium courgette
12 toothpicks

Preheat the air fryer to 182ºC. (If using a grill attachment, make sure it is inside the air fryer during preheating.)
In a small bowl, combine the feta, garlic, basil, capers, salt, red pepper flakes, and lemon juice.
Slice the courgette into ⅛-inch strips lengthwise. (Each courgette should yield around 6 strips.)
Spread 1 tablespoon of the cheese filling onto each slice of courgette, then roll it up and secure it with a toothpick through the middle.
Place the courgette roulades into the air fryer basket in a single layer, making sure that they don't touch each other.
Bake or grill in the air fryer for 10 minutes.
Remove the courgette roulades from the air fryer and gently remove the toothpicks before serving.

Chilli-Brined Fried Calamari

Prep time: 20 minutes | Cook time: 8 minutes | Serves 2

1 (227 g) jar sweet or hot pickled cherry peppers
227 g calamari bodies and tentacles, bodies cut into ½-inch-wide rings
1 lemon
475 ml plain flour
Rock salt and freshly ground
black pepper, to taste
3 large eggs, lightly beaten
Cooking spray
120 ml mayonnaise
1 teaspoon finely chopped rosemary
1 garlic clove, minced

Drain the pickled pepper brine into a large bowl and tear the peppers into bite-size strips. Add the pepper strips and calamari to the brine and let stand in the refrigerator for 20 minutes or up to 2 hours.
Grate the lemon zest into a large bowl then whisk in the flour and season with salt and pepper. Dip the calamari and pepper strips in the egg, then toss them in the flour mixture until fully coated. Spray the calamari and peppers liberally with cooking spray, then transfer half to the air fryer. Air fry at 204ºC, shaking the basket halfway into cooking, until the calamari is cooked through and golden brown, about 8 minutes. Transfer to a plate and repeat with the remaining pieces.
In a small bowl, whisk together the mayonnaise, rosemary, and garlic. Squeeze half the zested lemon to get 1 tablespoon of juice and stir it into the sauce. Season with salt and pepper. Cut the remaining zested lemon half into 4 small wedges and serve alongside the calamari, peppers, and sauce.

Shrimp Toasts with Sesame Seeds

Prep time: 15 minutes | Cook time: 6 to 8 minutes | Serves 4 to 6

230 g raw shrimp, peeled and deveined	1 to 2 teaspoons sriracha sauce
1 egg, beaten	1 teaspoon soy sauce
2 spring onions, chopped, plus more for garnish	½ teaspoon toasted sesame oil
2 tablespoons chopped fresh coriander	6 slices thinly sliced white sandwich bread
2 teaspoons grated fresh ginger	120 ml sesame seeds
	Cooking spray
	Thai chilli sauce, for serving

Preheat the air fryer to 204°C. Spritz the air fryer basket with cooking spray.

In a food processor, add the shrimp, egg, spring onions, coriander, ginger, sriracha sauce, soy sauce and sesame oil, and pulse until chopped finely. You'll need to stop the food processor occasionally to scrape down the sides. Transfer the shrimp mixture to a bowl.

On a clean work surface, cut the crusts off the sandwich bread. Using a brush, generously brush one side of each slice of bread with shrimp mixture.

Place the sesame seeds on a plate. Press bread slices, shrimp-side down, into sesame seeds to coat evenly. Cut each slice diagonally into quarters.

Spread the coated slices in a single layer in the air fryer basket.

Air fry in batches for 6 to 8 minutes, or until golden and crispy. Flip the bread slices halfway through. Repeat with the remaining bread slices.

Transfer to a plate and let cool for 5 minutes. Top with the chopped spring onions and serve warm with Thai chilli sauce.

Italian Rice Balls

Prep time: 20 minutes | Cook time: 10 minutes | Makes 8 rice balls

355 ml cooked sticky rice	tiny pieces (small enough to stuff into olives)
½ teaspoon Italian seasoning blend	2 eggs
¾ teaspoon salt, divided	80 ml Italian breadcrumbs
8 black olives, pitted	177 ml panko breadcrumbs
28 g Mozzarella cheese, cut into	Cooking spray

Preheat air fryer to 200°C.

Stuff each black olive with a piece of Mozzarella cheese. Set aside.

In a bowl, combine the cooked sticky rice, Italian seasoning blend, and ½ teaspoon of salt and stir to mix well. Form the rice mixture into a log with your hands and divide it into 8 equal portions. Mould each portion around a black olive and roll into a ball.

Transfer to the freezer to chill for 10 to 15 minutes until firm.

In a shallow dish, place the Italian breadcrumbs. In a separate shallow dish, whisk the eggs. In a third shallow dish, combine the panko breadcrumbs and remaining salt.

One by one, roll the rice balls in the Italian breadcrumbs, then dip in the whisked eggs, finally coat them with the panko breadcrumbs. Arrange the rice balls in the air fryer basket and spritz both sides with cooking spray.

Air fry for 10 minutes until the rice balls are golden brown. Flip the balls halfway through the cooking time.

Serve warm.

Roasted Mushrooms with Garlic

Prep time: 3 minutes | Cook time: 22 to 27 minutes | Serves 4

16 garlic cloves, peeled	⅛ teaspoon freshly ground black pepper
2 teaspoons olive oil, divided	
16 button mushrooms	1 tablespoon white wine or low-salt vegetable broth
½ teaspoon dried marjoram	

In a baking pan, mix the garlic with 1 teaspoon of olive oil. Roast in the air fryer at 176°C for 12 minutes.

Add the mushrooms, marjoram, and pepper. Stir to coat. Drizzle with the remaining 1 teaspoon of olive oil and the white wine.

Return to the air fryer and roast for 10 to 15 minutes more, or until the mushrooms and garlic cloves are tender. Serve.

Rumaki

Prep time: 30 minutes | Cook time: 10 to 12 minutes per batch | Makes about 24 rumaki

283 g raw chicken livers	60 ml low-salt teriyaki sauce
1 can sliced water chestnuts, drained	12 slices turkey bacon

Cut livers into 1½-inch pieces, trimming out tough veins as you slice.

Place livers, water chestnuts, and teriyaki sauce in small container with lid. If needed, add another tablespoon of teriyaki sauce to make sure livers are covered. Refrigerate for 1 hour.

When ready to cook, cut bacon slices in half crosswise.

Wrap 1 piece of liver and 1 slice of water chestnut in each bacon strip. Secure with toothpick.

When you have wrapped half of the livers, place them in the air fryer basket in a single layer.

Air fry at 200°C for 10 to 12 minutes, until liver is done, and bacon is crispy.

While first batch cooks, wrap the remaining livers. Repeat step 6 to cook your second batch.

Jalapeño Poppers

Prep time: 10 minutes | Cook time: 20 minutes | Serves 4

Oil, for spraying	parsley
227 g soft white cheese	½ teaspoon granulated garlic
177 ml gluten-free breadcrumbs, divided	½ teaspoon salt
2 tablespoons chopped fresh	10 jalapeño peppers, halved and seeded

Line the air fryer basket with parchment and spray lightly with oil.

In a medium bowl, mix together the soft white cheese, half of the breadcrumbs, the parsley, garlic, and salt.

Spoon the mixture into the jalapeño halves. Gently press the stuffed jalapeños in the remaining breadcrumbs.

Place the stuffed jalapeños in the prepared basket.

Air fry at 188°C for 20 minutes, or until the cheese is melted and the breadcrumbs are crisp and golden brown.

Homemade Sweet Potato Chips

Prep time: 5 minutes | Cook time: 15 minutes | Serves 2

1 large sweet potato, sliced thin
⅛ teaspoon salt

2 tablespoons olive oil

Preheat the air fryer to 192ºC.
In a small bowl, toss the sweet potatoes, salt, and olive oil together until the potatoes are well coated.
Put the sweet potato slices into the air fryer and spread them out in a single layer.
Fry for 10 minutes. Stir, then air fry for 3 to 5 minutes more, or until the chips reach the preferred level of crispiness.

Shrimp Pirogues

Prep time: 15 minutes | Cook time: 4 to 5 minutes | Serves 8

340 g small, peeled, and deveined raw shrimp
85 g soft white cheese, room temperature
2 tablespoons natural yoghurt
1 teaspoon lemon juice

1 teaspoon dried dill weed, crushed
Salt, to taste
4 small hothouse cucumbers, each approximately 6 inches long

Pour 4 tablespoons water in bottom of air fryer drawer.
Place shrimp in air fryer basket in single layer and air fry at 200ºC for 4 to 5 minutes, just until done. Watch carefully because shrimp cooks quickly, and overcooking makes it tough.
Chop shrimp into small pieces, no larger than ½ inch. Refrigerate while mixing the remaining ingredients.
With a fork, mash and whip the soft white cheese until smooth.
Stir in the yoghurt and beat until smooth. Stir in lemon juice, dill weed, and chopped shrimp.
Taste for seasoning. If needed, add ¼ to ½ teaspoon salt to suit your taste.
Store in refrigerator until serving time.
When ready to serve, wash and dry cucumbers and split them lengthwise. Scoop out the seeds and turn cucumbers upside down on paper towels to drain for 10 minutes.
Just before filling, wipe centres of cucumbers dry. Spoon the shrimp mixture into the pirogues and cut in half crosswise. Serve immediately.

Easy Spiced Nuts

Prep time: 5 minutes | Cook time: 25 minutes | Makes 3 L

1 egg white, lightly beaten
60 ml sugar
1 teaspoon salt
½ teaspoon ground cinnamon
¼ teaspoon ground cloves

¼ teaspoon ground allspice
Pinch ground cayenne pepper
240 ml pecan halves
240 ml cashews
240 ml almonds

Combine the egg white with the sugar and spices in a bowl.
Preheat the air fryer to 148ºC.
Spray or brush the air fryer basket with vegetable oil. Toss the nuts together in the spiced egg white and transfer the nuts to the air fryer basket.
Air fry for 25 minutes, stirring the nuts in the basket a few times during the cooking process. Taste the nuts (carefully because they will be very hot) to see if they are crunchy and nicely toasted. Air fry for a few more minutes if necessary.
Serve warm or cool to room temperature and store in an airtight container for up to two weeks.

Roasted Pearl Onion Dip

Prep time: 5 minutes | Cook time: 12 minutes | Serves 4

475 ml peeled pearl onions
3 garlic cloves
3 tablespoons olive oil, divided
½ teaspoon salt
240 ml non-fat plain Greek yoghurt

1 tablespoon lemon juice
¼ teaspoon black pepper
⅛ teaspoon red pepper flakes
Pitta chips, vegetables, or toasted bread for serving (optional)

Preheat the air fryer to 182ºC.
In a large bowl, combine the pearl onions and garlic with 2 tablespoons of the olive oil until the onions are well coated.
Pour the garlic-and-onion mixture into the air fryer basket and roast for 12 minutes.
Transfer the garlic and onions to a food processor. Pulse the vegetables several times, until the onions are minced but still have some chunks.
In a large bowl, combine the garlic and onions and the remaining 1 tablespoon of olive oil, along with the salt, yoghurt, lemon juice, black pepper, and red pepper flakes.
Cover and chill for 1 hour before serving with pitta chips, vegetables, or toasted bread.

Cheesy Courgette Tots

Prep time: 15 minutes | Cook time: 6 minutes | Serves 8

2 medium courgette (about 340 g), shredded
1 large egg, whisked
120 ml grated pecorino Romano cheese

120 ml panko breadcrumbs
¼ teaspoon black pepper
1 clove garlic, minced
Cooking spray

Using your hands, squeeze out as much liquid from the courgette as possible. In a large bowl, mix the courgette with the remaining ingredients except the oil until well incorporated.
Make the courgette tots: Use a spoon or cookie scoop to place tablespoonfuls of the courgette mixture onto a lightly floured cutting board and form into 1-inch logs.
Preheat air fryer to 192ºC. Spritz the air fryer basket with cooking spray.
Place the tots in the basket. You may need to cook in batches to avoid overcrowding.
Air fry for 6 minutes until golden brown.
Remove from the basket to a serving plate and repeat with the remaining courgette tots.
Serve immediately.

Beef and Mango Skewers

Prep time: 10 minutes | Cook time: 4 to 7 minutes | Serves 4

340 g beef sirloin tip, cut into 1-inch cubes	½ teaspoon dried marjoram
2 tablespoons balsamic vinegar	Pinch of salt
1 tablespoon olive oil	Freshly ground black pepper, to taste
1 tablespoon honey	1 mango

Preheat the air fryer to 200°C.

Put the beef cubes in a medium bowl and add the balsamic vinegar, olive oil, honey, marjoram, salt, and pepper. Mix well, then massage the marinade into the beef with your hands. Set aside.

To prepare the mango, stand it on end and cut the skin off, using a sharp knife. Then carefully cut around the oval pit to remove the flesh. Cut the mango into 1-inch cubes.

Thread metal skewers alternating with three beef cubes and two mango cubes.

Roast the skewers in the air fryer basket for 4 to 7 minutes, or until the beef is browned and at least 63°C.

Serve hot.

Stuffed Figs with Goat Cheese and Honey

Prep time: 5 minutes | Cook time: 10 minutes | Serves 4

8 fresh figs	1 tablespoon honey, plus more for serving
57 g goat cheese	1 tablespoon olive oil
¼ teaspoon ground cinnamon	

Preheat the air fryer to 182°C. Line an 8-by-8-inch baking dish with parchment paper that comes up the side so you can lift it out after cooking.

In a large bowl, mix together all of the ingredients until well combined.

Press the oat mixture into the pan in an even layer.

Place the pan into the air fryer basket and bake for 15 minutes.

Remove the pan from the air fryer and lift the granola cake out of the pan using the edges of the parchment paper.

Allow to cool for 5 minutes before slicing into 6 equal bars.

Serve immediately or wrap in plastic wrap and store at room temperature for up to 1 week.

Shrimp Egg Rolls

Prep time: 15 minutes | Cook time: 10 minutes per batch | Serves 4

1 tablespoon vegetable oil	60 ml hoisin sauce
½ head green or savoy cabbage, finely shredded	Freshly ground black pepper, to taste
240 ml shredded carrots	454 g cooked shrimp, diced
240 ml canned bean sprouts, drained	60 ml spring onions
1 tablespoon soy sauce	8 egg roll wrappers (or use spring roll pastry)
½ teaspoon sugar	Vegetable oil
1 teaspoon sesame oil	Duck sauce

Preheat a large sauté pan over medium-high heat. Add the oil and cook the cabbage, carrots and bean sprouts until they start to wilt, about 3 minutes. Add the soy sauce, sugar, sesame oil, hoisin sauce and black pepper. Sauté for a few more minutes. Stir in the shrimp and spring onions and cook until the vegetables are just tender. Transfer the mixture to a colander in a bowl to cool. Press or squeeze out any excess water from the filling so that you don't end up with soggy egg rolls.

Make the egg rolls: Place the egg roll wrappers on a flat surface with one of the points facing towards you so they look like diamonds. Dividing the filling evenly between the eight wrappers, spoon the mixture onto the centre of the egg roll wrappers. Spread the filling across the centre of the wrappers from the left corner to the right corner but leave 2 inches from each corner empty. Brush the empty sides of the wrapper with a little water. Fold the bottom corner of the wrapper tightly up over the filling, trying to avoid making any air pockets. Fold the left corner in toward the centre and then the right corner toward the centre. It should now look like an envelope. Tightly roll the egg roll from the bottom to the top open corner. Press to seal the egg roll together, brushing with a little extra water if need be. Repeat this technique with all 8 egg rolls.

Preheat the air fryer to 188°C.

Spray or brush all sides of the egg rolls with vegetable oil. Air fry four egg rolls at a time for 10 minutes, turning them over halfway through the cooking time.

Serve hot with duck sauce or your favourite dipping sauce.

Cheese Drops

Prep time: 15 minutes | Cook time: 10 minutes per batch | Serves 8

177 ml plain flour	60 ml butter, softened
½ teaspoon rock salt	240 ml shredded extra mature Cheddar cheese, at room temperature
¼ teaspoon cayenne pepper	
¼ teaspoon smoked paprika	
¼ teaspoon black pepper	Olive oil spray
Dash garlic powder (optional)	

In a small bowl, combine the flour, salt, cayenne, paprika, pepper, and garlic powder, if using.

Using a food processor, cream the butter and cheese until smooth. Gently add the seasoned flour and process until the dough is well combined, smooth, and no longer sticky. (Or make the dough in a stand mixer fitted with the paddle attachment: Cream the butter and cheese on medium speed until smooth, then add the seasoned flour and beat at low speed until smooth.)

Divide the dough into 32 equal-size pieces. On a lightly floured surface, roll each piece into a small ball.

Spray the air fryer basket with oil spray. Arrange 16 cheese drops in the basket. Set the air fryer to 164°C for 10 minutes, or until drops are just starting to brown. Transfer to a wire rack. Repeat with remaining dough, checking for doneness at 8 minutes.

Cool the cheese drops completely on the wire rack. Store in an airtight container until ready to serve, or up to 1 or 2 days.

Garlic-Parmesan Croutons

Prep time: 3 minutes | Cook time: 12 minutes | Serves 4

Oil, for spraying
1 L cubed French bread
1 tablespoon grated Parmesan cheese

3 tablespoons olive oil
1 tablespoon granulated garlic
½ teaspoon unsalted salt

Line the air fryer basket with parchment and spray lightly with oil.

In a large bowl, mix together the bread, Parmesan cheese, olive oil, garlic, and salt, tossing with your hands to evenly distribute the seasonings. Transfer the coated bread cubes to the prepared basket.

Air fry at 176ºC for 10 to 12 minutes, stirring once after 5 minutes, or until crisp and golden brown.

Chapter 10 Desserts

Chapter 10 Desserts

Cream Cheese Danish

Prep time: 20 minutes | Cook time: 15 minutes | Serves 6

70 g blanched finely ground almond flour
225 g shredded Mozzarella cheese
140 g full-fat cream cheese, divided

2 large egg yolks
75 g powdered sweetener, divided
2 teaspoons vanilla extract, divided

In a large microwave-safe bowl, add almond flour, Mozzarella, and 30 g cream cheese. Mix and then microwave for 1 minute.
Stir and add egg yolks to the bowl. Continue stirring until soft dough forms. Add 50 g sweetener to dough and 1 teaspoon vanilla.
Cut a piece of baking paper to fit your air fryer basket. Wet your hands with warm water and press out the dough into a ¼-inch-thick rectangle.
In a medium bowl, mix remaining cream cheese, remaining sweetener, and vanilla. Place this cream cheese mixture on the right half of the dough rectangle. Fold over the left side of the dough and press to seal. Place into the air fryer basket.
Adjust the temperature to 164ºC and bake for 15 minutes.
After 7 minutes, flip over the Danish.
When done, remove the Danish from baking paper and allow to completely cool before cutting.

Brown Sugar Banana Bread

Prep time: 20 minutes | Cook time: 22 to 24 minutes | Serves 4

195 g packed light brown sugar
1 large egg, beaten
2 tablespoons unsalted butter, melted
120 ml milk, whole or semi-skimmed
250 g plain flour

1½ teaspoons baking powder
1 teaspoon ground cinnamon
½ teaspoon salt
1 banana, mashed
1 to 2 tablespoons coconut, or avocado oil oil
30 g icing sugar (optional)

In a large bowl, stir together the brown sugar, egg, melted butter, and milk.
In a medium bowl, whisk the flour, baking powder, cinnamon, and salt until blended. Add the flour mixture to the sugar mixture and stir just to blend.
Add the mashed banana and stir to combine.
Preheat the air fryer to 176ºC. Spritz 2 mini loaf pans with oil.
Evenly divide the batter between the prepared pans and place them in the air fryer basket.
Cook for 22 to 24 minutes, or until a knife inserted into the middle of the loaves comes out clean.
Dust the warm loaves with icing sugar (if using).

Chocolate Peppermint Cheesecake

Prep time: 5 minutes | Cook time: 18 minutes | Serves 6

Crust:
110 g butter, melted
55 g coconut flour
2 tablespoons granulated sweetener
Cooking spray
Topping:

110 g unsweetened cooking chocolate
180 g mascarpone cheese, at room temperature
1 teaspoon vanilla extract
2 drops peppermint extract

Preheat the air fryer to 176ºC. Lightly coat a baking pan with cooking spray.
In a mixing bowl, whisk together the butter, flour, and sweetener until well combined. Transfer the mixture to the prepared baking pan.
Place the baking pan in the air fryer and bake for 18 minutes until a toothpick inserted in the center comes out clean.
Remove the crust from the air fryer to a wire rack to cool.
Once cooled completely, place it in the freezer for 20 minutes.
When ready, combine all the ingredients for the topping in a small bowl and stir to incorporate.
Spread this topping over the crust and let it sit for another 15 minutes in the freezer.
Serve chilled.

Double Chocolate Brownies

Prep time: 5 minutes | Cook time: 15 to 20 minutes | Serves 8

110 g almond flour
50 g unsweetened cocoa powder
½ teaspoon baking powder
35 g powdered sweetener
¼ teaspoon salt
110 g unsalted butter, melted

and cooled
3 eggs
1 teaspoon vanilla extract
2 tablespoons mini semisweet chocolate chips

Preheat the air fryer to 176ºC. Line a cake pan with baking paper and brush with oil.
In a large bowl, combine the almond flour, cocoa powder, baking powder, sweetener, and salt. Add the butter, eggs, and vanilla. Stir until thoroughly combined (the batter will be thick.) Spread the batter into the prepared pan and scatter the chocolate chips on top.
Air fry for 15 to 20 minutes until the edges are set (the center should still appear slightly undercooked.) Let cool completely before slicing. To store, cover and refrigerate the brownies for up to 3 days.

Chocolate Cake

Prep time: 10 minutes | Cook time: 20 to 23 minutes | Serves 8

100 g granulated sugar	¼ teaspoon salt
30 g plain flour, plus 3 tablespoons	1 egg
	2 tablespoons oil
3 tablespoons cocoa	120 ml milk
½ teaspoon baking powder	½ teaspoon vanilla extract
½ teaspoon baking soda	

Preheat the air fryer to 164ºC.
Grease and flour a baking pan.
In a medium bowl, stir together the sugar, flour, cocoa, baking powder, baking soda, and salt.
Add all other ingredients and beat with a wire whisk until smooth.
Pour batter into prepared pan and bake for 20 to 23 minutes, until toothpick inserted in center comes out clean, or with crumbs clinging to it.

Fried Cheesecake Bites

Prep time: 30 minutes | Cook time: 2 minutes | Makes 16 bites

225 g cream cheese, softened	divided
50 g powdered sweetener, plus 2 tablespoons, divided	½ teaspoon vanilla extract
	50 g almond flour
4 tablespoons heavy cream,	

In a stand mixer fitted with a paddle attachment, beat the cream cheese, 50 g of the sweetener, 2 tablespoons of the heavy cream, and the vanilla until smooth. Using a small ice-cream scoop, divide the mixture into 16 balls and arrange them on a rimmed baking sheet lined with baking paper. Freeze for 45 minutes until firm.
Line the air fryer basket with baking paper and preheat the air fryer to 176ºC.
In a small shallow bowl, combine the almond flour with the remaining 2 tablespoons of sweetener.
In another small shallow bowl, place the remaining 2 tablespoons cream.
One at a time, dip the frozen cheesecake balls into the cream and then roll in the almond flour mixture, pressing lightly to form an even coating. Arrange the balls in a single layer in the air fryer basket, leaving room between them. Air fry for 2 minutes until the coating is lightly browned.

Pecan Butter Cookies

Prep time: 5 minutes | Cook time: 24 minutes | Makes 12 cookies

125 g chopped pecans	150 g granulated sweetener, divided
110 g salted butter, melted	
55 g coconut flour	1 teaspoon vanilla extract

In a food processor, blend together pecans, butter, flour, 100 g sweetener, and vanilla 1 minute until a dough forms.
Form dough into twelve individual cookie balls, about 1 tablespoon each.

Cut three pieces of baking paper to fit air fryer basket. Place four cookies on each ungreased baking paper and place one piece baking paper with cookies into air fryer basket. Adjust air fryer temperature to 164ºC and set the timer for 8 minutes. Repeat cooking with remaining batches.
When the timer goes off, allow cookies to cool 5 minutes on a large serving plate until cool enough to handle. While still warm, dust cookies with remaining granulated sweetener. Allow to cool completely, about 15 minutes, before serving.

Vanilla Pound Cake

Prep time: 10 minutes | Cook time: 25 minutes | Serves 6

110 g blanched finely ground almond flour	1 teaspoon baking powder
	120 ml full-fat sour cream
55 g salted butter, melted	30 g full-fat cream cheese, softened
100 g granulated sweetener	
1 teaspoon vanilla extract	2 large eggs

In a large bowl, mix almond flour, butter, and sweetener.
Add in vanilla, baking powder, sour cream, and cream cheese and mix until well combined. Add eggs and mix.
Pour batter into a round baking pan. Place pan into the air fryer basket.
Adjust the temperature to 148ºC and bake for 25 minutes.
When the cake is done, a toothpick inserted in center will come out clean. The center should not feel wet. Allow it to cool completely, or the cake will crumble when moved.

Tortilla Fried Hand Pies

Prep time: 10 minutes | Cook time: 5 minutes per batch | Makes 12 pies

12 small flour tortillas (4-inch diameter)	2 tablespoons desiccated, unsweetened coconut
160 g fig jam	Coconut, or avocado oil for misting or cooking spray
20 g slivered almonds	

Wrap refrigerated tortillas in damp paper towels and heat in microwave 30 seconds to warm.
Working with one tortilla at a time, place 2 teaspoons fig jam, 1 teaspoon slivered almonds, and ½ teaspoon coconut in the center of each.
Moisten outer edges of tortilla all around.
Fold one side of tortilla over filling, to make a half-moon shape, and press down lightly on center. Using the tines of a fork, press down firmly on edges of tortilla to seal in filling.
Mist both sides with oil or cooking spray.
Place hand pies in air fryer basket, close, but not overlapping. It's fine to lean some against the sides and corners of the basket. You may need to cook in 2 batches.
Air fry at 200ºC for 5 minutes, or until lightly browned. Serve hot.
Refrigerate any leftover pies in a closed container. To serve later, toss them back in the air fryer basket and cook for 2 to 3 minutes to reheat.

Simple Pineapple Sticks

Prep time: 5 minutes | Cook time: 10 minutes | Serves 4

½ fresh pineapple, cut into sticks

25 g desiccated coconut

Preheat the air fryer to 204ºC.
Coat the pineapple sticks in the desiccated coconut and put each one in the air fryer basket.
Air fry for 10 minutes.
Serve immediately

Funnel Cake

Prep time: 10 minutes | Cook time: 5 minutes | Serves 4

Coconut, or avocado oil, for spraying
110 g self-raising flour, plus more for dusting

240 ml fat-free vanilla Greek yogurt
½ teaspoon ground cinnamon
¼ cup icing sugar

Preheat the air fryer to 192ºC. Line the air fryer basket with baking paper, and spray lightly with oil.
In a large bowl, mix together the flour, yogurt and cinnamon until the mixture forms a ball.
Place the dough on a lightly floured work surface and knead for about 2 minutes.
Cut the dough into 4 equal pieces, then cut each of those into 6 pieces. You should have 24 pieces in total.
Roll the pieces into 8- to 10-inch-long ropes. Loosely mound the ropes into 4 piles of 6 ropes.
Place the dough piles in the prepared basket, and spray liberally with oil. You may need to work in batches, depending on the size of your air fryer.
Cook for 5 minutes, or until lightly browned.
Dust with the icing sugar before serving.

Apple Hand Pies

Prep time: 15 minutes | Cook time: 25 minutes | Serves 8

2 apples, cored and diced
60 ml honey
1 teaspoon ground cinnamon
1 teaspoon vanilla extract
⅛ teaspoon ground nutmeg

2 teaspoons cornflour
1 teaspoon water
1 sheet shortcrust pastry cut into 4
Cooking oil spray

Insert the crisper plate into the basket and the basket into the unit. Preheat the unit to 204ºC.
In a metal bowl that fits into the basket, stir together the apples, honey, cinnamon, vanilla, and nutmeg.
In a small bowl, whisk the cornflour and water until the cornflour dissolves.
Once the unit is preheated, place the metal bowl with the apples into the basket.
cook for 2 minutes then stir the apples. Resume cooking for 2 minutes.

Remove the bowl and stir the cornflour mixture into the apples. Reinsert the metal bowl into the basket and resume cooking for about 30 seconds until the sauce thickens slightly.
When the cooking is complete, refrigerate the apples while you prepare the piecrust.
Cut each piecrust into 2 (4-inch) circles. You should have 8 circles of crust.
Lay the piecrusts on a work surface. Divide the apple filling among the piecrusts, mounding the mixture in the center of each round.
1Fold each piecrust over so the top layer of crust is about an inch short of the bottom layer. (The edges should not meet.) Use the back of a fork to seal the edges.
1Insert the crisper plate into the basket and the basket into the unit. Preheat the unit 204ºC again.
1Once the unit is preheated, spray the crisper plate with cooking oil, line the basket with baking paper, and spray it with cooking oil. Working in batches, place the hand pies into the basket in a single layer.
1Cook the pies for 10 minutes.
1When the cooking is complete, let the hand pies cool for 5 minutes before removing from the basket. 1Repeat steps 12, 13, and 14 with the remaining pies.

Dark Brownies

Prep time: 10 minutes | Cook time: 11 to 13 minutes | Serves 4

1 egg
115 g granulated sugar
¼ teaspoon salt
½ teaspoon vanilla
55 g unsalted butter, melted
30 g plain flour, plus 2 tablespoons

30 g cocoa
Cooking spray
Optional:
Vanilla ice cream
Caramel sauce
Whipped cream

Beat together egg, sugar, salt, and vanilla until light.
Add melted butter and mix well.
Stir in flour and cocoa.
Spray a baking pan with raised sides lightly with cooking spray.
Spread batter in pan and bake at 164ºC for 11 to 13 minutes. Cool and cut into 4 large squares or 16 small brownie bites.

Cinnamon-Sugar Almonds

Prep time: 5 minutes | Cook time: 8 minutes | Serves 4

150 g whole almonds
2 tablespoons salted butter, melted

1 tablespoon granulated sugar
½ teaspoon ground cinnamon

In a medium bowl, combine the almonds, butter, sugar, and cinnamon. Mix well to ensure all the almonds are coated with the spiced butter.
Transfer the almonds to the air fryer basket and shake so they are in a single layer. Set the air fryer to 148ºC, and cook for 8 minutes, stirring the almonds halfway through the cooking time.
Let cool completely before serving.

Pecan and Cherry Stuffed Apples

Prep time: 10 minutes | Cook time: 20 minutes | Serves 4

4 apples (about 565 g)	3 tablespoons brown sugar
40 g chopped pecans	¼ teaspoon allspice
50 g dried tart cherries	Pinch salt
1 tablespoon melted butter	Ice cream, for serving

Cut off top ½ inch from each apple; reserve tops. With a melon baller, core through stem ends without breaking through the bottom. (Do not trim bases.)

Preheat the air fryer to 176°C. Combine pecans, cherries, butter, brown sugar, allspice, and a pinch of salt. Stuff mixture into the hollow centers of the apples. Cover with apple tops. Put in the air fryer basket, using tongs. Air fry for 20 to 25 minutes, or just until tender.

Serve warm with ice cream.

Peaches and Apple Crumble

Prep time: 10 minutes | Cook time: 10 to 12 minutes | Serves 4

2 peaches, peeled, pitted, and chopped	plain flour
1 apple, peeled and chopped	2 tablespoons unsalted butter, at room temperature
2 tablespoons honey	3 tablespoons packed brown sugar
45 g quick-cooking oats	½ teaspoon ground cinnamon
45 g whole-wheat pastry, or	

Preheat the air fryer to 192°C.

Mix together the peaches, apple, and honey in a baking pan until well incorporated.

In a bowl, combine the oats, pastry flour, butter, brown sugar, and cinnamon and stir to mix well. Spread this mixture evenly over the fruit.

Place the baking pan in the air fryer basket and bake for 10 to 12 minutes, or until the fruit is bubbling around the edges and the topping is golden brown.

Remove from the basket and serve warm.

Halle Berries-and-Cream Cobbler

Prep time: 10 minutes | Cook time: 25 minutes | Serves 4

340 g cream cheese, softened	unsalted butter, cut into pieces
1 large egg	¼ teaspoon fine sea salt
75 g powdered sweetener	Frosting:
½ teaspoon vanilla extract	55 g cream cheese, softened
¼ teaspoon fine sea salt	1 tablespoon powdered sweetener
120 g sliced fresh raspberries or strawberries	1 tablespoon unsweetened, unflavored almond milk or
Biscuits:	heavy cream
3 large egg whites	Fresh raspberries or strawberries, for garnish
70 g blanched almond flour	
1 teaspoon baking powder	
2½ tablespoons very cold	

Preheat the air fryer to 204°C. Grease a pie pan.

In a large mixing bowl, use a hand mixer to combine the cream cheese, egg, and sweetener until smooth. Stir in the vanilla and salt. Gently fold in the raspberries with a rubber spatula. Pour the mixture into the prepared pan and set aside.

Make the biscuits: Place the egg whites in a medium-sized mixing bowl or the bowl of a stand mixer. Using a hand mixer or stand mixer, whip the egg whites until very fluffy and stiff.

In a separate medium-sized bowl, combine the almond flour and baking powder. Cut in the butter and add the salt, stirring gently to keep the butter pieces intact.

Gently fold the almond flour mixture into the egg whites. Use a large spoon or ice cream scooper to scoop out the dough and form it into a 2-inch-wide biscuit, making sure the butter stays in separate clumps. Place the biscuit on top of the raspberry mixture in the pan. Repeat with remaining dough to make 4 biscuits.

Place the pan in the air fryer and bake for 5 minutes, then lower the temperature to 164°C and bake for another 17 to 20 minutes, until the biscuits are golden brown.

While the cobbler cooks, make the frosting: Place the cream cheese in a small bowl and stir to break it up. Add the sweetener and stir. Add the almond milk and stir until well combined. If you prefer a thinner frosting, add more almond milk.

Remove the cobbler from the air fryer and allow to cool slightly, then drizzle with the frosting. Garnish with fresh raspberries.

Store leftovers in an airtight container in the refrigerator for up to 3 days. Reheat the cobbler in a preheated 176°C air fryer for 3 minutes, or until warmed through.

Pumpkin Cookie with Cream Cheese Frosting

Prep time: 10 minutes | Cook time: 7 minutes | Serves 6

50 g blanched finely ground almond flour	½ teaspoon pumpkin pie spice
50 g powdered sweetener, divided	2 tablespoons pure pumpkin purée
2 tablespoons butter, softened	½ teaspoon ground cinnamon, divided
1 large egg	40 g low-carb, sugar-free chocolate chips
½ teaspoon unflavored gelatin	85 g full-fat cream cheese, softened
½ teaspoon baking powder	
½ teaspoon vanilla extract	

In a large bowl, mix almond flour and 25 gsweetener. Stir in butter, egg, and gelatin until combined.

Stir in baking powder, vanilla, pumpkin pie spice, pumpkin purée, and ¼ teaspoon cinnamon, then fold in chocolate chips.

Pour batter into a round baking pan. Place pan into the air fryer basket.

Adjust the temperature to 148°C and bake for 7 minutes.

When fully cooked, the top will be golden brown, and a toothpick inserted in center will come out clean. Let cool at least 20 minutes.

To make the frosting: mix cream cheese, remaining ¼ teaspoon cinnamon, and remaining 25 g sweetener in a large bowl. Using an electric mixer, beat until it becomes fluffy. Spread onto the cooled cookie. Garnish with additional cinnamon if desired.

Carrot Cake with Cream Cheese Icing

Prep time: 10 minutes | Cook time: 55 minutes | Serves 6 to 8

155 g plain flour
1 teaspoon baking powder
½ teaspoon baking soda
1 teaspoon ground cinnamon
¼ teaspoon ground nutmeg
¼ teaspoon salt
3 to 4 medium carrots or 2 large, grated
150 g granulated sugar
50 g brown sugar

2 eggs
175 ml canola or vegetable oil
Icing:
225 g cream cheese, softened at room temperature
8 tablespoons butter, softened at room temperature
120 g icing sugar
1 teaspoon pure vanilla extract

Grease a cake pan.
Combine the flour, baking powder, baking soda, cinnamon, nutmeg, and salt in a bowl. Add the grated carrots and toss well. In a separate bowl, beat the sugars and eggs together until light and frothy. Drizzle in the oil, beating constantly. Fold the egg mixture into the dry ingredients until everything is just combined and you no longer see any traces of flour. Pour the batter into the cake pan and wrap the pan completely in greased aluminum foil.
Preheat the air fryer to 176°C.
Lower the cake pan into the air fryer basket using a sling made of aluminum foil (fold a piece of aluminum foil into a strip about 2-inches wide by 24-inches long). Fold the ends of the aluminum foil into the air fryer, letting them rest on top of the cake. Air fry for 40 minutes. Remove the aluminum foil cover and air fry for an additional 15 minutes or until a skewer inserted into the center of the cake comes out clean and the top is nicely browned.
While the cake is cooking, beat the cream cheese, butter, icing sugar and vanilla extract together using a hand mixer, stand mixer or food processor (or a lot of elbow grease!).
Remove the cake pan from the air fryer and let the cake cool in the cake pan for 10 minutes or so. Then remove the cake from the pan and let it continue to cool completely. Frost the cake with the cream cheese icing and serve.

Vanilla and Cardamon Walnuts Tart

Prep time: 5 minutes | Cook time: 13 minutes | Serves 6

240 ml coconut milk
60 g walnuts, ground
60 g powdered sweetener
55 g almond flour
55 g butter, at room temperature

2 eggs
1 teaspoon vanilla essence
¼ teaspoon ground cardamom
¼ teaspoon ground cloves
Cooking spray

Preheat the air fryer to 184°C. Coat a baking pan with cooking spray.
Combine all the ingredients except the oil in a large bowl and stir until well blended. Spoon the batter mixture into the baking pan.
Bake in the preheated air fryer for approximately 13 minutes. Check the tart for doneness: If a toothpick inserted into the center of the tart comes out clean, it's done.
Remove from the air fryer and place on a wire rack to cool. Serve immediately.

Pumpkin Spice Pecans

Prep time: 5 minutes | Cook time: 6 minutes | Serves 4

125 g whole pecans
50 g granulated sweetener
1 large egg white

½ teaspoon ground cinnamon
½ teaspoon pumpkin pie spice
½ teaspoon vanilla extract

Toss all ingredients in a large bowl until pecans are coated. Place into the air fryer basket.
Adjust the temperature to 148°C and air fry for 6 minutes.
Toss two to three times during cooking.
Allow to cool completely. Store in an airtight container up to 3 days.

Brownies for Two

Prep time: 5 minutes | Cook time: 15 minutes | Serves 2

50 g blanched finely ground almond flour
3 tablespoons granulated sweetener
3 tablespoons unsweetened cocoa powder

½ teaspoon baking powder
1 teaspoon vanilla extract
2 large eggs, whisked
2 tablespoons salted butter, melted

In a medium bowl, combine flour, sweetener, cocoa powder, and baking powder.
Add in vanilla, eggs, and butter, and stir until a thick batter forms.
Pour batter into two ramekins greased with cooking spray and place ramekins into air fryer basket. Adjust the temperature to 164°C and bake for 15 minutes. Centers will be firm when done. Let ramekins cool 5 minutes before serving.

Coconut-Custard Pie

Prep time: 10 minutes | Cook time: 20 to 23 minutes | Serves 4

240 ml milk
50 g granulated sugar, plus 2 tablespoons
30 g scone mix
1 teaspoon vanilla extract

2 eggs
2 tablespoons melted butter
Cooking spray
50 g desiccated, sweetened coconut

Place all ingredients except coconut in a medium bowl.
Using a hand mixer, beat on high speed for 3 minutes.
Let sit for 5 minutes.
Preheat the air fryer to 164°C.
Spray a baking pan with cooking spray and place pan in air fryer basket.
Pour filling into pan and sprinkle coconut over top.
Cook pie for 20 to 23 minutes or until center sets.

Chocolate Bread Pudding

Prep time: 10 minutes | Cook time: 10 to 12 minutes | Serves 4

Nonstick, flour-infused baking spray	2 tablespoons cocoa powder
1 egg	3 tablespoons light brown sugar
1 egg yolk	3 tablespoons peanut butter
175 ml chocolate milk	1 teaspoon vanilla extract
	5 slices firm white bread, cubed

Spray a 6-by-2-inch round baking pan with the baking spray. Set aside.

In a medium bowl, whisk the egg, egg yolk, chocolate milk, cocoa powder, brown sugar, peanut butter, and vanilla until thoroughly combined. Stir in the bread cubes and let soak for 10 minutes. Spoon this mixture into the prepared pan.

Insert the crisper plate into the basket and the basket into the unit. Preheat the unit to 164°C.

cook the pudding for about 10 minutes and then check if done. It is done when it is firm to the touch. If not, resume cooking.

When the cooking is complete, let the pudding cool for 5 minutes. Serve warm.

Fried Oreos

Prep time: 7 minutes | Cook time: 6 minutes per batch | Makes 12 cookies

Coconut, or avocado oil for misting, or nonstick spray	120 ml water, plus 2 tablespoons
120 g ready-made pancake mix	12 Oreos or other chocolate sandwich biscuits
1 teaspoon vanilla extract	1 tablespoon icing sugar

Spray baking pan with oil or nonstick spray and place in basket. Preheat the air fryer to 200°C.

In a medium bowl, mix together the pancake mix, vanilla, and water.

Dip 4 cookies in batter and place in baking pan.

Cook for 6 minutes, until browned.

Repeat steps 4 and 5 for the remaining cookies.

Sift icing sugar over warm cookies.

Chocolate and Rum Cupcakes

Prep time: 5 minutes | Cook time: 15 minutes | Serves 6

150 g granulated sweetener	⅛ teaspoon salt
140 g almond flour	120 ml milk
1 teaspoon unsweetened baking powder	110 g butter, at room temperature
3 teaspoons cocoa powder	3 eggs, whisked
½ teaspoon baking soda	1 teaspoon pure rum extract
½ teaspoon ground cinnamon	70 g blueberries
¼ teaspoon grated nutmeg	Cooking spray

Preheat the air fryer to 176°C. Spray a 6-cup muffin tin with cooking spray.

In a mixing bowl, combine the sweetener, almond flour, baking powder, cocoa powder, baking soda, cinnamon, nutmeg, and salt and stir until well blended.

In another mixing bowl, mix together the milk, butter, egg, and rum extract until thoroughly combined. Slowly and carefully pour this mixture into the bowl of dry mixture. Stir in the blueberries.

Spoon the batter into the greased muffin cups, filling each about three-quarters full.

Bake for 15 minutes, or until the center is springy and a toothpick inserted in the middle comes out clean.

Remove from the basket and place on a wire rack to cool. Serve immediately.

Boston Cream Donut Holes

Prep time: 30 minutes | Cook time: 4 minutes per batch | Makes 24 donut holes

200 g bread flour	Vegetable oil
1 teaspoon active dry yeast	Custard Filling:
1 tablespoon granulated sugar	95 g box French vanilla instant pudding mix
¼ teaspoon salt	
120 ml warm milk	175 ml whole milk
½ teaspoon pure vanilla extract	60 ml heavy cream
2 egg yolks	Chocolate Glaze:
2 tablespoons unsalted butter, melted	170 g chocolate chips
	80 ml heavy cream

Combine the flour, yeast, sugar, and salt in the bowl of a stand mixer. Add the milk, vanilla, egg yolks and butter. Mix until the dough starts to come together in a ball. Transfer the dough to a floured surface and knead the dough by hand for 2 minutes. Shape the dough into a ball, place it in a large, oiled bowl, cover the bowl with a clean kitchen towel and let the dough rise for 1 to 1½ hours or until the dough has doubled in size.

When the dough has risen, punch it down and roll it into a 24-inch log. Cut the dough into 24 pieces and roll each piece into a ball. Place the dough balls on a baking sheet and let them rise for another 30 minutes.

Preheat the air fryer to 204°C.

Spray or brush the dough balls lightly with vegetable oil and air fry eight at a time for 4 minutes, turning them over halfway through the cooking time.

While donut holes are cooking, make the filling and chocolate glaze. Make the filling: Use an electric hand mixer to beat the French vanilla pudding, milk and ¼ cup of heavy cream together for 2 minutes.

Make the chocolate glaze: Place the chocolate chips in a medium-sized bowl. Bring the heavy cream to a boil on the stovetop and pour it over the chocolate chips. Stir until the chips are melted and the glaze is smooth.

To fill the donut holes, place the custard filling in a pastry bag with a long tip. Poke a hole into the side of the donut hole with a small knife. Wiggle the knife around to make room for the filling. Place the pastry bag tip into the hole and slowly squeeze the custard into the center of the donut. Dip the top half of the donut into the chocolate glaze, letting any excess glaze drip back into the bowl. Let the glazed donut holes sit for a few minutes before serving

Sweet Potato Donut Holes

Prep time: 10 minutes | Cook time: 4 to 5 minutes per batch | Makes 18 donut holes

125 g plain flour
65 g granulated sugar
¼ teaspoon baking soda
1 teaspoon baking powder
⅛ teaspoon salt

125 g cooked & mashed purple sweet potatoes
1 egg, beaten
2 tablespoons butter, melted
1 teaspoon pure vanilla extract
Coconut, or avocado oil for misting or cooking spray

Preheat the air fryer to 200°C.
In a large bowl, stir together the flour, sugar, baking soda, baking powder, and salt.
In a separate bowl, combine the potatoes, egg, butter, and vanilla and mix well.
Add potato mixture to dry ingredients and stir into a soft dough.
Shape dough into 1½-inch balls. Mist lightly with oil or cooking spray.
Place 9 donut holes in air fryer basket, leaving a little space in between. Cook for 4 to 5 minutes, until done in center and lightly browned outside.
Repeat step 6 to cook remaining donut holes.

Cardamom Custard

Prep time: 10 minutes | Cook time: 25 minutes | Serves 2

240 ml whole milk
1 large egg
2 tablespoons granulated sugar, plus 1 teaspoon

¼ teaspoon vanilla bean paste or pure vanilla extract
¼ teaspoon ground cardamom, plus more for sprinkling

In a medium bowl, beat together the milk, egg, sugar, vanilla, and cardamom.
Place two ramekins in the air fryer basket. Divide the mixture between the ramekins. Sprinkle lightly with cardamom. Cover each ramekin tightly with aluminum foil. Set the air fryer to 176°C and cook for 25 minutes, or until a toothpick inserted in the center comes out clean.
Let the custards cool on a wire rack for 5 to 10 minutes.
Serve warm or refrigerate until cold and serve chilled.

Chocolate Chip Cookie Cake

Prep time: 5 minutes | Cook time: 15 minutes | Serves 8

4 tablespoons salted butter, melted
65 g granular brown sweetener
1 large egg
½ teaspoon vanilla extract

110 g blanched finely ground almond flour
½ teaspoon baking powder
40 g low-carb chocolate chips

In a large bowl, whisk together butter, sweetener, egg, and vanilla. Add flour and baking powder and stir until combined.
Fold in chocolate chips, then spoon batter into an ungreased round nonstick baking dish.
Place dish into air fryer basket. Adjust the temperature to 148°C and set the timer for 15 minutes. When edges are browned, cookie cake will be done.
Slice and serve warm.

Chapter 11 Family Favorites

Chapter 11 Family Favorites

Bacon-Wrapped Hot Dogs

Prep time: 5 minutes | Cook time: 10 minutes | Serves 4

Oil, for spraying
4 bacon slices
4 beef hot dogs
4 hot dog buns
Toppings of choice

Line the air fryer basket with parchment and spray lightly with oil.
Wrap a strip of bacon tightly around each hot dog, taking care to cover the tips so they don't get too crispy.
Secure with a toothpick at each end to keep the bacon from shrinking.
Place the hot dogs in the prepared basket.
Air fry at 192°C for 8 to 9 minutes, depending on how crispy you like the bacon. For extra-crispy, cook the hot dogs at 204°C for 6 to 8 minutes.
Place the hot dogs in the buns, return them to the air fryer, and cook for another 1 to 2 minutes, or until the buns are warm.
Add your desired toppings and serve.

Pecan Rolls

Prep time: 20 minutes | Cook time: 20 to 24 minutes | Makes 12 rolls

475 ml plain flour, plus more for dusting
2 tablespoons granulated sugar, plus 60 ml, divided
1 teaspoon salt
3 tablespoons butter, at room temperature
180 ml milk, whole or semi-skimmed
60 ml packed light brown sugar
120 ml chopped pecans, toasted
1 to 2 tablespoons oil
60 ml icing sugar (optional)

In a large bowl, whisk the flour, 2 tablespoons granulated sugar, and salt until blended.
Stir in the butter and milk briefly until a sticky dough forms.
In a small bowl, stir together the brown sugar and remaining 60 ml granulated sugar.
Place a piece of parchment paper on a work surface and dust it with flour.
Roll the dough on the prepared surface to ¼ inch thickness.
Spread the sugar mixture over the dough. Sprinkle the pecans on top. Roll up the dough jelly roll-style, pinching the ends to seal. Cut the dough into 12 rolls.
Preheat the air fryer to 160°C.
Line the air fryer basket with parchment paper and spritz the parchment with oil.
Place 6 rolls on the prepared parchment. Bake for 5 minutes. Flip the rolls and bake for 5 to 7 minutes more until lightly browned.
Repeat with the remaining rolls.
Sprinkle with icing sugar (if using).

Pork Stuffing Meatballs

Prep time: 10 minutes | Cook time: 12 minutes | Makes 35 meatballs

Oil, for spraying
680 g minced pork
235 ml breadcrumbs
120 ml milk
60 ml minced onion
1 large egg
1 tablespoon dried rosemary
1 tablespoon dried thyme
1 teaspoon salt
1 teaspoon freshly ground black pepper
1 teaspoon finely chopped fresh parsley

Line the air fryer basket with parchment and spray lightly with oil.
In a large bowl, mix together the minced pork, breadcrumbs, milk, onion, egg, rosemary, thyme, salt, black pepper, and parsley.
Roll about 2 tablespoons of the mixture into a ball.
Repeat with the rest of the mixture. You should have 30 to 35 meatballs.
Place the meatballs in the prepared basket in a single layer, leaving space between each one. You may need to work in batches, depending on the size of your air fryer.
Air fry at 200°C for 10 to 12 minutes, flipping after 5 minutes, or until golden brown and the internal temperature reaches 72°C.

Pork Burgers with Red Cabbage Salad

Prep time: 20 minutes | Cook time: 7 to 9 minutes | Serves 4

120 ml Greek yoghurt
2 tablespoons low-salt mustard, divided
1 tablespoon lemon juice
60 ml sliced red cabbage
60 ml grated carrots
450 g lean minced pork
½ teaspoon paprika
235 ml mixed baby lettuce greens
2 small tomatoes, sliced
8 small low-salt wholemeal sandwich buns, cut in half

In a small bowl, combine the yoghurt, 1 tablespoon mustard, lemon juice, cabbage, and carrots; mix and refrigerate.
In a medium bowl, combine the pork, remaining 1 tablespoon mustard, and paprika. Form into 8 small patties.
Put the sliders into the air fryer basket. Air fry at 204°C for 7 to 9 minutes, or until the sliders register 74°C as tested with a meat thermometer.
Assemble the burgers by placing some of the lettuce greens on a bun bottom.
Top with a tomato slice, the burgers, and the cabbage mixture.
Add the bun top and serve immediately.

Filo Vegetable Triangles

Prep time: 15 minutes | Cook time: 6 to 11 minutes | Serves 6

3 tablespoons minced onion
2 garlic cloves, minced
2 tablespoons grated carrot
1 teaspoon olive oil
3 tablespoons frozen baby peas, thawed

2 tablespoons fat-free soft white cheese, at room temperature
6 sheets frozen filo pastry, thawed
Olive oil spray, for coating the dough

In a baking pan, combine the onion, garlic, carrot, and olive oil.
Air fry at 200°C for 2 to 4 minutes, or until the vegetables are crisp-tender.
Transfer to a bowl.
Stir in the peas and soft white cheese to the vegetable mixture.
Let cool while you prepare the dough.
Lay one sheet of filo on a work surface and lightly spray with olive oil spray.
Top with another sheet of filo.
Repeat with the remaining 4 filo sheets; you'll have 3 stacks with 2 layers each.
Cut each stack lengthwise into 4 strips (12 strips total).
Place a scant 2 teaspoons of the filling near the bottom of each strip.
Bring one corner up over the filling to make a triangle; continue folding the triangles over, as you would fold a flag. Seal the edge with a bit of water.
Repeat with the remaining strips and filling.
Air fry the triangles, in 2 batches, for 4 to 7 minutes, or until golden brown.
Serve.

Meringue Cookies

Prep time: 15 minutes | Cook time: 1 hour 30 minutes | Makes 20 cookies

Oil, for spraying
4 large egg whites

235 ml sugar
Pinch cream of tartar

Preheat the air fryer to 60°C.
Line the air fryer basket with parchment and spray lightly with oil.
In a small heatproof bowl, whisk together the egg whites and sugar.
Fill a small saucepan halfway with water, place it over medium heat, and bring to a light simmer.
Place the bowl with the egg whites on the saucepan, making sure the bottom of the bowl does not touch the water.
Whisk the mixture until the sugar is dissolved.
Transfer the mixture to a large bowl and add the cream of tartar.
Using an electric mixer, beat the mixture on high until it is glossy and stiff peaks form.
Transfer the mixture to a piping bag or a zip-top plastic bag with a corner cut off.
Pipe rounds into the prepared basket. You may need to work in batches, depending on the size of your air fryer. Cook for 1 hour 30 minutes.
Turn off the air fryer and let the meringues cool completely inside.
The residual heat will continue to dry them out.

Chinese-Inspired Spareribs

Prep time: 30 minutes | Cook time: 8 minutes | Serves 4

Oil, for spraying
340 g boneless pork spareribs, cut into 3-inch-long pieces
235 ml soy sauce
180 ml sugar
120 ml beef or chicken stock

60 ml honey
2 tablespoons minced garlic
1 teaspoon ground ginger
2 drops red food colouring (optional)

Line the air fryer basket with parchment and spray lightly with oil.
Combine the ribs, soy sauce, sugar, beef stock, honey, garlic, ginger, and food colouring (if using) in a large zip-top plastic bag, seal, and shake well until completely coated.
Refrigerate for at least 30 minutes.
Place the ribs in the prepared basket. Air fry at 192°C for 8 minutes, or until the internal temperature reaches 74°C.

Coconut Chicken Tenders

Prep time: 10 minutes | Cook time: 12 minutes | Serves 4

Oil, for spraying
2 large eggs
60 ml milk
1 tablespoon hot sauce
350 ml sweetened flaked or desiccated coconut

180 ml panko breadcrumbs
1 teaspoon salt
½ teaspoon freshly ground black pepper
450 g chicken tenders

Line the air fryer basket with parchment and spray lightly with oil.
In a small bowl, whisk together the eggs, milk, and hot sauce.
In a shallow dish, mix together the coconut, breadcrumbs, salt, and black pepper.
Coat the chicken in the egg mix, then dredge in the coconut mixture until evenly coated.
Place the chicken in the prepared basket and spray liberally with oil.
Air fry at 204°C for 6 minutes, flip, spray with more oil, and cook for another 6 minutes, or until the internal temperature reaches 74°C.

Veggie Tuna Melts

Prep time: 15 minutes | Cook time: 7 to 11 minutes | Serves 4

2 low-salt wholemeal English muffins, split
1 (170 g) can chunk light low-salt tuna, drained
235 ml shredded carrot
80 ml chopped mushrooms

2 spring onions, white and green parts, sliced
80 ml fat-free Greek yoghurt
2 tablespoons low-salt wholegrain mustard
2 slices low-salt low-fat Swiss cheese, halved

Place the English muffin halves in the air fryer basket.
Air fry at 172°C for 3 to 4 minutes, or until crisp.
Remove from the basket and set aside.
In a medium bowl, thoroughly mix the tuna, carrot, mushrooms, spring onions, yoghurt, and mustard.
Top each half of the muffins with one-fourth of the tuna mixture and a half slice of Swiss cheese.
Air fry for 4 to 7 minutes, or until the tuna mixture is hot and the cheese melts and starts to brown.
Serve immediately.

Fried Green Tomatoes

Prep time: 15 minutes | Cook time: 6 to 8 minutes | Serves 4

4 medium green tomatoes
80 ml plain flour
2 egg whites
60 ml almond milk
235 ml ground almonds

120 ml panko breadcrumbs
2 teaspoons olive oil
1 teaspoon paprika
1 clove garlic, minced

Rinse the tomatoes and pat dry.
Cut the tomatoes into ½-inch slices, discarding the thinner ends.
Put the flour on a plate.
In a shallow bowl, beat the egg whites with the almond milk until frothy.
And on another plate, combine the almonds, breadcrumbs, olive oil, paprika, and garlic and mix well.
Dip the tomato slices into the flour, then into the egg white mixture, then into the almond mixture to coat.
Place four of the coated tomato slices in the air fryer basket.
Air fry at 204°C for 6 to 8 minutes or until the tomato coating is crisp and golden brown.
Repeat with remaining tomato slices and serve immediately.

Chapter 12 Holiday Specials

Chapter 12 Holiday Specials

Hearty Honey Yeast Rolls

Prep time: 10 minutes | Cook time: 20 minutes | Makes 8 rolls

60 ml whole milk, heated to 46°C in the microwave
½ teaspoon active dry yeast
1 tablespoon honey
160 ml plain flour, plus more for dusting
½ teaspoon rock salt
2 tablespoons unsalted butter, at room temperature, plus more for greasing
Flaky sea salt, to taste

In a large bowl, whisk together the milk, yeast, and honey and let stand until foamy, about 10 minutes.
Stir in the flour and salt until just combined. Stir in the butter until absorbed.
Scrape the dough onto a lightly floured work surface and knead until smooth, about 6 minutes.
Transfer the dough to a lightly greased bowl, cover loosely with a sheet of plastic wrap or a kitchen towel, and let sit until nearly doubled in size, about 1 hour.
Uncover the dough, lightly press it down to expel the bubbles, then portion it into 8 equal pieces.
Prep the work surface by wiping it clean with a damp paper towel (if there is flour on the work surface, it will prevent the dough from sticking lightly to the surface, which helps it form a ball).
Roll each piece into a ball by cupping the palm of the hand around the dough against the work surface and moving the heel of the hand in a circular motion while using the thumb to contain the dough and tighten it into a perfectly round ball.
Once all the balls are formed, nestle them side by side in the air fryer basket.
Cover the rolls loosely with a kitchen towel or a sheet of plastic wrap and let sit until lightly risen and puffed, 20 to 30 minutes.
Preheat the air fryer to 132°C.
Uncover the rolls and gently brush with more butter, being careful not to press the rolls too hard.
Air fry until the rolls are light golden brown and fluffy, about 12 minutes.
Remove the rolls from the air fryer and brush liberally with more butter, if you like, and sprinkle each roll with a pinch of sea salt.
Serve warm.

Air Fried Spicy Olives

Prep time: 10 minutes | Cook time: 5 minutes | Serves 4

340 g pitted black extra-large olives
60 ml plain flour
235 ml panko breadcrumbs
2 teaspoons dried thyme
1 teaspoon red pepper flakes
1 teaspoon smoked paprika
1 egg beaten with 1 tablespoon water
Vegetable oil for spraying

Preheat the air fryer to 204°C.

Drain the olives and place them on a paper towel–lined plate to dry.
Put the flour on a plate.
Combine the panko, thyme, red pepper flakes, and paprika on a separate plate.
Dip an olive in the flour, shaking off any excess, then coat with egg mixture.
Dredge the olive in the panko mixture, pressing to make the crumbs adhere, and place the breaded olive on a platter.
Repeat with the remaining olives.
Spray the olives with oil and place them in a single layer in the air fryer basket. Work in batches if necessary so as not to overcrowd the basket.
Air fry for 5 minutes until the breading is browned and crispy.
Serve warm

Simple Air Fried Crispy Brussels Sprouts

Prep time: 5 minutes | Cook time: 20 minutes | Serves 4

¼ teaspoon salt
⅛ teaspoon ground black pepper
1 tablespoon extra-virgin olive oil
450 g Brussels sprouts, trimmed and halved
Lemon wedges, for garnish

Preheat the air fryer to 176°C.
Combine the salt, black pepper, and olive oil in a large bowl. Stir to mix well.
Add the Brussels sprouts to the bowl of mixture and toss to coat well.
Arrange the Brussels sprouts in the preheated air fryer.
Air fry for 20 minutes or until lightly browned and wilted.
Shake the basket two times during the air frying.
Transfer the cooked Brussels sprouts to a large plate and squeeze the lemon wedges on top to serve.

Garlicky Baked Cherry Tomatoes

Prep time: 5 minutes | Cook time: 4 to 6 minutes | Serves 2

475 ml cherry tomatoes
1 clove garlic, thinly sliced
1 teaspoon olive oil
⅛ teaspoon rock salt
1 tablespoon freshly chopped basil, for topping
Cooking spray

Preheat the air fryer to 182°C.
Spritz the air fryer baking pan with cooking spray and set aside.
In a large bowl, toss together the cherry tomatoes, sliced garlic, olive oil, and rock salt.
Spread the mixture in an even layer in the prepared pan.
Bake in the preheated air fryer for 4 to 6 minutes, or until the tomatoes become soft and wilted.
Transfer to a bowl and rest for 5 minutes.
Top with the chopped basil and serve warm.

Honey Bartlett Pears with Lemony Ricotta

Prep timeHoney Bartlett Pears with Lemony Ricotta

2 large Bartlett or Anjou pears, peeled, cut in half, cored
3 tablespoons melted butter
½ teaspoon ground ginger
¼ teaspoon ground cardamom
3 tablespoons brown sugar
120 ml whole-milk ricotta cheese
1 teaspoon pure lemon extract
1 teaspoon pure almond extract
1 tablespoon honey, plus additional for drizzling

Preheat the air fryer to 192ºC.
Toss the pears with butter, ginger, cardamom, and sugar in a large bowl. Toss to coat well.
Arrange the pears in the preheated air fryer, cut side down.
Air fry for 5 minutes, then flip the pears and air fry for 3 more minutes or until the pears are soft and browned.
In the meantime, combine the remaining ingredients in a separate bowl.
Whip for 1 minute with a hand mixer until the mixture is puffed.
Divide the mixture into four bowls, then put the pears over the mixture and drizzle with more honey to serve.

Kale Salad Sushi Rolls with Sriracha Mayonnaise

Prep time: 10 minutes | Cook time: 10 minutes | Serves 12

Kale Salad:
350 ml chopped kale
1 tablespoon sesame seeds
¾ teaspoon soy sauce
¾ teaspoon toasted sesame oil
½ teaspoon rice vinegar
¼ teaspoon ginger
⅛ teaspoon garlic powder
Sushi Rolls:
3 sheets sushi nori
1 batch cauliflower rice
½ avocado, sliced
Sriracha Mayonnaise:
60 ml Sriracha sauce
60 ml vegan mayonnaise
Coating:
120 ml panko breadcrumbs

Preheat the air fryer to 200ºC.
In a medium bowl, toss all the ingredients for the salad together until well coated and set aside.
Place a sheet of nori on a clean work surface and spread the cauliflower rice in an even layer on the nori. Scoop 2 to 3 tablespoon of kale salad on the rice and spread over.
Place 1 or 2 avocado slices on top. Roll up the sushi, pressing gently to get a nice, tight roll.
Repeat to make the remaining 2 rolls.
In a bowl, stir together the Sriracha sauce and mayonnaise until smooth.
Add breadcrumbs to a separate bowl.
Dredge the sushi rolls in Sriracha Mayonnaise, then roll in breadcrumbs till well coated.
Place the coated sushi rolls in the air fryer basket and air fry for 10 minutes, or until golden brown and crispy. Flip the sushi rolls gently halfway through to ensure even cooking.
Transfer to a platter and rest for 5 minutes before slicing each roll into 8 pieces.
Serve warm.

South Carolina Shrimp and Corn Bake

Prep time: 10 minutes | Cook time: 18 minutes | Serves 2

1 ear corn, husk and silk removed, cut into 2-inch rounds
227 g red potatoes, unpeeled, cut into 1-inch pieces
2 teaspoons Old Bay or all-purpose seasoning, divided
2 teaspoons vegetable oil, divided
¼ teaspoon ground black pepper
227 g large shrimps (about 12 shrimps), deveined
170 g andouille or chorizo sausage, cut into 1-inch pieces
2 garlic cloves, minced
1 tablespoon chopped fresh parsley

Preheat the air fryer to 204ºC.
Put the corn rounds and potatoes in a large bowl.
Sprinkle with 1 teaspoon of seasoning and drizzle with vegetable oil. Toss to coat well.
Transfer the corn rounds and potatoes on a baking sheet, then put in the preheated air fryer.
Bake for 12 minutes or until soft and browned. Shake the basket halfway through the cooking time.
Meanwhile, cut slits into the shrimps but be careful not to cut them through.
Combine the shrimps, sausage, remaining seasoning, and remaining vegetable oil in the large bowl. Toss to coat well.
When the baking of the potatoes and corn rounds is complete, add the shrimps and sausage and bake for 6 more minutes or until the shrimps are opaque. Shake the basket halfway through the cooking time.
When the baking is finished, serve them on a plate and spread with parsley before serving.

Crispy Green Tomato Slices

Prep time: 10 minutes | Cook time: 8 minutes | Makes 12 slices

120 ml plain flour
1 egg
120 ml buttermilk
235 ml cornmeal
235 ml panko breadcrumbs
2 green tomatoes, cut into ¼-inch-thick slices, patted dry
½ teaspoon salt
½ teaspoon ground black pepper
Cooking spray

Preheat the air fryer to 204ºC.
Line the air fryer basket with parchment paper.
Pour the flour in a bowl.
Whisk the egg and buttermilk in a second bowl.
Combine the cornmeal and panko breadcrumbs in a third bowl.
Dredge the tomato slices in the bowl of flour first, then into the egg mixture, and then dunk the slices into the cornmeal mixture. Shake the excess off.
Transfer the well-coated tomato slices in the preheated air fryer and sprinkle with salt and ground black pepper.
Spritz the tomato slices with cooking spray.
Air fry for 8 minutes or until crispy and lightly browned.
Flip the slices halfway through the cooking time.
Serve immediately.

Simple Butter Cake

Prep time: 25 minutes | Cook time: 20 minutes | Serves 8

235 ml plain flour
1¼ teaspoons baking powder
¼ teaspoon salt
120 ml plus 1½ tablespoons granulated white sugar
9½ tablespoons butter, at room temperature

2 large eggs
1 large egg yolk
2½ tablespoons milk
1 teaspoon vanilla extract
Cooking spray

Preheat the air fryer to 164°C.
Spritz a cake pan with cooking spray.
Combine the flour, baking powder, and salt in a large bowl. Stir to mix well.
Whip the sugar and butter in a separate bowl with a hand mixer on medium speed for 3 minutes.
Whip the eggs, egg yolk, milk, and vanilla extract into the sugar and butter mix with a hand mixer.
Pour in the flour mixture and whip with hand mixer until sanity and smooth.
Scrape the batter into the cake pan and level the batter with a spatula.
Place the cake pan in the preheated air fryer.
Bake for 20 minutes or until a toothpick inserted in the centre comes out clean. Check the doneness during the last 5 minutes of the baking.
Invert the cake on a cooling rack and allow to cool for 15 minutes before slicing to serve.

Easy Air Fried Edamame

Prep time: 5 minutes | Cook time: 7 minutes | Serves 6

680 g unshelled edamame
2 tablespoons olive oil

1 teaspoon sea salt

Preheat the air fryer to 204°C.
Place the edamame in a large bowl, then drizzle with olive oil. Toss to coat well.
Transfer the edamame to the preheated air fryer.
Cook for 7 minutes or until tender and warmed through.
Shake the basket at least three times during the cooking.
Transfer the cooked edamame onto a plate and sprinkle with salt.
Toss to combine well and set aside for 3 minutes to infuse before serving.

Chapter 13 Staples, Sauces, Dips, and Dressings

Chapter 13 Staples, Sauces, Dips, and Dressings

Pepper Sauce

Prep time: 10 minutes | Cook time: 20 minutes | Makes 1 L

2 red hot fresh chillies, seeded
2 dried chillies
½ small brown onion, roughly chopped

2 garlic cloves, peeled
475 ml water
475 ml white vinegar

In a medium saucepan, combine the fresh and dried chillies, onion, garlic, and water.
Bring to a simmer and cook for 20 minutes, or until tender.
Transfer to a food processor or blender.
Add the vinegar and blend until smooth.

Mushroom Apple Gravy

Prep time: 5 minutes | Cook time: 10 minutes | Serves 4

475 ml vegetable broth
120 ml finely chopped mushrooms
2 tablespoons wholemeal flour
1 tablespoon unsweetened apple sauce

1 teaspoon onion powder
½ teaspoon dried thyme
¼ teaspoon dried rosemary
⅛ teaspoon pink Himalayan salt
Freshly ground black pepper, to taste

In a non-stick saucepan over medium-high heat, combine all the ingredients and mix well.
Bring to a boil, stirring frequently, reduce the heat to low, and simmer, stirring constantly, until it thickens.

Green Basil Dressing

Prep time: 10 minutes | Cook time: 0 minutes | Makes 235 ml

1 avocado, peeled and pitted
60 ml sour cream
60 ml extra-virgin olive oil
60 ml chopped fresh basil
1 tablespoon freshly squeezed

lime juice
1 teaspoon minced garlic
Sea salt and freshly ground black pepper, to taste

Place the avocado, sour cream, olive oil, basil, lime juice, and garlic in a food processor and pulse until smooth, scraping down the sides of the bowl once during processing.
Season the dressing with salt and pepper.
Keep the dressing in an airtight container in the refrigerator for 1 to 2 weeks.

Peanut Sauce with black pepper

Prep time: 5 minutes | Cook time: 0 minutes | Serves 4

80 ml peanut butter
60 ml hot water
2 tablespoons soy sauce
2 tablespoons rice vinegar

Juice of 1 lime
1 teaspoon minced fresh ginger
1 teaspoon minced garlic
1 teaspoon black pepper

In a blender container, combine the peanut butter, hot water, soy sauce, vinegar, lime juice, ginger, garlic, and pepper.
Blend until smooth.
Use immediately or store in an airtight container in the refrigerator for a week or more.

Hemp Dressing

Prep time: 5 minutes | Cook time: 0 minutes | Makes 12 tablespoons

120 ml white wine vinegar
60 ml tahini
60 ml water
1 tablespoon hemp seeds
½ tablespoon freshly squeezed lemon juice
1 teaspoon garlic powder

1 teaspoon dried oregano
1 teaspoon dried basil
1 teaspoon red pepper flakes
½ teaspoon onion powder
½ teaspoon pink Himalayan salt
½ teaspoon freshly ground black pepper

In a bowl, combine all the ingredients and whisk until mixed well.

Sweet Ginger Teriyaki Sauce

Prep time: 5 minutes | Cook time: 0 minutes | Serves 4

60 ml pineapple juice
60 ml low-salt soy sauce
2 tablespoons packed brown sugar

1 tablespoon arrowroot powder or cornflour
1 tablespoon grated fresh ginger
1 teaspoon garlic powder

Mix together all the ingredients in a small bowl and whisk to incorporate.
Serve immediately, or transfer to an airtight container and refrigerate until ready to use.

Apple Cider Dressing

Prep time: 5 minutes | Cook time: 0 minutes | Serves 2

2 tablespoons apple cider vinegar
⅓ lemon, juiced

⅓ lemon, zested
Salt and freshly ground black pepper, to taste

In a jar, combine the vinegar, lemon juice, and zest.
Season with salt and pepper, cover, and shake well.

Lemony Tahini

Prep time: 5 minutes | Cook time: 0 minutes | Serves 4

180 ml water
120 ml tahini
3 garlic cloves, minced

Juice of 3 lemons
½ teaspoon pink Himalayan salt

In a bowl, whisk together all the ingredients until mixed well.

Tzatziki

Prep time: 10 minutes | Cook time: 0 minutes | Serves 4

1 large cucumber, peeled and grated (about 475 ml)
235 ml plain Greek yoghurt
2 to 3 garlic cloves, minced
1 tablespoon tahini (sesame paste)

1 tablespoon fresh lemon juice
½ teaspoon rock salt, or to taste
Chopped fresh parsley or dill, for garnish (optional)

In a medium bowl, combine the cucumber, yoghurt, garlic, tahini, lemon juice, and salt.
Stir until well combined.
Cover and chill until ready to serve.
Right before serving, sprinkle with chopped fresh parsley, if desired.

Cauliflower Alfredo Sauce

Prep time: 2 minutes | Cook time: 0 minutes | Makes 1 L

2 tablespoons olive oil
6 garlic cloves, minced
700 ml unsweetened almond milk
1 (450 g) head cauliflower, cut into florets

1 teaspoon salt
¼ teaspoon freshly ground black pepper
Juice of 1 lemon
4 tablespoons Engevita yeast flakes

In a medium saucepan, heat the olive oil over medium-high heat.
Add the garlic and sauté for 1 minute or until fragrant.
Add the almond milk, stir, and bring to a boil.
Gently add the cauliflower.
Stir in the salt and pepper and return to a boil.
Continue cooking over medium-high heat for 5 minutes or until the cauliflower is soft. Stir frequently and reduce heat if needed to prevent the liquid from boiling over.
Carefully transfer the cauliflower and cooking liquid to a food processor, using a slotted spoon to scoop out the larger pieces of cauliflower before pouring in the liquid.
Add the lemon and yeast flakes and blend for 1 to 2 minutes until smooth.
Serve immediately.

Appendix 2 Recipes Index

Printed in Great Britain
by Amazon

12938012R00061